MEDIA AT WAR

Radio's Challenge to the Newspapers, 1924–1939

Gwenyth L. Jackaway

Westport, Connecticut
London

Library of Congress Cataloging-in-Publication Data

Jackaway, Gwenyth L.
    Media at war : radio's challenge to the newspapers, 1924–1939 /
Gwenyth L. Jackaway.
        p.   cm.
    Includes bibliographical references and index.
    ISBN 0–275–95257–6 (alk. paper)
    1. Newspapers—History—20th century.   2. Radio journalism—
History—20th century.   I. Title.
PN4815.J27   1995
070.9′09042—dc20   95–13919

British Library Cataloguing in Publication Data is available.

Library of Congress Catalog Card Number: 95–13919
ISBN: 0–275–95257–6

First published in 1995

Praeger Publishers, 88 Post Road West, Westport, CT 06881
An imprint of Greenwood Publishing Group, Inc.

Printed in the United States of America

The paper used in this book complies with the
Permanent Paper Standard issued by the National
Information Standards Organization (Z39.48–1984).

10 9 8 7 6 5 4 3 2 1

To my mother, Rita Freedman

Contents

Acknowledgments

Media At War is a project that I have been working on, in various forms, for nearly a decade. During that time I received many kinds of support from a variety of sources, and it is with great pleasure that I take this opportunity to say thank you.

As this has been primarily an intellectual endeavor, my first debt is to the teachers with whom I had the privilege of studying, and who had a profound influence in shaping my development as a scholar. Long ago, when I was in high school, Eric Rothschild kindled my love of history, and showed me that the study of the past can be filled with passion and discovery. I am an historian today because of him. When I got to college, Eviatar Zerubavel opened the door for me to a whole new world of theory and ideas, and it was sitting in his classroom, rapt in fascination and wonder, that I chose to pursue an academic life. In graduate school, Carolyn Marvin inspired, challenged, and shaped me as my teacher and mentor. She taught me how to ask questions about the social response to new media, and pushed me to new levels of responsible scholarship. Throughout the various stages of this project she has been a tremendously supportive source of guidance. Her ideas continue to shape my own research, and I will always consider myself her student.

Colleagues as well as teachers provided assistance along the way, and I am indebted to several people in particular. Daniel Czitrom, Susan Douglas, and Susan Smulyan corresponded with me in the early stages of the research, each of them sharing ideas and articles. Garth Jowett provided invaluable encouragement at a crucial point in the project, and has helped me in many ways over the years. Robert McChesney was been an endless source of support. He offered me his hospitality, his feedback, and his consistently valuable advice on the publishing process. I am honored to have been the recipient of assistance from media historians of such caliber.

All works of scholarship are dependent in various ways on the institutions that make academic life possible, and this book is no exception. My first debt of institutional gratitude goes to the Annenberg School for Communication at the University of Pennsylvania, for providing me with the outstanding training that prepared me for this research, as well as the financial support for my education. Once the project was underway, my work took me to various archives and libraries, where I always found people willing to help me locate materials. Thanks to the staffs at the Columbia School of Journalism Library, Fordham University Library, the Lincoln Center Branch of the New York Public Library, The Oral History Collection at Columbia University, The University of Pennsylvania Library, and the Wisconsin State Historical Society at the University of Wisconsin, Madison.

For the past six years, Fordham University has been my institutional home. I am grateful to my colleagues in the Fordham Communication Department for providing me with a supportive environment in which to complete this work. Special thanks go to: Edward Wachtel for his unfailing support and friendship during his time as Department Chair; Ron Jacobson, who, as Assistant Chair gave me a teaching schedule that allowed me to write, Robin Andersen for her encouragement, and Roger Musgrave for listening. Our Department Secretary, Rose Muccioli, saved the day by graciously allowing me to use her computer at a critical point in the final stage of the project.

Over the years, various people have read drafts of the manuscript or served as sounding boards, providing crucial feedback at key points. In the early stages of the project, Julia Dobrow and Rita Freedman gave valuable suggestions. Later, Edward Wachtel and Benyamin Lichtenstein listened as I worked out the basic model of the argument. And when it was time to make final changes, Debra Hochman and Paul Lustgarten offered their valuable editorial skills.

In addition to help on the content of the book, I also received technical assistance. Edward Wachtel and Thomas McLaughlin provided key computer support. Arana averted a disaster and recovered a dysfunctional hard drive. Helen Hunt generously allowed me to borrow a laptop, making it possible for me to work out of town at a crucial point in the editing. There were also those who offered help of a more therapeutic nature. Leslie Kaminoff and William LeSassier kept my body functioning when too many hours at the computer took their toll. Dr. Jack Soltanoff helped me back to health after a long illness, and Sharami Kerr joined me in truly transformational work.

Every book is, ultimately, reliant on the kindness of editors to find its way into print, and this one is no exception. Thanks to Dan Eades, acquisitions editor at Praeger Publishers, for recognizing the potential in the original manuscript, and to Liz Leiba, my production editor, for her infinite patience with a first-time author.

And then there are my friends. Without them this book might never have existed, for they are the ones who supplied the nurturing and the love that got me through the long process of producing this work. James Ramos gets special acknowledgment for providing almost daily support throughout the entire period during which I transformed my dissertation into this book. He is a constant source of inspiration, and teaches me not to settle for anything less than my best. Thank you James, for everything. Elizabeth Neustadter has been my partner on an astounding journey of exploration and discovery, in which we continue to learn ever more about the true meaning of friendship. Arana brought, as he always does, an endless supply of tenderness, understanding, magic and love. Benyamin Lichtenstein gave me a unique combination of emotional and intellectual support, for he is ever willing and able to listen on all levels. Lisamichelle Davis offered the empathy that can only come from having shared similar levels of professional pressure, while providing me with an inspirational model of strength and courage in her fierce survivor spirit. In the final stages of the project I was joined by two wonderful new friends: Eric Canny gifted me with the nurturing, patience, and kindness that makes his friendship so precious. And Marc Fenty, my trusty dance partner, was always there, with the joy of the music, the companionship, and the laughter, that we share everyday. Finally, my new roommate, Randy Bullard, tolerated the last few months of manuscript production with good humor, and joined me in creating a wonderful household filled with good feelings, great music, and fabulous parties.

Above all, however, it is my family that has made everything possible. My grandparents, Martin and Adele Freedman have been a constant source of love, pride and great generosity. My brother, Adam Jackaway, has taught me important lessons about balancing work and play, and taking things lightly. Stan Josephson always lets me know how much he cares. Ultimately, however, it is to my mother, Rita Freedman, that I owe the deepest thanks. Her support for my professional development has been unceasing. She taught me to believe in myself and to follow my dreams. It is to her that I dedicate this book.

MEDIA AT WAR

1

Media Wars and Resistance
to New Technologies

This is an age of constant innovation in the realm of communication technologies. Scarcely a day goes by, it seems, without news of yet another media-related development. Headlines forecast the arrival of the latest innovation and herald the wonders of cyberspace. As Americans, seemingly so fascinated with all that is "new and improved," and we tend to welcome such innovations, anticipating that they will help us communicate better, faster, more efficiently, give us more personal control, greater flexibility, greater access, and more information. Yet with all change comes disruption. Familiar, established patterns of communication must give way to make room for the new. New media touch many areas of our lives. They change the way we do business, conduct our personal lives and run our political system. They also have an impact on existing media industries. Like so many of us trying to cope with an ever changing world, established media institutions must face the challenge of responding to the arrival of new communication technologies, and they do not always respond with enthusiasm.

Media wars are battles waged between old and new media. They are inter-industry conflicts between existing and emerging media industries that take place at the time of technological innovation in communication. They have happened with the introduction of almost every new medium in this century. The newspapers fought the introduction of radio. Hollywood fought the introduction of television. Broadcast television struggled against the introduction of cable TV. Both newspapers and cable companies have fought the phone companies. What are these media wars about? What is at stake in these battles for control over the channels of communication, and why are the same battles fought over and over again?

Adapting to the constant stream of technological innovations and the social change that goes with them is perhaps one of the greatest challenges of our age. Adjusting to change is difficult, for with all change comes disruption. No matter how much we say we want things to improve, it is hard to let go of familiar, established ways of doing things. This is particularly true when the change has a direct impact on things we hold dear, like our sense of self, our jobs, or our level of power in the society. When such things are in jeopardy, there is a tendency to react with fearful protectiveness. The survival instinct comes into play, and the new force is seen as malevolent, something to be battled and conquered. We appear to be trapped in a repeating cycle of innovation and resistance, pouring millions of dollars and countless hours of labor each year into research and development, and then balking when the time comes to let go of the old way of doing things.

Technological innovation in communications is inevitable. Therefore, what is needed is a better understanding of our own resistance to changes in the communication environment, and of the issues that arise when existing media struggle to make room for new competition. It is to this end that this book is dedicated. *Media At War* is an exploration of the nature of conflicts between established and emerging media. Offered here is a model for understanding the issues and tactics that are characteristic of such battles. The route to this model is an in-depth case study of one particular inter-industry conflict: The Press-Radio War. Fought between the established newspaper industry and the emergent broadcast industry in the early days of radio, the Press-Radio War was a battle waged on the part of the print journalists to defend their territory from the newcomers. It was a war that the newspapers lost, but not before putting up a ten-year struggle to block the development of broadcast journalism. It is a story that has much to teach about media wars, the issues over which they are fought, and the tactics with which they are waged.

MEDIA HISTORY: THE COMMUNICATION LENS

As an in-depth study of one particular media war, this book is an exercise in media history. Like all histories, it is informed by contemporary concerns and conducted with the goal of using events of yesterday to help shed light on issues of today. Like all histories, therefore, it is at best only partial in its construction of the story. It is no longer novel to acknowledge the inherently biased nature of historical accounts. Indeed, if anything, writing in an age so heavily influenced by cultural relativism and theories of deconstruction makes it impossible to put forth a book titled *the* history of anything. The question is, rather, which history? Whose history? From what perspective is this history being told, and to what end?

If we think about the historian as a photographer, for whom the choice of lens determines the view of the past, traditional historians have viewed the Press-Radio War through an economic lens. This is a perspective, highly influenced by the works of Marx and Weber, that sees human relations as being governed by struggles for control over the means and modes of production. In the case of the conflict between radio and newspapers, it yields an argument that this media war was fought on the part of the press to defend its advertising and newsstand revenue.[1] On one level, of course, this seems a logical and obvious analysis. Old media *are* economically threatened by new media. The competition and danger of obsolescence are real.

There are other lenses, however, that can be put on Clio's camera to reveal another historical terrain. Anthropologist Jack Goody has suggested that what is needed is "to shift part of the emphasis put on the means and modes of *production* in explaining human history to the means and modes of *communication.*"[2] What does this mean? What happens when media wars of yesterday are viewed through an communication lens rather than an economic one? How might this shift our understanding of social and institutional reactions to new media?

To view conflicts between existing and emergent media industries as strictly economic in nature is to ignore the true nature of communication technologies and the crucial feature that differentiates them from the other machinery. The key word here is *communication.* The difference between communication technologies and other inventions is that these media are inextricably linked to the very stuff of culture. These are the devices that help us to create symbols, define meaning, and therefore construct our social realities. When a new form of communication arrives, therefore, the impact is not only upon the economic sphere. If meaning is socially constructed and arrived at through the process of communication, then new media are potentially threatening to the very way in which we define social reality.

Every culture has written and unwritten rules governing the flow of information in society. These are the rules of social discourse: rules that cover who should speak to whom about what; rules about what should be said, the way it should be said, and the circumstances in which it should be said; and rules about who should have and control access to information, and which sources of information are considered legitimate. These rules shape much of our experience of the world, on a personal and professional level.

New media can disrupt these established patterns of communication. With their capacity to transmit and receive information in new ways, new media often render the old rules obsolete or impossible to enforce. The new technology may open new doors to entirely new means of interacting. With their ability to send information through new channels, in new ways, at greater speeds with higher efficiency, new media demand that we alter our familiar ways of communicating with each other. To accommodate these new communication technologies, we must adopt new practices. The old ways of sending and receiving messages, of storing and retrieving information, no longer make sense in the new communicative environment.

How does this affect media industries that have been established to support existing communication technologies? At worst, it threatens to render them obsolete. At best, even if they manage to survive the disruption of the established patterns of communication, their place in the larger stream of social discourse will be redefined. They must now share the communicative environment with a new channel, one that may well perform the same or a similar function, and probably does it in a way that offers new options of speed, efficiency, or control on the part of the user. Thus, new communication technologies threaten to displace older media from their established role in the stream of social discourse.

Beyond struggles for economic survival, what are media wars about? They are battles to control the channels of communication, to determine the form and content of messages and to identify who gets to deliver them. They are battles over access to and ownership of information. They are battles to preserve established roles and patterns in the social communication process. Control over the channels of communication brings not only profits, but power over the domain of meaning-making, power to shape the cultural agenda, public opinion, and the nature of social discourse. It is the power, to some degree, to determine the way millions of people define and experience reality, and for many, that is a power worth fighting for.

THE THREATS OF NEW MEDIA

It is not enough, however, to state simply that media wars are fought to retain control over the channels of communication. To fully understand these inter-industry conflicts, more information is needed about the particular ways in which new media threaten the role of old media in the stream of social discourse. In what ways, specifically, do new communication technologies pose a danger to the power of existing media? The story of the Press-Radio War suggests that new media are threatening to established media institutions on at least three levels: *institutional identity, institutional structure, and institutional function.*

Institutional identity is the "personality" of an institution. In much the way that personal identity differentiates people from each other, institutional identity is composed of those qualities or characteristics that distinguish an institution from other institutions. Frequently this is determined by the way in which the institution does its job. Often a set of standards or guidelines governs job performance, earning a particular institution a certain reputation. For example, people expect a different level of production value from cinema than they do from prime-time broadcast television. Indeed, this is one of the main distinctions between these two media institutions. The arrival of a new communication technology can be quite disruptive to the established identity of existing media institutions. When a new medium is introduced, with its capacity to process information in new ways, older media are faced with the challenge of differentiating themselves from the new competition. If the new technology can do much of what the older one could, but does it faster, better and more efficiently, what distinguishes the two?

In recent years, for example, there has been a considerable blurring of the boundaries between telephones and computers, or between entertainment and information service providers. It is hard to tell, after a while, where the job of one media institution leaves off and another begins. To differentiate itself from the competing medium, the older institution must grapple with questions of who it is, and how it does its job. Debates about institutional identity become an important way to distinguish the old medium from the new. At the time of the introduction of a new communication technology, established media may be called upon to assess what they are, what they do, and what makes their work unique in the field of communications. Changes in the communication environment may prompt institutional identity reassessment.

Today, faced with competition from a number of new sources, newspapers are busy trying to redefine themselves and determine what their new role will be in the context of an on-line, multimedia society. Similarly, the introduction of radio forced print journalists of the 1930s to grapple with a number of questions pertaining to their own identity in the context of a changing communication environment. In response to the presence of a new channel of information and new messengers, print journalists were faced with fundamental questions of identity. What or who is a journalist? What is news? How should the news be delivered? What are the rules regarding the form and content of an acceptable news message? As they wrestled with these issues, they ultimately wrestled with the definition and boundaries of their profession.

New communication technologies also pose a threat to the *institutional structure* of established media. Like all businesses, media institutions develop ways of doing things that help their work run smoothly. Institutions that have been in existence for some time have generally developed patterns that are designed to maximize profits and efficiency. Usually these patterns involve a carefully devised division of labor in which different players in the industry carry out different roles in the production and distribution of media content to the public. The arrival of a new means of information dissemination can be quite disruptive to this established institutional structure.

Recent media history offers numerous examples of this phenomenon. By making it difficult to enforce rules regarding the duplication and distribution of information, for instance, various new communication technologies have rendered rules governing intellectual property rights hard to enforce. This has led to efforts within the music industry, for example, to block the introduction of digital audio tape (DAT) technology, out of concern that this new medium would disrupt the established structure of music production and distribution. This issue has also raised considerable concern within the publishing and computer software industries. When new technologies make the high-quality reproduction of information open to anyone, certain players in the institutional structure lose their role, fundamentally disrupting the established order of business.

In the case of the Press-Radio War, radio posed a threat to the long-standing relationship between the wire services and the newspapers. By opening a channel through which news could flow directly from the wire services to the people, radio made it possible for news to bypass the newspapers altogether, a development about which print journalists were not pleased. The broadcasters could also steal the news from the newspapers and read it over the air, raising questions of violation of intellectual property rights. Thus, in addition to challenging the familiar definition of news and journalist, radio also threatened the established institutional structure of the journalism industry and the longstanding patterns of news flow through the culture.

Finally, new media can also pose a threat to the established *institutional function* of existing media. The function of an institution is defined by the role or roles it plays in society. Just as different communication institutions have different identities, so too do they each serve different communication functions in the larger stream of social discourse. It is as if there is a division of labor among the various channels of communication in society, each playing a distinct role in the job of keeping everyone in the culture connected, informed, educated, and entertained. When a new medium comes along, there is the possibility that its technological capacities make it better suited to do the work that another medium has previously been doing. This means that the old medium may be displaced, and its institutional function may be assumed by the new medium.

Media history offers numerous examples of this. One is the displacement of the telegraph by the telephone. Another is the transformation of radio programming in the wake of the introduction of television. A third is the redefinition of the telephone as its capacities have been expanded by such technologies as the answering machine, call waiting and voice mail. Sometimes the older medium becomes extinct; sometimes it merely transforms, taking on a new role. In each case, its former place in the social communication process is lost, the old role having been taken over or transformed by a new medium.

In the case of radio and the press, the live transmission capabilities of broadcasting raised the specter of radio replacing newspapers as the primary channel of news distribution in this country. Prior to the advent of radio there were only a few ways people could obtain political information: attending political speeches or rallies, talking to friends, and reading the newspaper. Newspapers were a critical element in the process of shaping public opinion. As the principal news medium of the nation for over a century, therefore, newspapers had long enjoyed several crucial roles in the democratic political process: they served the function of helping to create and maintain an informed electorate, and acted (at least at times) as the fourth estate, serving as a watchdog of the government.[3] Indeed, these communication functions were seen as being so crucial to the survival of a democracy that the Constitutional framers reserved a special place for the press in the Bill of Rights, in order to ensure that the press would have the freedom necessary to perform these functions properly.

But information in the newspaper is inherently out of date by the time the paper is delivered. Therefore, the arrival of a medium with the capacity to broadcast live threatened to render the newspaper obsolete, or at least significantly decrease its importance in the process of keeping the nation informed. Radio was potentially quite dangerous to the powerful role that newspapers had long occupied in the political process, and the print journalists of the 1930s were quite concerned about having their role usurped. They also made grim predictions about the dire consequences that our country would suffer if the balance of power in the political communication process was disrupted.

Thus, the story of the Press-Radio War suggests that new media threaten old media in several key ways. On the level of *institutional identity*, there is the question of institutional definition. On the level of *institutional structure*, there is the issue of division of labor and other procedural patterns that govern the way in which the job gets carried out. Finally, on the level of *institutional function*, there is the issue of the place of the institution in society at large. On all three levels, new media threaten to disrupt the communication status quo. When the communication status quo is disrupted, those who enjoyed power as a result of their previous role may find themselves displaced. Therefore, when established media wage war on emergent media, such battles can be seen as efforts on the part of the older media institution to preserve their role in the larger stream of social discourse.

THE INVOCATION OF SACRED RHETORIC

When people or institutions experience things that they hold dear as being in danger, they tend to respond in a self-protective manner. The aim, of course, is to preserve what is important to them. There are many ways to respond to being threatened. The way in which people and institutions choose to defend themselves or their turf can reveal as much about them as the fact that they feel threatened. Approaches to self-defense can be heavily laden with philosophical implications regarding beliefs about the nature of conflict and social change. In the case of media wars, self-defense tactics may also have much to reveal about the way in which media industries perceive themselves and the role in society.

In the battle between radio and the press, one of the most common tactics employed by print journalists in their efforts at institutional self-defense against the invasion of broadcasting was the invocation of sacred rhetoric. When making their arguments about the dangers of this new technology, they frequently called upon one of the hallowed ideals of the culture, claiming that this sacred value would in some way be endangered if radio took over the job of journalism. Radio journalism, they warned, posed a threat to the journalistic ideals of objectivity, the social ideals of public service, the capitalist ideals of property rights, and the political ideals of democracy. In the name of preserving these ideals, print journalists argued that they, and not the broadcasters, were the only ones suited to gather and disseminate news in this country. Thus, as a means of defending their own interests they invoked the interests of the nation.

The invocation of cultural ideals as a form of self-defense is an interesting tactic. Existing media waging war against emerging media have to solve the tactical challenge of winning support from the rest of the culture to hold back technological progress. While the new medium may be a threat to the old one, it may hold many attractions for everyone else. The tactic of calling upon sacred cultural values serves two important functions. On a public relations level, it creates the impression that the besieged medium is not just acting out of self-interest but is actually concerned about the greater public good. It also serves the function of linking the needs of the established medium with the interests of the nation as a whole. By arguing that the culture's cherished ideals may be threatened if the new medium is allowed to flourish, the old medium makes its own concerns suddenly relevant to everyone.

Elevating the established communication patterns to sacred status makes their violation a sacrilege. This then justifies taking action to prevent the invasion of the industry by the newcomers with their new technologies and their new ways. Now they are no longer simply annoying competitors; they are invaders who pose a threat to some of the culture's most sacred ideals. In the name of protecting these values, the besieged industry is then justified in taking regulatory or legal steps to attempt to block the invaders. Whether this sacred rhetoric is spoken with any degree of sincerity, of course, is difficult to determine. It is impossible to know if the print journalists of the 1930s actually believed that radio was a threat to democracy. What we do know, however, is that they apparently felt that this would be the most effective way to protect their place in the social communication process. One need only listen to the arguments of the American Newspaper Publishers Association (ANPA) in its fight against the Baby Bells in the 1980s to know that this tactic is still being used in contemporary media wars.

What follows, then, is a history of the Press-Radio War, told from a communications perspective. Examined here are the kinds of objections the print journalists of the 1930s had to radio, as voiced in their public statements and on the pages of their trade journals. An in-depth textual and discourse analysis of the print journalists' sentiments about the dangers of radio provides access to the kinds of issues and concerns they had about the potential impact of this new medium upon their industry. The study covers the period from 1924, the year in which the first election returns were reported on the air, through 1939, the year that the Associated Press finally lifted its ban on the provision of news briefs to radio, thereby officially ending the Press-Radio War.

Moving beyond the traditional economic interpretation of this conflict, this book argues that the Press-Radio War was fought by the print journalists to retain control over 'their' portion of the channels of communication. This battle was not just fought over money, but over power. At stake was the power to control the channels of news distribution in America, a role that carries with it the power to shape public opinion and set the national political agenda. It is a role that carries with it the power to define the nature, form and content of news. It also carries with it the power to determine whose voices are heard, and what issues get addressed in the collective cultural conversation. And it is a role that the print journalists were not enthusiastic about sharing with the new medium of radio.

In waging war against radio, the print journalists were attempting to protect several key areas of their domain that were essential to preserving the power they derived from controlling the channels of news distribution: the institutional identity of the press, the institutional structure of the journalism industry, and the institutional function of the press in the democratic political process. At stake in this struggle was the definition and nature of news and the identity of its messengers, the process by which news is disseminated through the culture, and the role of the news messengers in the larger political context. Examining this particular media war may offer insight into the kinds of objections that established media make against newer channels of communication, and provide information about the institutional self-defense tactics they employ to preserve the communication status quo.

A word of clarification is needed about the terminology used in this book. I have chosen to use the word *institution* rather than *industry* when referring to a group of organizations that are all in a particular media-related business. Thus, throughout the book I refer to "the institution of journalism" rather than "the journalism industry." The institution of journalism, in this case, would be comprised of all print and electronic sources of news and information. This would include, of course, newspapers, magazines, radio and television news divisions, wire services, and today, on-line news services.

Although this institutional terminology may be jarring and unfamiliar for some readers, it is used for a very specific reason. The term industry is a business-oriented term that evokes images of the manufacturing and distribution of a product. While the media are indeed businesses, they are in the business of facilitating human communication. As explained earlier, it is the goal of this book to shift the analytic focus of the story of the Press-Radio War from an economic to a communication perspective. The term "institution" is more sociological than economic. It has been chosen for this analysis because it better conveys the sense of media organizations as well-established and structured systems. Since it is the argument of this book that new media disrupt established communication systems, "institution" is the better term for the purposes of this analysis.

The organization of this book is as follows. After an initial chapter in which the story of the Press-Radio War is told, the bulk of the text consists of three chapters, each dealing with one of the three areas threatened by new media: institutional identity, institutional structure, and institutional function. Chapter 3 explores the ways in which radio challenged the identity of print journalism, raising questions about standards and quality of reporting. Chapter 4 examines radio's challenge to established procedures that had long constituted the structure of print journalism, disrupting the relationship between the wire services and the newspapers. Chapter 5 discusses the threat posed by radio to the established function of print journalism in the process of political communication in our democracy, disrupting the familiar channels of communication between the politicians and the people. Finally, the epilogue offers some speculations on the lessons that the Press-Radio War has to offer about adapting to technological innovation in communications.

NOTES

1. See for example, Eric Barnouw, *The Golden Web* (New York: Oxford University Press, 1968); Giraud Chester, "The Press-Radio War: 1933-1935," *Public Opinion Quarterly*, (Summer 1949): 252-264; Sammy Danna, "The Rise of Radio News," in Lawrence Lichty and Malachi Topping, *American Broadcasting: A Source Book on the History of Radio and Television* (New York: Hastings House, 1975); Edwin Emery, *The History of the ANPA* (Minneapolis: University of Minnesota, 1950); Edwin and Michael Emery, *The Press and America* (Englewood Cliffs: Prentice Hall, 7th edition, 1992); Russell Hammargren, "The Origin of Press-Radio Conflict," *Journalism Quarterly*, Volume 13; George Lott, "The Press-Radio War of the 1930s," *Journal of Broadcasting*, 1970; Frank Luther Mott, *American Journalism: A History, 1690-1960* (New York: Macmillan, 1962); Rudolph Michael, "History and Criticism of Press-Radio Relationships," *Journalism Quarterly*, (Spring   1938); Robert R. Smith, "The Origins of Radio Network News Commentary," *Journal of Broadcasting*, 9:2:113-122.

2. Jack Goody, *The Logic of Writing and the Organization of Society* (Cambridge:Cambridge University Press, 1986), 11.

3. Fred Siebert, Ted Peterson, Wilbur Schramm, *Four Theories of the Press* (Urbana: University of Illinois Press, 1956), chapter one.

2

The Press-Radio War:
A Battle in Three Stages

We cannot hope to sweep back the ocean with a broom...
Radio is here to stay.[1]

J.R. Knowland, publisher
Oakland Tribune, 1929

The Press-Radio War unfolded in stages as the institution of journalism went through various phases in its response to the emergence of radio. Initially, there was a period of internal conflict, during which the print journalists were divided over how to handle the new competition. This first phase was one of assessment. It was necessary to determine the level of threat posed by the new arrival in order to decide what response, if any, was needed. In the second stage, the various groups of journalists put aside their differences to work together against what they had decided was a common enemy. Having achieved internal consensus, they were then able to unite and take action in an attempt to block the development of the new competition. Finally, unsuccessful in their efforts, the print journalists eventually concede to the inevitability of technological progress and began forming economic links with radio. In what might be called a tactic of alliance and acquisition, many newspapers dropped their combative stance and elected to cash in on the new profits to be made from broadcasting. This chapter traces the story of the Press-Radio War. Explored here are the various stages that the print journalists went through in their response to the arrival of radio as an established media institution adapted to technological changes in the communication environment. (See Figure 1 for a timeline of the main events in each stage.) While this is only the tale of one media war, it offers insights into larger patterns characteristic of struggles between old and new media.

Figure 1
Timeline of the Press-Radio War

STAGE ONE: INTERNAL CONFLICT

1922: Associated Press warns member papers about broadcasting AP news.

1924: *April*--Radio listed by AP as chief topic of concern at annual meeting.

November--Conflict within AP over provision of election returns to
station-owning papers.
--AP allows news of transcendent importance to be aired.

1926: National Broadcasting Company (NBC) established.

Publisher's Association of New York votes to eliminate all sponsor
names from program logs.

1927: Columbia Broadcasting Company (CBS) established.

New York papers abandon program log boycott.

1928: *November*-- UP, INS, and AP provide election returns to radio.

1929: *October*--Wall Street Crash.

1931: *April*--ANPA passes resolution that program logs must be handled
as paid advertising.

1931: Harold Davis, editor, *Ventura Free Press,* launches campaign
against radio ads.

1932: Elezy Roberts quits post as ANPA Radio Committee Chair over inability
to unify ANPA on radio issue. He is replaced by Edward Harris.

March--Lindbergh baby kidnapping.

November--National elections, controversy over AP provision of returns
--Edward Harris forms Publisher's National Radio Committee.

December--ANPA Board of Directors recommends that wire services
stop providing radio with news.

1933: *February* --AP v. KSOO. First news piracy suit is filed, against a station in Sioux Falls, South Dakota.
--AP survey finds majority of its membership is opposed to providing radio with news.

March --Attempted assassination of FDR, covered live by radio.
--FDR's first fireside chat.

STAGE TWO: UNITY AND ACTION

1933: *April*--Wire services decide to cease providing news to networks.
--ANPA resolution to cease carrying program logs.

June --Four New Orleans papers file a news piracy suit against WDSU.

Summer --Networks form own news gathering services.

Fall--CBS applies for access to Congressional press galleries.

November--Networks appeal to publishers for peace.

December--Biltmore Conference., Press-Radio Agreement formed.
Press-Radio Bureau created.

1934: *March*--Press Radio Bureau, Transradio Press Service, and Yankee News Service commence operations

June--Modifications made to Press Radio Bureau restrictions.

Fall--AP files suit against KVOS, a station in Bellingham, Washington.

STAGE THREE: ALLIANCE AND ACQUISITION

1935: *April*--At ANPA convention, additional modifications made to Press Radio Bureau restrictions.
-- UP and INS decide to sell news to independent radio stations.

1936: *January*--Edward Harris unsuccessfully appeals to publishers to save agreement, tries to stop UP and INS from selling news.

April-- Feud essentially ended. Radio Committee says future welfare of both institutions is closely aligned.

1938: Press Radio Bureau discontinued.

1939: *May*--AP lifts ban on sponsored newscasts of its services.

STAGE ONE: INTERNAL CONFLICT

Stage One of the Press-Radio War began slowly. In the very early years of press-radio relations, newspapers were not at all hostile toward broadcasting. In fact, newspapers were very helpful in promoting radio to the public. In the early 1920s, radio was the latest craze, a novelty item with a large following among amateurs building crystal sets at home. Many newspaper publishers, far from feeling threatened at this stage, recognized in this new area of interest the opportunity to draw readers, by featuring stories about the new technology.

As radio became a subject of growing interest to the public, newspapers responded by running more stories about it. Some papers went even further, devoting several pages, or even, on the weekends, an entire magazine section to radio.[2] These special sections would offer a range of information to the ham radio enthusiast, including technical diagrams and instructions for building sets, "reports on last night's reception" and strategies for tuning in to distant stations. There were also pages devoted exclusively to answering the letters from readers with technical questions about radio construction. Writers from science publications or physics professors from local universities would frequently be brought on staff to provide the technical expertise necessary to address the mysteries of broadcasting.[3] As *Editor and Publisher* put it, "Newspapers helped build the new plaything of the nation."[4]

Some of the larger, urban papers took their involvement with radio one step further, buying or affiliating with local stations. What were their motives? Initially these stations were seen not as channels of news delivery, but as promotional devices for the newspaper that owned them. When news bulletins were put on the air, they were brief, and always urged the listener to purchase the paper for the full story.[5] The advertising function served by these stations is evident from their call letters. For instance, WGN, the station of the *Chicago Tribune*, proudly announced that the *Tribune* was the "World's Greatest Newspaper."[6] For most of the early station-owning newspapers, station acquisition was motivated by self-promotion. The airwaves were simply another way of attracting potential readers.[7]

Just how many papers were linked with radio at this time is hard to say, exactly, because the figures vary significantly by year and source consulted. For example, the U.S. Department of Commerce reported that by the end of 1922 there were sixty-nine papers owning radio stations.[8] That same year, however, the American Newspaper Publisher's Association (ANPA) estimated that the number was over 100.[9] Nonetheless, it seems safe to say that of the roughly 500 stations on the air in the early to mid 1920s, somewhere between fifty and 100 stations were owned by or affiliated with newspapers. This represents, of course, only a small fraction of the nearly 1900 newspapers that were being published in the nation at the time.[10] Why were so few papers involved with radio? It was simply too expensive. The only newspapers that were able to afford an affiliation with radio tended to be the larger and more powerful papers of the country, such as *The Chicago Tribune*, *The Los Angeles Times*, *The Boston Post*, and *The Brooklyn Eagle*. In addition, most of the newspapers of the Hearst chain were linked in some way with radio stations.[11] Thus during the 1920s there were two groups of newspapers in the country, those with connections to radio, and those without. The majority of the nation's papers fell into the latter category, while the former group was composed of a handful of the larger, more powerful papers. This split would later become an important factor in the story of press-radio relations.

But in these early days, the relationship between radio and the press was quite amicable. Radio provided newspapers with a popular new topic to cover that drew readers. Newspapers provided the radio with free publicity, helping to create a new subculture of ham radio enthusiasts and informing the public about this new medium. The peaceful coexistence of these two media would not last long, however. As radio became more popular and began to move past the stage of being a mere hobby, forces within the journalism industry became concerned. What had started as an enjoyable pastime for young boys in their basements was becoming a medium to reckon with. It was not long before some journalists began to rethink their initial support of this new competition.

The Debate over Supplying Radio with News

By the mid-1920s many journalists were expressing concerns that radio posed a serious threat to their business. At first glance this may seem odd, because at this stage, the broadcasters were doing very little original news programming. While stations would occasionally cover special sporting events, parades, or political speeches,[12] they lacked the staff, equipment and funds required to do their own regular news gathering. This meant that there was no real competition between radio and newspapers at this point over the business of gathering and distributing news. Most broadcasters were quite dependent upon the newspaper industry for their news. A radio station that wanted to air a regularly scheduled newscast had only two real options. The first was to read the news directly from the pages of a newspaper, over the air. The problem with this was that it meant giving the public stale news that had already been published. The other alternative, if they wanted to air fresh news, was to turn to the wire services for news bulletins.

The prospect of wire service provision of news to radio was quite upsetting to some print journalists. It was this issue that evoked the initial anti-radio sentiments from the press. One of the earliest expressions of concern over this issue was in 1922, when the Associated Press issued a notice to its members informing them that AP news bulletins were not to be used for the purposes of broadcasting.[13] Not all print journalists, however, objected to giving radio wire service news bulletins. There were some who approved of the practice and willingly participated in it. Thus, at this stage, the Press-Radio War was really more of an intra- rather than an inter-institutional battle. On one side were those who felt that they stood to gain from an alliance with radio, and on the other were those who felt that they did not.

Two key factors determined the position of print journalists on the issue of radio during the early to mid-1920s. One was whether their newspaper was affiliated with a radio station. The other was the wire service to which their newspaper subscribed. It is not surprising that those papers that had financial ties to broadcasting tended to be in favor of providing radio with news. For these papers, the issue of being "scooped" by radio was not a concern. They simply used the news bulletins to promote their own paper, urging listeners to turn to the newspaper for further details on stories that broke over the air. Those newspapers without a radio affiliation, on the other hand, were opposed to wire service provision of news to radio. Since they had no opportunity to broadcast themselves, they were helpless in the face of this new medium that could air news faster than they could print it. They objected that if stations were allowed to air news bulletins, their own papers would be outdated by the time they hit the news stands.

The non-broadcasting newspapers were not the only ones, however, that objected to supplying radio with news bulletins. They were joined by the other group of anti-radio papers, those belonging to the Associated Press. There were three major wire services at this time: the Associated Press (AP), the United Press (UP) and International News Service (INS). The wire services themselves were split on the issue of radio. While the UP and INS were willing to supply the broadcasters with news, AP, the largest and most successful of the three, was not. The explanation for this difference in positions on the radio question lies in important structural differences between the organization and operation of the different wire services. The Associated Press is a collective news-gathering agency. Its papers are members of a cooperative system by which each paper contributes its own news and is then entitled to the news of all other papers on the system. AP news is therefore considered property of all AP member papers. UP and INS, on the other hand, did their own news gathering, and simply sold the bulletins to client papers.

These structural differences translated into very different positions on the issue of providing radio with news. For the Associated Press, the problem was that radio could bring news to the air faster than papers could publish it. This meant that if the AP allowed their bulletins to be broadcast, their member papers would be 'scooped' by their own news. These concerns can be heard, for example, in the words of one AP member, who complained that

> [t]he smaller newspaper cannot maintain a broadcasting station. Yet should important news develop in his circulation territory, it would be carried by wire to a broadcasting station of a larger member, and before he could be in type and on the street with the story, the radio public in his city would have it all. [14]

Clearly, then, the non-broadcasting members of the Associated Press had good reasons to object to the airing of AP copy. It was a practice that threatened to disrupt the long standing relationship between the Associated Press and its members.[15] The anti-radio camp was largely composed of smaller papers unable to own or affiliate with a radio station, and newspapers that were Associated Press members. Given the fact that the expenses involved with broadcasting were well beyond the reach of most papers, and given that the AP was by far the dominant wire service of the day, the majority of the nation's papers fell into the anti-radio camp.

Of course, if UP or INS provided radio with news, their newspaper clients would be similarly scooped. The difference, however, was that newspapers subscribing to these services had merely purchased the news bulletins. Unlike the AP members, they had not supplied any of their own news into the system, and thus had no proprietary claim over the bulletins. This gave the UP and INS a bit more freedom to negotiate with radio. Both of these wire services had a very compelling reason to offer their news to the broadcasters. It was a great way to compete with the larger and more powerful Associated Press. Since station-owning papers could not get news for their broadcasts from AP, they were forced to turn to one of the two other wire services. In addition, supplying these newspaper-owned stations with bulletins was seen as a way to promote good relations with these papers, in the hopes that they would then become loyal customers of these wire services. As Karl Bickel, head of the United Press put it, "Radio, if properly used, can be made a great asset for building good will with broadcasting newspapers."16

Indeed, the UP and INS were so confident of the promotional value of these news bulletins that they gave them to the stations for free, in exchange for on-air credit. This arrangement was described by H. V. Kaltenborn, one of the nation's first news commentators. Kaltenborn had a news program on WAHG, a station owned by the *Brooklyn Eagle*. As he put it, "I gave the United Press credit for important news stories and they seemed to regard that as sufficient *quid pro quo*. They were also negotiating with the *Brooklyn Eagle* for UP service and were creating good will." Apparently they were quite successful, for Kaltenborn claimed to have used nothing but UP service for his entire thirty years on the air.17

Initially, the Associated Press leadership sided with the non-broadcasting papers, stating that it was against AP policy to allow member papers to use AP news on the air. As early as 1922, the AP issued a notice to its 1200 members, observing that "it has escaped the attention of a few members that the broadcasting of news by wireless telephone and telegraph makes it possible for those to receive it who are not entitled to do so." The bulletin went on to remind all members that news of the Associated Press, "is delivered to members solely for publication in their newspapers, and that members shall not permit any other use to be made of it. Members are bound to supply their local news exclusively to the Associated Press and its members."18 This last point was particularly important. Not only were member papers forbidden from using AP wire service copy, but, since their own local news, gathered by their own staffs, was also considered AP property, even that news could not be aired. Failure to observe the rules could result in a fine, suspension of membership, or expulsion from the association.19

Violations did occur, and several papers were disciplined for breaking the rule.20 No action on the part of the AP, however, could prevent stations from obtaining news from the UP, INS, or any other source, which was the real weakness in the AP's position. This became clear in 1924, when a furor arose over the issue of broadcasting election returns.

A few weeks before the elections, the *Chicago Tribune* announced that it planned to challenge the Associated Press' policy of restricting news broadcasting by AP members. Claiming that the Associated Press was "attempting to monopolize news and prevent its dissemination by means of radio," the *Tribune* declared its intentions to air the election returns gathered by its own reporters.21 That same week, Karl Bickel, president of the United Press, announced that the UP would furnish election returns to its clients for broadcasting purposes, "in recognition of the fact that the era of radio had come." Noting the importance of national elections, Bickel explained that he felt it was the duty of a press association to provide the American people with election returns as quickly as possible. The policy of the UP was to permit "its client newspapers on events of great importance to use the radio."22 The International News Service took a similar position.

When it came time to broadcast on election night, the *Chicago Tribune* did not challenge the Associated Press policy, but joined 28 other papers, many of them AP members, in turning directly to the United Press for election returns to put on the air.23 Other newspaper-owned stations obtained their election returns through the International News Service or through their own arrangements with the headquarters of local political parties.24 Thus, the Associated Press' policy had backfired, leading some of its own members to turn to the competition for service.

The lesson of the 1924 elections was not lost on the Associated Press. Stations wishing to broadcast news would find a way to obtain it, and if they couldn't use AP copy, they'd get it somewhere else. When the members of the Associated Press came together in April 1925 for their annual meeting, they voted to modify the restriction on radio broadcasting. The resolution passed by the membership noted that the public's great interest in the results of the presidential elections, as well as other events of national importance, had "raised the question of the advisability and wisdom of permitting the limited and restricted use of Associated Press matter in the broadcasting of such special and outstanding events." It was therefore resolved that the AP would henceforth "permit the broadcast of such news of the Association as it shall deem of transcendent, national and international importance, and which cannot by its very nature be exclusive..." The resolution concluded with the requirement that in the case of such broadcasts, it was imperative that "proper credit in each and every instance be accorded the Associated Press."25

In the first round of the struggle over what to do about radio news, the pro-radio journalists were clearly the winners. The Associated Press had adopted a modified version of the policies of the United Press and the International News Service, thus serving the interests of the station-owning papers. This new position would hold through the end of the 1920s. The 1928 presidential elections were marked by a relative absence of overt tension between radio and the newspapers. While there was some conflict once again within the ranks of the Associated Press over the wisdom of cooperating with radio, [26] all three wire services did air election returns in exchange for on-air credit.

Although the 1925 resolution solved the problem for a short time, the deeper split dividing the two groups of journalists had not been healed. The bigger question of what to do about radio remained unsolved. Battle lines were drawn between those newspapers that had a vested interest in promoting radio news and those that did not. The great division between these two camps over the issue of providing radio with news bulletins was noted by a number of journalists at the time. An ANPA Radio Committee Report explained, for example, that "[n]ewspapers owning their own broadcasting stations believe this practice does not hurt the quality or freshness of the news," while "the vast bulk of newspapers are unwilling to have the freshness of their news destroyed."[27]

Frank Miller, editor of the *South Bend Tribune* observed that "the viewpoint of a newspaper publisher on the issue of radio news is influenced by the possession or non-possession of a broadcasting station."[28]   Similarly, *Editor and Publisher* noted that when the topic of radio came up, "*the usual abyss of opinion between newspapers which operate their own stations and those which have no radio relations was apparent.*"[29]

Ultimately, this split caused Elezy Roberts, the ANPA Radio Committee chair, to resign in 1932, frustrated over his inability to bring the two camps to some sort of agreement. Roberts felt that "it is idle to oppose radio while so many newspapers are themselves engaged in it or striving to get into the field."[30] In his letter of resignation Roberts complained that the ANPA was divided into two groups, with the radio-owning newspapers having the dominant influence over the association's policies, "not owing to numbers but to activity." He predicted that "until these two groups admit the dissimilarity of their interests and desire to go their separate ways, I see no hope of protective action on radio by the ANPA."[31]

Roberts was right. There were two camps, and two positions over the issue of radio. They were divided because their interests lay in different places. Only common concerns could bring them together, which is exactly what happened in the next stage of the Press-Radio War. Within a year of Roberts' resignation, in fact, these groups agreed to put aside their differences and unify against radio. But it was an alliance that would not last. The conflict between the two camps would continue to hinder the efforts of the anti-radio publishers to block the growing competition from radio, and would contribute to their eventual loss of the Press-Radio War.

STAGE TWO: UNITY AND ACTION

While the rift between the different groups of journalists would never disappear, there was a brief period when the various factions within the journalistic community agreed to set aside their differences and truly wage war against radio. During the early 1930s a number of forces converged to bring the print journalists together, allowing them to pool their energies to fight against radio, rather than among themselves. This second stage of the Press-Radio War was one of unity and action, in which the various factions of the press came together to move against their now common enemy, radio.

One crucial factor that helped unite the journalists was the Depression. Prior to the crash there had been little serious talk about radio as a real economic threat because newspapers were doing fairly well during the 1920s. The economy was strong and there seemed to be enough ad revenue to go around for everyone. But that all changed. Newspapers, like most businesses of the time, were hard hit by the severe economic conditions. Advertising revenue began to fall rapidly, and continued to plummet for several years. Between 1929 and 1933, estimated annual advertising revenue for the nation's newspapers was cut almost in half, dropping from a national total of $800 million before October 1929, down to $450 million in 1933.[32] Suddenly, with the nation in an economic crisis, radio began to look like a very real threat indeed, one with which newspapers would have to compete for the rapidly dwindling advertising dollar.

To make matters worse, while everyone else was losing money, radio, which had been in a period of steady growth and expansion throughout the 1920s, continued to enjoy an increase in profits during the first few years of the Depression. In the first three years after the crash, the estimated annual advertising revenue for radio doubled, from $40 million per year in 1929 to $80 million in 1932.[33] Although radio would eventually be moderately affected by the economic slump as well, it never suffered the degree of revenue loss that newspapers experienced during the same time period.[34] This disparity between the two media during a period of severe economic hardship deepened a growing rift. Those journalists who already had several arguments against broadcasting now had another very compelling reason to feel quite hostile toward this new medium.

The growing economic competition between radio and the press, however, was not the only source of friction between radio and the press. Other key events of this time also served to heighten the tension, such as the kidnapping of Charles and Anne Morrow Lindbergh's infant son on March 1, 1932, and the attempted assassination of President-elect Franklin D. Roosevelt almost exactly one year later. In addition to marking the boundaries of what would be a pivotal year in press-radio relations, these two events had several important things in common. Both involved violence toward public figures, both were major news stories on which radio scooped the newspapers, and both served to further aggravate the relationship between the two media. Given the economic climate facing newspapers at the time, being beaten by the broadcasters on stories with the potential to boost circulation was not good news.

The Lindbergh baby kidnapping was a particularly crucial event in the story of press-radio relations because it was one of the first major news events that radio covered on its own, without help or bulletins from the press. While there had been some live coverage of sporting events, parades and political speeches, this was much more of a hard news story, involving a kidnapping and a murder. At this point neither the networks nor most independent stations had their own news divisions, but when news of the kidnapping came over the wires, the broadcasters responded immediately. The celebrity status of the baby's father ensured that this would be a big story, and radio was there to cover it. In fact, the nationwide coverage radio provided during the initial days after the kidnapping was one of the first real national debuts of serious broadcast journalism.

Radio stations from the New York area sent members of their press-relations staff, many of whom were former newspaper reporters, to the Lindbergh estate in New Jersey to cover the story. The radio coverage was continuous and extensive. Radio reporters maintained a vigil for days, with local and network stations broadcasting hundreds of bulletins in the first week after the child was taken.[35] The press was not pleased about all of this. They criticized the quality of coverage and accused the announcers of failing to adhere to professional journalistic standards in their reporting of the tragedy. They also complained that the extensive radio coverage of the event was cutting into newspaper sales.[36] That the broadcast coverage of the kidnapping increased the level of hostility on the part of print journalists toward radio was evident from comments that appeared in *Editor and Publisher* in the weeks following the kidnapping. One article noted that the "problem of spot news broadcasting" and the "*amount of harm caused by the frequent radio bulletins on the Lindbergh story*" were the focus of increasing debate among newspaper executives.[37] Another observed that "*the situation* [between newspapers and radio] *has been aggravated by the recent spot broadcasting of news of the Lindbergh kidnapping* by radio corporations with announcers at the scene of the activity."[38]   Later that year another event further exacerbated what was becoming an increasingly volatile situation. The fall of 1932 brought another presidential election, and with it came a revival of old questions regarding the provision of news to the networks. This time, however, a complex dance took place among the various press associations as each jockeyed to see the position the other would take on the issue. Once again the split between the AP and the other two wire services was an important theme, but this time there was evidence that formerly pro-radio journalists were beginning to shift their position.

Four years earlier, the election returns had been provided to the broadcasters by all three wire services. But that was before the crash, before the Lindbergh kidnapping, and before the networks began making so much money. By the election of 1932, many print journalists were beginning to have a change of heart about giving the returns to radio for free. The United Press, in particular, decided it was time to charge the broadcasters for its services. A month before the elections the United Press went to the networks and offered to sell them the returns for the nominal fee of $1,000. NBC officials declined the offer, saying they felt the arrangement of 1928 should be continued. The Associated Press let it be known that their news was not available to any chain that purchased news from another service.[39]

CBS accepted the United Press proposal, but then the UP had second thoughts. After consulting a number of its clients, the United Press decided that unless the broadcasters paid a much higher fee, one that more realistically reflected the costs of gathering and distributing the returns, it would be financially unfeasible to provide radio with the election service.[40] A week before the elections, UP said that it would supply election returns only if the network agreed to pay 50 percent of the election coverage costs. The fee, which was expected to be somewhere between $35,000 and $60,000, "would be applied to cutting down the extra charges publishers must pay for election service."[41] Not surprisingly, CBS declined the offer. At this point, with the elections just days away, neither of the networks had arrangements set up for election night. The International News Service was no longer an option either, having decided to follow the example of the United Press, stating flatly that "it would neither sell nor give its service to radio." According to INS president J. V. Connolly, INS had decided that it "had no business furnishing material to the radio that could be used in competition with the client newspapers."[42] Clearly, by this point, both INS and UP had had a significant change of heart on the issue of providing radio with news.

What followed was a rather comical, confused sequence of events. Once it was clear that no press associations would be receiving a fee for providing radio with election news, the Associated Press made a last-minute offer to give the returns to the broadcasters for free. Upon hearing about this, United Press reconsidered its position, for although UP didn't want to anger its client papers, it also did not want the AP to walk away with all the credit.[43] On election night, the United Press printers, already installed in network headquarters, were "mysteriously" turned on. As it turned out, INS reports were also aired, because, as a back-up plan, CBS had made an arrangement with the *New York Evening Journal*, a paper that obtained some of its election service through the International News Service.[44]

Thus in the end, just as in 1928, the election returns from all three wire services were aired by the networks. This time, however, all of the press associations had displayed far more ambivalence in handling the coverage. This new ambivalence was a symptom of the increasing hostility toward radio on the part of journalists associated with all three wire services. The longstanding split between the different wire services was beginning to heal. The confusion over the 1932 election coverage marks the beginnings of the shift from the first to the second stage of the Press-Radio War. The internal conflict that had divided the different groups of journalists in stage one was beginning to resolve. The two camps were starting to move toward unity. Once they were all on the same side, in opposition to radio, they would be free to take action.

At this point, however, no internal consensus had been reached. For in the end, all three wire services did decide to provide the returns, much to the displeasure of many journalists around the country. The Associated Press, in particular, was inundated with hostile letters from its member papers.[45] The letters, many of which came from small newspapers, complained that by providing news of the elections to the broadcasters, the AP "had entered its service into direct competition with member newspapers."[46] In response to the flood of protests that came in following the provision of election returns to the networks, the Associated Press conducted a poll of its members to determine the extent of their opposition to radio newscasting.[47]   The poll brought an enormous response, with replies received from over 90 percent of the domestic members of the Associated Press. The results were quite revealing. Over 70 percent responded by stating that they were opposed to supplying the broadcasting chains with AP bulletins, even on occasions of "transcendent importance." It is not surprising that those opposed to providing radio with news were the smaller papers, without ties to radio.[48] Since all papers, large and small, held equal power in voting on matters of this kind, the results of this survey predicted fairly clearly what the outcome would be when the membership brought this issue to a vote at its annual meeting in April.

The ANPA also received complaints from its membership on the way the election coverage was handled. In response, the ANPA board announced the formation of a nationwide committee with the purpose of formulating "a united newspaper policy in regard to radio competition." In an effort to bring the different groups of publishers together around the negotiating table, the committee was made up of representatives from both broadcasting and non-broadcasting newspapers. It was hoped that "through this large nation-wide committee the groups of publishers without radio affiliation and those with them may be brought closer together."[49] Here, at last, was the first attempt at alliance building within the journalistic community around the issue of radio. It seems to have worked, for only a few weeks after the formation of the new committee on radio, the ANPA board of directors announced that it had adopted a series of resolutions on the issue of radio.

The resolutions recommended that press associations neither sell nor give news bulletins to radio in advance of their publication in newspapers. They also suggested that papers owning or affiliated with stations should limit their use of news on the radio to brief bulletins, and that proper credit should always be given on the air to the appropriate news-gathering organization. In addition, the ANPA urged publishers to take any legal action necessary to protect their property rights in the news.[50] These recommendations were intended as a guide for the formation of more official policies when the AP and ANPA had their annual meetings the following spring.[51] Clearly, the tide had turned in press-radio relations. A committee made up of journalists from both "sides" had been able to work together, and more important, it had devised a set of policies that was firmly in the interest of the non-broadcasting newspapers. The time was finally ripe for the journalists of the nation to unite against radio. They expressed enthusiastic support for the ANPA's anti-radio resolutions and urged more formal action. As Joseph Daniel, editor of the *Raleigh News and Observer*, put it, "The question [of radio] should have first place on the agenda at the spring meetings of the ANPA and Associated Press."[52]

Just prior to the much anticipated annual meetings in April, several more events contributed to the ever growing tensions between radio and the press. All of them, appropriately enough, involved Franklin Roosevelt, the man who would come to be known as the "radio president." The first was the attempted assassination of the president-elect in Miami, just before his inauguration in March 1933. On the night of the shooting, Roosevelt excused the team of reporters that had been traveling with him, assuring them that he would say nothing but pleasantries at the reception he would be attending that night, and told them to catch up with him later that evening at the train station. As a result, the print journalists were all at the train depot when an assassin's bullet narrowly missed Roosevelt, wounding the mayor of Chicago instead. Only a local radio station was there, covering the event live. A CBS official, Ed Cohan, vacationing in Florida, happened to be driving nearby in a car equipped with a short-wave radio. Listening to the broadcast of the reception ceremony, he heard the sounds of the gunfire and the local announcer describing the   scene. He quickly phoned CBS headquarters, and within minutes the news was broadcast over a nationwide hookup, hours before any newspaper could publish the story.[53] Radio had scooped the newspaper on a story of true national and political significance.

Soon after his narrow escape, Roosevelt was sworn into office, with radio listeners across the country tuned in to the   broadcast. The press was quite concerned about this extensive radio coverage and made a special effort to do a very thorough job of handling the inauguration because newspapers knew they were competing with radio. In an article headlined "Press Coverage of Inauguration Spurred by Radio Plans," Washington correspondent George Manning noted that "the knowledge that radio will play a large part in the inauguration is keying up members of the press corps here to their highest notch of efficiency and speed." [54] The following week Roosevelt reached out to a national audience in the first of what would become a regular series of "fireside chats." A new era had dawned in American politics. Important news involving the president of the United States could now reach the people without the help of the newspapers. National leaders could now bypass the press and go directly to the public. This disruption in the established flow of political information was quite disturbing to many journalists, as will be discussed further in Chapter 5.

"War" Is Declared

April finally came, and the nation's journalists gathered in Washington for the annual meetings of the Associated Press and the American Newspaper Publisher's Association. After years of internal conflict over the radio question, the events of the previous year, in combination with the worsening national economy, had finally persuaded the various factions within the press to take a unified position against radio. Following the meeting, *Broadcasting* magazine announced in no uncertain terms that a new stage in press-radio relations had begun. The front-page banner headline declared: "AP and ANPA

Declare War on Radio."[55] After what was reported to be a very heated debate, the majority of the Associated Press members voted to cease supplying the networks with news of any kind. In addition, they decided that member papers would have to limit their newscasts to occasional, unsponsored, thirty-word bulletins. Any member paper engaged in local broadcasting would henceforth be charged an additional assessment.[56] For its part in this "declaration of war," the ANPA issued a resolution that henceforth radio program logs would be treated as advertising matter and would be published only when paid for.[57] Prior to this, many newspapers had printed the program logs as a service to their readers, without charging the broadcasters.[58]

Despite the *Broadcasting* headline that both the AP and the ANPA had declared war on radio, it was actually the AP decision that was of real significance. The Associated Press resolution was mandatory, and all AP members were obliged to follow the rules or suffer fines or expulsion from the association. The ANPA resolution, on the other hand, was merely a recommendation. Since the ANPA had no power to govern the behavior of its members, the resolution carried weight only as the "official opinion" of the body as a whole. Furthermore, since the ANPA had passed similar resolutions in the past about the treatment of program logs, there was no reason to believe that this one would be any more binding.[59]

Initially, even the AP resolution had little effect because, at first, both UP and INS were still providing broadcasters with bulletins. But soon, facing pressure from their non-broadcasting customers, these two wire services followed the lead of the Associated Press and placed similar restrictions on the use of their news by their customers. They also stopped selling news directly to stations.[60] At last all forces within the institution of print journalism had aligned themselves against their common enemy. The various wire services and newspapers with and without ties to broadcasting had united against radio. The war had truly begun.

Cut off from the wire services, the networks and independent radio stations now faced three options when it came to news: (1) They could simply abandon the practice of providing regular newscasts; (2) They could "steal" the news from the newspapers; or 3) They could start doing their own news gathering. Some stations took the first option. For example, a few weeks after the AP voted to stop providing stations with news, the *Indianapolis Star* announced that it was discontinuing its evening newscasts, explaining that the brief bulletins it was still allowed to air were insufficient to provide listeners with satisfactory service.[61] There were at least a few instances in which other broadcasters risked the second option, and "lifted" the news from the newspapers or directly off the wires, only to be met with lawsuits charging them with violation of property rights.[62] The networks opted for the third choice: gathering the news on their own. This was the development that would finally bring the tensions between the two industries to their peak.

During the summer of 1933, both networks began to develop their own methods of obtaining news, relying heavily on "the newspaper trained members of their publicity and spot news broadcasting staffs."[63] CBS established a full-scale news division, the Columbia News Service, with bureaus in New York, Washington, Chicago, Los Angeles, and London, under the leadership of Paul White, a former United Press editor.[64] According to *Broadcasting*, the formation of this news division was "a direct answer by CBS to the recent edict of the Associated Press, which the other press associations are following."[65]

At NBC, efforts were on a smaller scale. Instead of establishing a news division, NBC assigned a few people to the job of getting news to put on the air. Most of it was handled by one man, Abe Schechter. Like his counterpart at CBS, Paul White, Schechter also had a background in print journalism. Working almost exclusively by telephone, he became a one-man news organization, single-handedly gathering the material for Lowell Thomas' newscasts. Schechter got his stories through the extensive network of contacts he developed with key city, government, and publicity heads. He discovered that by placing a call and identifying himself as speaking for the News Department at NBC, he could "get practically anyone on the telephone," even while newspaper reporters waited unsuccessfully outside closed doors for an official statement. With such direct access to sources, it was not unusual for NBC to scoop the papers even on major stories.[66]

The response to this new competition from the press was less than enthusiastic. While NBC's small operation was not viewed with much concern, the large-scale nature of the growing news organization at CBS was another matter. Edward Harris, chair of the ANPA Radio Committee, announced that the establishment of the CBS news service indicated that "a general attack has been launched by broadcasters against newspapers."[67] In response to this perceived threat, many papers stopped publishing CBS's program listings, while continuing to print those of other stations.[68] Despite the ANPA resolution in April, many papers were still publishing radio program logs at this point, and they could therefore still use the threat of withholding the logs as a weapon. In addition, both networks were placed under strict observation, with press associations and leading newspapers keeping stenographic records of broadcasts to determine whether any news items had been stolen from the press.[69]

Further indication of just how threatened the newspapers felt came when CBS filed an application with the National Press Club in Washington requesting that its radio reporters be given admission to the Congressional Press Galleries. Since the regulations of the National Press Club specified that only persons representing "daily newspapers or newspaper associations" could be allowed access to the galleries, an amendment to the rules would be necessary to include the broadcasters. For many print journalists, the concept of sharing the press gallery with broadcasters was unacceptable. So strongly did they feel about this matter that they launched a protest campaign. Over 100 letters and telegrams from print journalists around the country poured into Washington objecting to the proposed amendment. The campaign was successful: the appeal from CBS was denied.[70] The doors to the Congressional Press Gallery would remain closed to radio until August 1939, when, after another appeal, the broadcasters were finally granted admission and a separate Radio Gallery was opened for their use.[71] But by then, the hostilities between radio and the press were essentially over.

In the fall of 1933, however, the battle was far from over. Tensions were so high that by early December, only a few months after they had truly begun their own news-gathering efforts, the broadcasters sued for peace. The appeal came in the form of a telegram from CBS president William Paley to the representatives of the ANPA National Radio Committee. Paley requested a meeting between representatives of the networks and representatives of the publishers for the purpose of ending "the long standing dispute as to news broadcasting." He suggested that perhaps it would be possible to work out a plan "whereby the broadcasters may have access to news without gathering it themselves and under arrangements that would be mutually satisfactory."[72] The ANPA accepted the invitation, and plans for a meeting were quickly made.

The Biltmore Agreement

On December 11 and 12, 1933, a conference between representatives from the broadcasting and newspaper industries was held at the Hotel Biltmore in New York City. Present at the meeting were the presidents of both networks and representatives from the three wire services, the ANPA and the National Association of Broadcasters.[73] After two days of negotiations, most of those at the meeting agreed upon a plan that would come to be known as "the Biltmore Agreement," or, "the Press-Radio Plan." It was hoped that this plan would satisfy the needs of the broadcasters for news bulletins while protecting the interests of the press.[74] The points of the agreement are outlined in Figure 2.

In essence, The Biltmore Agreement was a plan by which the broadcasters agreed to cease gathering their own news in exchange for a limited bulletin service to be provided by the wire services, with restrictions to prevent these news broadcasts from competing in any way with the newspapers. Just why the networks sued for peace, and why they agreed to such a one-sided plan is explored in Chapter 4. While the majority of those attending the meeting expressed their willingness to participate in the plan, there was no formal signing of an agreement. This was on the advice of ANPA lawyer Elisha Hanson, who warned of the danger that the plan might be attacked as an "agreement in restraint of trade."[75] Thus, it was decided that the plan would be carried out on instead on a purely "*modus operandi* basis," that is, an arrangement enforceable only by the good faith of all parties.[76]

Although the publishers obtained agreement to the plan from the two networks, they were not as successful in gaining compliance from the independent stations. The president of the National Association of Broadcasters, Alfred McCosker, representing the independents at the meeting, said that he could not commit the NAB to the plan until he consulted with the membership. Thus, when the Administrative Committee overseeing the activities of the PRB was established, a seat was left open for a representative

Figure 2
Main Points of the Biltmore Agreement

1. The networks were to cease gathering their own news. CBS would dismantle its news-gathering service and NBC would refrain from developing one.

2. In exchange, the three wire services would each provide brief news bulletins that would be rewritten into radio news announcements by the Press-Radio Bureau (PRB). The PRB would be a kind of central clearing house that would receive the news bulletins from the wire services and would create from them the newscasts, that would then be given to the broadcasters.

3. A number of rules would govern the use of this news:

  * The PRB bulletins could total no longer than five minutes in length.

  * The morning bulletins could not be aired before 9:30 A.M., and the evening bulletins could only be aired after 9 P.M., well after the morning and evening editions of the papers were on the newsstands.

  * The bulletins could not be aired with commercial sponsorship.

4. The broadcasters would pay the costs of the PRB.

5. In the event of news of "transcendent importance," the bureau was authorized to issue special bulletins, urging listeners to consult the newspapers for further details.

6. Radio commentators were prohibited from covering headlines or any material less than twelve hours old, and their presentations had to be limited to "generalization and background of general news situations." They were also required to eliminate "the practice of the recital of spot news."

7. Newspaper-owned stations were to limit their broadcasting of news "on a basis comparable to the schedule set up for the radio chains."

8. The Press-Radio Plan would be administered by a committee consisting of representatives from each of the publishing and broadcasting organizations that agreed to be a part of the plan. All actions of the committee would be subject to the approval of the ANPA Radio Committee.[77]

from the NAB.[78] As the NAB annual meeting was not to take place until the following September, the Press-Radio Bureau would start without the participation of the independent stations. Ultimately, the independent stations never did agree to the conditions of the Biltmore program, a fact that would contribute greatly to its eventual failure.

The Press-Radio Bureau and Its Competition

Despite the fact that it seemed as if the newspapers had won, there were serious problems with the Press-Radio Plan. One was the fact the independent stations had not consented to it. Since only 150 of the 600 stations in the country were network-owned or affiliated, this gave the independents tremendous power to help bring about the dissolution of the Press-Radio Bureau. The other limitation of the plan was that it had no power to prevent the emergence of new, independent news services willing to provide the independent stations with news on their own terms.

On March 1, 1934, the PRB began operations out of New York City, under the direction of James W. Barnett, former city editor of the *New York World*. Starting with 125 network subscribers when it first went on the air, the bureau was serving over 160 stations within six months.[79] The daily task of the small staff of writers working under Barnett was to take the AP, UP, and INS wire service copy and create two five-minute newscasts that would then be used by the networks.[80]   Each newscast consisted of about twenty bulletins of approximately thirty words a piece.[81] According to the terms of the Press-Radio agreement, the bulletins were to be written "in such a manner as to stimulate public interest in the reading of newspapers."[82]

By the time its first bulletins were on the air, however, the Bureau already had competition. The independent stations, unwilling to participate in the Press-Radio Plan, needed a new source for their news, and several independent news-gathering agencies quickly formed to fill the vacuum. These were essentially wire services for radio, consisting of teams of reporters who gathered their own news and provided bulletins to the broadcasters by telegraph and teletype. Unlike the PRB, these services placed no limitations on the time of day the newscasts could be aired, and did not prohibit the stations from airing the news with commercials.

By April 1934, a number of these independent services in operation: the Yankee Network in Boston, the Continental Radio News Service in Washington, and the Radio News Association in Los Angeles. The most successful, however, was the Transradio Press Service. Transradio was founded by Herbert Moore, a former United Press writer who, until the Press-Radio Plan, had been the news editor at CBS. When operations at CBS were discontinued as part of the Biltmore Agreement, Moore organized many of the former CBS news staff into a highly successful, independent news-gathering organization. Backed by several major financial investors, Moore was able to establish a large-scale operation. Within nine months of commencing operations, he claimed to have reporters in all key cities and stringers in over 700 smaller towns, correspondents in many major European and Central American capitals, and over 150 stations subscribing to his service.[83]

The committee in charge of the Press-Radio Bureau took several steps in response to the growing competition. One was to establish a second branch of the Bureau on the West Coast. This second office, based in Los Angeles, was created to "fight west coast independent radio stations which are broadcasting news in opposition to the ANPA agreement," by offering West Coast subscribers a substantial savings in the cost of the long-distance wire tolls.[84] Furthermore, various aspects of the Biltmore Agreement were amended to allow the Press-Radio Bureau to compete more effectively against the independent stations. Rules regarding the length of the bulletins and the time of day in which they could be broadcast were relaxed.[85] So too were the policies regarding the conditions under which special bulletins could be released. As H. V. Kaltenborn put it, the creation of the independent radio news services forced the Bureau to liberalize its news policy, "leading to a more broad-minded interpretation of the word "transcendent" in connection with exceptional news stories."[86]

In addition to competition from the independent stations, the Press-Radio Bureau had another challenge to face during its first year of operations: an enemy in Washington. Senator Clarence Dill, one of the authors of both the 1927 Radio Act and the newly passed 1934 Communications Act, took a strong stand against the Bureau. Dill's complaint was that the Biltmore Agreement was far too one-sided, and that in consenting to it, the networks had surrendered their "birthright" to freely broadcast the news. He argued that the newspaper chains and wire services had a monopolistic control over the flow of news and accused the print journalists of abusing press freedom. The solution, and the key to continued public service in the realm of news, he concluded, lay in the formation of an independent, national wire service exclusively for radio.[87] His plan was to establish an organization structured along the lines of the Associated Press, a non-profit radio wire service that would be owned and run by the member stations. So dedicated to this plan was he that Dill announced he would not seek re-election and would step down from public office to start this new radio news service instead.[88]

While Dill's proposal received overwhelming support from the nation's broadcasters,[89] the journalists responded with hostility and anger.[90] The proposed radio news service was attacked as "repugnant to Americanism," and there were complaints that since broadcasters are under the jurisdiction of the Federal Communications Commission (FCC) and dependent upon the federal government for the renewal of their licenses, a national radio news service would be nothing less than a government-controlled news service and was therefore highly unacceptable.[91] As it turned out, Dill's plan for a national radio news service never materialized. Before he had a chance to begin putting it into motion, several key members of the Biltmore Agreement began to back out of the arrangement. With the fall of the Press Radio Bureau, the senator's proposal was superfluous.

STAGE THREE: ALLIANCE AND ACQUISITION

In the first stage of the Press-Radio War, the conflict was largely between two different groups of journalists: those who stood to gain from the development of radio news, and those for whom the new competition was a threat. In the second stage, as discussed, these different camps put aside their differences to unite in action against radio, which had come to be seen by the majority of the nation's press as a common enemy. This internal unity did not last for long, however. Within little more than a year after the establishment of the Press-Radio Bureau, there were signs that old tensions between the different groups of journalists over radio were re-emerging. Thus began the third phase of the Press-Radio War. In this stage, press unity on the issue of radio rapidly disintegrated. As the benefits of working with rather than against radio became more apparent, the stance of many journalists toward radio shifted from a position of hostility to one of alliance and acquisition.

By the spring of 1935, there were signs that a growing number of broadcasters and publishers were becoming increasingly dissatisfied with the Biltmore Agreement. As the independent radio news services brought in more and more advertising, those wire services and newspapers that were adhering to the terms of the Agreement prohibiting the sponsorship of news found themselves excluded from this new source of revenue. At this point the old split between the different groups of journalists reappeared. On one side was the Associated Press and the non-broadcasting newspapers, which were still staunchly opposed to providing radio with news or allowing the bulletins of the Press-Radio Bureau to be aired with commercials. On the other side were the station-owning papers, along with the United Press and the International News Service. For this group, selling news to sponsors was an increasingly attractive prospect, that promised to bring in new income. Given the state of the economy at the time, any additional source of money was welcome; thus, forming an economic alliance with the broadcasters was once again becoming quite appealing.

Just prior to the annual meetings of the AP and ANPA that year, there were rumblings that the United Press and International News Service were interested in modifying the Biltmore Agreement to permit sponsorship of the news bulletins. Similar suggestions were coming from the station-owning papers.[92] There was also discussion of the possibility that the UP and INS might drop out of the Press-Radio Bureau altogether in order to free themselves to compete directly with Transradio Press and the other independent radio news services.[93] When the ANPA members met that spring, they modified the rules governing the Press-Radio Bureau, increasing the amount of news available to subscribers and the frequency with which such news could be aired.[94] The Radio Committee took a strong stand, however, against commercial sponsorship of news, continuing its staunch opposition to the practice.

This left the United Press and International New Service with little choice but to take matters into their own hands. Within a month the two services announced that they had changed their policies and that their newspaper clients could now use UP and INS news bulletins for commercially sponsored newscasts.[95] Soon this offer was extended to all radio stations, even those not affiliated with newspapers. Now these two wire services were free to compete with the independent radio news services for the advertising revenue that could be earned through selling news for broadcasting. By late July, the United Press was claiming nearly forty clients.[96]

In addition to the formation of wire service alliances with radio, another shift took place during this period: An increasing number of newspapers began to buy or affiliate with radio stations. The longstanding division between broadcasting and non-broadcasting newspapers had returned once again, but this time, more newspapers chose acquisition over antagonism. As radio commentator Boake Carter put it, "Today keen newspaper publishers have switched their ground. Instead of now trying to block radio news they are acquiring as many radio stations as they can lay their hands on."[97] In the period between 1934, when the Press-Radio Bureau began, and 1938, when it was disbanded, the number of newspaper-owned or affiliated stations more than doubled, from 100 to 211.[98] This was a jump from approximately 15 percent to nearly 30 percent of the total stations in the country having ties to newspapers. In the year 1936 alone, the FCC approved nearly twice as many newspaper stations as it had during the previous year.[99] During this period numerous papers made the choice to control radio by owning it, and when the UP and INS began selling news to radio, these new paper-owned stations were there as customers.

Once the UP and INS abandoned the Biltmore Agreement, it was not long before others followed suit. Soon the networks were expressing interest in offering advertisers the opportunity to sponsor newscasts. While CBS and NBC agreed to continue using Press Radio Bureau news without sponsorship on their affiliated stations, both networks began negotiating with UP and INS to purchase news for sponsorship over their owned and operated stations in order to compete against the Transradio Press in certain cities.[100] By the end of June 1935, CBS had signed a deal with the United Press, arranging for five of its owned and operated stations to receive full news reports to be used in sponsored newscasts.[101] The print journalists' united front against radio had crumbled, and the networks were departing from the original terms of the Biltmore Agreement. It was just a matter of time before the entire agreement was abandoned.[102]

By the end of the summer, the Pacific Coast office of the Press-Radio Bureau had ceased operations. Things were starting to break down rapidly. The decision on the part of the UP and INS to sell news directly to radio had "nullified, in great measure" the attempt to make the Press-Radio Bureau a "panacea for press-radio ills."[103] In the spring of 1936, Edward Harris made one last attempt to keep the fight alive by encouraging journalists to bring pressure against the INS and UP to reverse their policy. He made an impassioned speech before the Pennsylvania Newspaper Publishers' Association, recommending that publishers dealing with either the UP or INS insist on a contractual clause ensuring that news purchased from these press associations would not be sold to radio.[104] His efforts were unsuccessful. The tide had shifted, and too many of the papers using the news of these two wire services were involved in broadcasting with no intention of giving up a lucrative source of advertising revenue.[105]   The alliance between the different groups of journalists was broken. The pro-radio faction, it seems, had abandoned the fight, and without its support, the war was essentially over.

By the following spring, at the annual AP and ANPA meetings, the change in relations between radio and the press was quite evident. Radio received far less focus at these gatherings than it had in previous years. As *Broadcasting* described it, there was "hardly a word raised against the 'broadcast menace' that aroused such serious antagonisms and bitter debates in previous sessions."[106] While the ANPA membership did vote to continue the Press-Radio Bureau for another year, it seemed that the major tensions had come to an end. A year later it was clear that the war between the two institutions had truly ended. In the spring of 1937, the headlines in *Broadcasting* announced, "Newspapers End Antagonism to Radio," explaining that the publishers and editors had accepted radio as an "established institution." Indeed, the annual meetings that year were described as being "noteworthy in their lack of critical outbursts against radio" in contrast with the "decidedly antagonistic attitude towards radio" that had characterized previous gatherings.[107]

The Press-Radio Bureau, which by this point was being supplied with bulletins only by the Associated Press, finally "died quietly" in December 1938.[108] The obituary for the Bureau took the form of a small, four-paragraph column that ran in *Editor and Publisher* under the headline "Networks Discontinue Press-Radio News." The article offered no explanation as to why this decision had been made but noted that the networks were now obtaining their news from   UP and INS.[109] Finally, in the spring of 1939,   the Associated Press lifted its ban on the sale of AP news for sponsored broadcasts.[110] That same year, broadcast journalists were at last given access to their own radio galleries in Congress. By this point war had begun in Europe and radio was beginning to make its own name in news coverage, with Edward R. Murrow and William Shirer broadcasting live reports from the battlefields. It was not long before both networks re-established their own news divisions. The Press-Radio War was over.

Why the Press Lost the War

Why did the publishers seemingly abandon the fight that they had initiated? There are several reasons. One was the virtual unenforceability of the Biltmore plan. Since it was never a signed agreement, none of the players involved in its formation were legally bound to cooperate with its implementation. The effects of this became evident when the United Press and the International News Service decided to pull out of the deal. Furthermore, in many ways, the plan was doomed from the start when its originators failed to gain the cooperation of the independent radio stations. Since the independents outnumbered the network-affiliated stations by a margin of three to one, they had the power necessary to thwart the print journalists' attempt to retain control over radio news. Without the participation of the independent stations in the Press-Radio Plan, there was no real way it could work. The independents' need for news created the market for Transradio Press and the other radio wire services, and in order to compete with these independent radio news services, UP and INS defected from the alliance. Thus, the independent stations were the real Achilles heel of the plan.

Another factor contributing to the dissolution of the plan was most certainly the economy. Given the hard times facing broadcasters and publishers alike in the early 1930s, the prohibition against selling the Press-Radio Bureau's news bulletins for sponsorship could not have made participation in the plan particularly appealing. Taking news from any of the independent radio services, or, later, from UP and INS, provided a new stream of advertising revenue, something that was much needed at this time.

Finally, the re-emergence of the longstanding split between the broadcasting and non-broadcasting newspapers was a key factor. Similarly, the organizational and structural differences between the Associated Press and its competitors, UP and INS, made it highly unlikely that the Biltmore Agreement could have been upheld for very long. The different camps of journalists simply had different stakes in the radio game. It was not possible for them to preserve the internal alliance that they had achieved in their brief attempt at unity. And without internal unity they could not effectively wage war against the competition. Ultimately, the collapse of the print journalists' united front contributed significantly to their loss of the battle with radio news.

Although for a time the various factions within the journalistic community had been able to put aside their differences and wage war on the new competing medium, it was an alliance that was not to last. The war between two media disintegrated as old conflicts on one side of the battlefield returned to divide the attacking forces. The intra-industry split between the broadcasting and non-broadcasting journalists proved too deep to heal. There was just too much money to be made in radio. Trying to block technological progress in communication had proven futile. Clearly, the only way to beat radio was to own it, or at least join in and invest in the development of a medium that was obviously not going away. Those with the means to make the investment in broadcasting were no longer willing to stand aside and let somebody else enjoy the profits.

This chapter has traced the story of the Press-Radio War. The tale reveals that battles of institutional self-defense may be fought in a sequence of stages. During each stage the established media institution is engaged in an attempt to respond to the changing communication environment. In the chapters that follow, the issues underlying such battles between old and new media are explored in greater depth, as are the motives and tactics of those trying to defend their institution.

NOTES

1. "Giving News to Radio Viewed as Menace to Newspapers by Many Editors," *Editor and Publisher*, (December 22, 1928):4.

2. Joseph Haeffner, *Reminiscences*, Broadcast Pioneers Project, (New York: Columbia University Oral History Collection, 1950).

3. Everett Bragdon, *Reminiscences*, Broadcast Pioneers Project, (New York, Columbia University Oral History Collection, 1950), 20.

4. Robert S. Mann, "Dailies Aided Greatly in Building Popularity of Broadcasting," *Editor and Publisher*, (February 14, 1931): 34.

5. Eric Barnouw, *A Tower in Babel* (New York: Oxford University Press, 1966), 138.

6. Edward Bliss, *Now the News: The Story of Broadcast Journalism* (New York: Columbia University Press, 1991), 14.

7. Mitchell Charnley, *News by Radio* (New York: Macmillan, 1948), 4.

8. Harvey Levin, *Broadcast Regulation and Joint Ownership of Media* (New York: New York University Press, 1960).

9. Report of the ANPA Committee on Radio, *Editor and Publisher*, (April 25, 1925) 25.

10. *Editor and Publisher Annual Yearbook*, 1925.

11. Karl Bikel, *New Empires: The Newspapers and the Radio* (Philadelphia, J. P. Lippincott, 1930), 81-85.

12. George Lott, "The Press-Radio War of the 1930s," *Journal of Broadcasting*, Vol 14, No. 3 (Summer 1970):277.

13. "Chicago Tribune Defies Associated Press Rule to Radio Election Returns," *Editor and Publisher*, (October 25, 1924):1.

14. "AP Modifies Rule On Radio Broadcasting", *Editor and Publisher*, (April 25, 1925):11.

15. For further discussion about radio's threat to the relationship between the Associated Press and its members, see Gwenyth Jackaway, *The Press-Radio War, 1924-1937: A Battle to Defend the Professional, Institutional and Political Power of the Press*, (Ph.D. dissertation., University of Pennsylvania, 1992), chap. 5.

16. "Press Radiocasting of Election Returns Gives Journalism New Ally," *Editor and Publisher*, (November 8, 1924): 3.

17. H. V. Kaltenborn, *Reminiscences*, Broadcast Pioneers Project, (New York: Columbia University Oral History Collection, 1950), 187.

18. "Chicago Tribune Defies Associated Press Rule to Radio Election Returns," *Editor and Publisher*, (October 25, 1924): 1.

19. Ibid.

20. "A.P. Plans to Detect and Punish Possible Radio Rule Violators," *Editor and Publisher*, (November 15, 1924).

21. "Chicago Tribune Defies Associated Press Rule," *Editor and Publisher*, (October 25, 1924) 1.

22. Ibid.

23. "A.P. Radio Violators Before Directors", *Editor and Publisher*, (January 24, 1925).

24. Ibid.

25. "A.P. Modifies Rule on Radio Broadcasting", *Editor and Publisher*, (April 25, 1925): 11.

26. "Giving News to Radio Viewed as Menace to Newspapers by Many Editors," *Editor and Publisher*, (December 22, 1928): 4. See also, John Roche, "AP to Continue News Broadcasting," *Editor and Publisher,* (April 27, 1929): 11.

27. Report of the ANPA Radio Committee, *Editor and Publisher*, (April 26, 1930), 68, emph added.

28. Frank Miller, "Radio War on Newspaper Would Only Harm Radio, Says Editor," *Editor and Publisher*, (November 25, 1933): 36.

29. Arthur Robb, "Keep News from Radio, SNPA Urges," *Editor and Publisher*, (July 23,1932): 7.

30. "Idle Opposition," *Broadcasting*, (May 15, 1932): 18.

31. John Perry, "Showdown on Radio Problem Expected as ANPA, AP Act on Protests," *Editor and Publisher*, (December 10, 1932): 6.

32. McCann-Erickson, Inc. for *Printer's Ink*, March 1, 1940.

33. Ibid. For further details on radio's economic impact on newspapers, see Jackaway, *The Press-Radio War, 1924-1937: A Battle to Defend the Professional, Institutional and Political Power of the Press*, (Ph.D. Dissertation, University of Pennsylvania, 1992), Chap. 5.

34. Ibid.

35. "Radio Covers Lindbergh Kidnapping," *Broadcasting*, (March 15, 1932): 6.

36. "Editor's Views on Lindbergh Coverage," *Editor and Publisher*, (April 16, 1932): 8, (emphasis added).

37. "Press Service Policies Differ On Giving News to Radio," *Editor and Publisher*, (March 26, 1932): 15, (emphasis added).

38. "Economy Measures and Radio Competition Chief Topics of New York Conventions," *Editor and Publisher*, (April 23, 1932): 3.

39. Perry, "Showdown on Radio Problem Expected," 3.

40. "AP Gives Radio Election Data; UP and INS Off the Air," *Editor and Publisher*, (November 12, 1932): 8.

41. Ibid.

42. Ibid.

43. Bliss, *Now the News*, 41.

44. "AP Gives Radio Election Data," 8.

45. Ibid.

46. "ANPA Acts to Frame Radio Policy," *Editor and Publisher*, (November 19, 1932): 7.

47. "Majority of AP Members Oppose Giving News to Radio Stations," *Editor and Publisher*, (April 15, 1933): 8.

48. Ibid.

49. "ANPA Acts to Frame Radio Policy," *Editor and Publisher,* (November

19, 1932): 7.

50. "ANPA Resolution Hits News by Radio," *Broadcasting*, (December 15, 1932): 24.

51. Perry, "Showdown on Radio Problem Expected," 3.

52. Ibid.

53. Allen Raymond, "The Coming Fight Over News," *New Outlook*, 161, (June 1933): 15.

54. John Perry, "AP News Is Barred from Radio Chains; Members' Use Held to Brief Bulletins," *Editor and Publisher*, (April 29, 1933): 3.

55. "AP and ANPA Declare War on Radio," *Broadcasting*, (May 1 1933): 5.

56. Perry, "AP News is Barred from Radio Chains," 3.

57. "AP and ANPA Declare War on Radio," 5.

58. For further discussion of the program log issue, see Chap. 4.

59. Ibid.

60. Mitchell Charnley, *News by Radio* (NY: Macmillan, 1948): 15.

61. "Indiana Daily Drops News Broadcasts," *Editor and Publisher*, (May 20, 1933): 6.

62. For details on the property rights suits between the Associated Press and various radio stations, see Jackaway, *The Press-Radio War*, Chap. 5.

63. "News Service for Radio Organized," *ANPA Bulletin*, (September 21, 1933): 507.

64. Danna, "The Rise of Radio News," 342.

65. "CBS News Bureaus Serving Net Sponsors, Commentators," *Broadcasting*, (October 15, 1933): 10.

66. Abe Schechter, *I Live On Air* (New York: Stokes 1941), 1.

67. "Radio News Service Seen as Threat," *Editor and Publisher*, (October 7, 1933).

68. Barnouw, The Golden Web., 20; Chester, "The Press-Radio War," 256; Danna, "The Rise of Radio News," 342.

69. Schechter, I Live on Air, 1.

70. "Publishers Oppose Gallery Rights for Radio Reporters," *Editor and Publisher*, (December 2, 1933), 8.

71. "Galleries Opened in House, Senate," *Broadcasting*, (August 1, 1939): 30; "Gate Crasher," *Newsweek*, (August 1939).

72. "Press-Radio Parley In New York December 11," *Editor and Publisher*, (December 9, 1933).

73. Representing Broadcasting: Merlin Aylesworth, president of NBC; Alfred J. McCosker, president of the National Association of Broadcasters (NAB); William S Paley, President of CBS.

Representing Publishing: Karl Bickel, president of United Press; Harry Bitner of Hearst Newspapers; Edward Harris, chair ANPA Radio Committee and four members of the Committee; Roy Howard of Scripps-Howard Newspapers; J.H. Gortatowsky of INS; L.B. Palmer, general manager of the ANPA; Lloyd Stratton, executive assistant to Kent Cooper, president of the Associated Press. Charnley, *News by Radio*, 17.

74. Ibid.

75. Martin Codel, "News Plan to End Radio-Press War," *Broadcasting*, (January 1, 1934): 10.

76. Rudolph Michael, "History and Criticism of Press-Radio Relationships," *Journalism Quarterly*, (Fall 1938): 179.

77. "Radio-News Program in Final Stage," *Broadcasting*, (February 1, 1934): 7.

78. "Report of Radio Committee," *ANPA Bulletin*, (May 3, 1934): 283.

79. Charnley, 19.

80. Bliss, 43.

81. "Radio-Press Arrangment Stirs Dissention", *Broadcasting*, (March 1, 1934): 9.

82. "Radio-Press Plan Starts March 1; News Bureau Will Be Set Up," *Editor and Publisher*, (February 3, 1934): 6.

83. Herbert Moore, "The News War in the Air," *Journalism Quarterly*, (Fall 1935), 50.

84. "Radio News Service Started on Coast," *Editor and Publisher*, (March 24, 1934).

85. "Early News Period Found Satisfactory," *Broadcasting*, (August 1, 1934): 26.

86. "Press-Radio Situation Is Aired Before Ohio Education Institute," *Broadcasting*, (May 15, 1934), 17. This meant that in addition to its regularly scheduled news broadcasts, the Bureau was releasing an impressive number of "extra" news flashes, 4,670 in its first year alone. See Charnley, *News by Radio*, 22.

87. "Press Radio Pact Has Failed, Says Dill," *Editor and Publisher*, (September 22, 1934): 7.

88. "Dill Plans Big Radio News Service," *Editor and Publisher*, (August 18, 1934): 7.

89. "Dill Plans Big Radio News Service," 5.

90. "News by Radio," *Broadcasting*, (October 1, 1934), 30.

91. "Keep an Eye on Dill," *Editor and Publisher*, (September 22, 1934), 26.

92. "Fate of Radio-Press Situation Awaits Meeting of Publishers," *Broadcasting*, (March 15, 1933): 43; "News Flashes Grown Favor -- Sponsors Showing Interest," *Broadcasting*, (April 1, 1935): 20.

93. "UP and INS May Sell Radio News," *Broadcasting*, (April 15, 1935): p. 11.

94. "UP and INS Offer News to Radio," *Broadcasting*, (May 15, 1935): 11.

95. Ibid.

96. "Press Radio Drops Pacific Coast Unit," *Broadcasting*, (August 1, 1935): 7.

97. "Hits Newspaper Control of Radio," *Editor and Publisher*, (October 3, 1936): 9.

98. "Newspaper-Radio Legislation Delayed," *Broadcasting*, (March 15,

1937), 22; "Dailies Must Oppose Use of Radio to Impair Democracy," *Editor and Publisher*, (April 30, 1938), 18.

99. "Newspaper-Radio Legislation Delayed," 22.

100. "Sponsored News Programs Spreading," *Broadcasting*, (June 15, 1935), 11.

101. "Five CBS Stations Take Up; Three More Acquired by INS", *Broadcasting*, (July 1, 1935): 48.

102. Danna, "The Rise of Radio News", 347. There was really only one last burst of hostilities between the two industries. This time the attack came from the broadcasters' side of the field. In May of 1935, the Transradio Press Service, and Radio News Service, its shortwave subsidiary, filed an anti-trust suit against all parties that had agreed to the Press-Radio Plan: the AP, INS, UP, ANPA, CBS and NBC. Herbert Moore of the Transradio Press sued the defendants for more than a million dollars, charging that the Press-Radio agreement constituted a violation of the Sherman and Clayton Anti-Trust Acts and the Federal Communications Act. Moore claimed that the alliance formed between the various defendants constituted a conspiracy in restraint of trade, preventing Transradio Press from selling its news services to the broadcasting networks. He also charged that the press-radio agreement violated broadcast regulations, since the Communications Act required that broadcasters operate in the "public interest, convenience and necessity," and that any arrangement limiting the amount of news available to the people is not, according to Moore, in the best interest of the public. The figure of one million dollars was arrived at by calculating the amount of revenue that Moore estimated he had lost by being unable to do business freely with all broadcasters in the nation.

The ANPA filed a response to the suit, denying all charges. The publishers argued that since the news of the Press Radio Bureau was not sold for commercial sponsorship, it did not constitute commerce and therefore could not be held as a violation of any anti-trust acts. Further, they pointed out that Transradio Press was not in existence at the time that the plans for the Bureau were made, and therefore the press-radio agreement could not be held as a conspiracy against Transradio. The ultimate outcome of this suit is unclear. Several sources indicate that the case dragged on for some time, but that Moore never collected any damages. "News Services Clamor for Radio Clients," *Broadcasting*, (June 1, 1935):9; "Transradio Press Service v. ANPA et al," *ANPA Bulletin*, (June 26, 1935): 456. See also, Danna, "The Rise of Radio News,", 347, and Michael, "History and Criticism of Press-Radio Relationships," 181.

103. "Harris Rebukes Agencies Selling News For Radio Sponsorship," *Editor and Publisher*, (January 25, 1936).

104. Ibid.

105. "Radiocasts Viewed As Newspaper Aid," *Broadcasting*, (March 1, 1936): 51.

106. "Press Drops Cudgels, Ends Radio Feud," *Broadcasting*, (May 1, 1936): 9.

107. "Newspapers End Antagonism to Radio," *Broadcasting*, (May 1,

1937): 15.

108. Emery, 204.

109. "Networks Discontinue Press-Radio News," *Editor and Publisher*, (December 31, 1938).

110. "AP Paves Way for Use of News in Sponsored Radio Broadcasts," *Editor and Publisher*, (April 29, 1939): 11.

3

Radio's Threat to the Institutional Identity of the Press

The newspapers of the country, through their own trained representatives and through the respective news organizations, are the only ones equipped to do and accurate, honest job of news reporting.[1]

James Stahlman
Chair, Southern Newspapers Association 1933

There is much talk these days about the blurring of the boundaries between media institutions. Every day, it seems, the headlines bring news of yet another media merger. Telephone and cable companies are forming alliances; film studios are starting broadcast networks. Predictions of the future forecast an interactive, multi-media environment in which a host of information and entertainment services will be available at the touch of a button through the magic of fiber optics. In our homes, we are told, there will be a single, multipurpose device that will serve our various needs, from telecommunications through video programming to computing. Futuristic ads promise that all of these services will be brought to us by the same company. Gone are the days of autonomous and distinct communication institutions like radio, cinema, and television. In fact, it no longer makes sense to speak in media-bound categories at all. Today's media corporations are all in the business of processing information and entertainment (categories that are themselves becoming increasingly indistinguishable), and they bring it to us in a variety of forms.

This institutional blurring of boundaries has been made possible largely through technological innovation. New communication technologies facilitate the dissolution of barriers between communication institutions, allowing established media institutions to function in new ways. Connecting a computer to the telephone redefines the boundaries of telephony. Suddenly an older medium can perform new tricks. Indeed, the definition of the medium itself, and the institution that supports it, may well be challenged by the arrival of a new medium. It becomes difficult to determine where one institution ends and the next begins. Thus, *new communication technologies pose a potential threat to the established institutional identity of existing media industries.*

But what is institutional identity? Just as personal identity distinguishes people, institutional identity distinguishes institutions. Media institutions may serve very similar communication functions, and yet have distinct identities. For example, both cable and broadcast television serve the function of providing video entertainment, but they do so in different ways. The programming available from these two sources differs enough to render them distinct institutions. Similarly, both newspapers and magazines provide news and information in a printed form, but each does the job in a different way. Interpersonal communication services are provided by a number of institutions: phone companies, the U.S. Postal System, private mail carriers, and on-line computer services. Each serves a similar function, but does it in a very different way. The identity of a communication institution, then, is determined by the way in which the institution performs its communication function.

Institutional identity is not determined in a vacuum. Just as people often define themselves in relation to others, so do institutions. Media institutions exist in a larger context of other communication institutions. To survive in a competitive marketplace, each must have their own identity. One way to achieve a unique identity is to adopt a characteristic way of doing things. Different media institutions each have certain rules, either explicit or implicit, that govern the way they do their job. They also each have different guidelines that govern whom they hire to perform their services. Thus, for example, the postal system operates according to certain guidelines, utilizing a certain type of personnel. The journalism industry works within a different set of professional guidelines and very different hiring codes. There have been times in media history when communication institutions have done this in a formal, conscious way, establishing codes or standards governing the job performance. This was done, for example, by the film industry during the 1930s with the adoption of the Hays Code. Similarly, during the 1980s, the recording industry was pressured to develop its own set of codes governing the labeling of popular music. During the 1990s, the television industry has faced considerable pressure to establish a set of codes governing violent programming.

Usually, however, the development of recognizable production patterns is a less formal process and occurs in a more organic way. Over time, a way of doing things simply emerges. After a while, there is a predictable pattern to the way that the job gets done. Codes of message production, either formal or informal, are established. Certain formats are adopted and then become signature styles of particular industries. The disc jockey format, for example, has become a characteristic feature of FM radio. The "talking head" format has long been the identifying style of network news presentation. The inverted pyramid style of news writing is one of the unwritten rules of print journalism. These informal codes become the guidelines that help those working within a particular media institution to create the right kind of messages. These codes help us distinguish the products of various institutions. They help us distinguish news from entertainment, tabloid from mainstream journalism, and programs from advertising. The style of message creation or message delivery adopted by the institution becomes a fundamental element of its identity.

An examination of the history of mass media in this century quickly reveals that these institutionally defined communication codes evolve and change over time. The institution of cinema has adopted and abandoned several sets of production codes over the course of this century. Radio today is nothing like it was in the 1930s, and contemporary television bears little resemblance to TV in its "Golden Age." Institutional identity, like personal identity, may be transformed over time, going through various stages throughout the life of an industry. Indeed, if a communication institution is to survive in the face of ongoing technological change, this kind of periodic identity reassessment may be essential.

In fact, the emergence of a new communication technology may be precisely the catalyst for this type of identity reassessment, because new media are often capable of outperforming older media at their own job. New media offer new ways to perform familiar communication functions. The new medium may deliver the message faster or with greater efficiency than the older medium. It may reach a wider audience. Or it may allow people greater control over their interpersonal interactions. In some way, it does what the old medium or communication institution does, but does it better.

Faced with this new kind of competition, older media are forced to redefine themselves in the context of a new communication environment. Their institutional identity must be sufficiently distinct from the newly emergent industry to be able to compete with the new and improved version available from the newer industry. Today, for example, the interpersonal communication options available are quite numerous. The public is faced with a similar range of choices in the realm of news and entertainment as well. Ultimately, whether seeking to meet their interpersonal or mass communication needs, consumers contemplating this array of choices will base their decisions on the apparent differences between these various communication channels.

The emergence of a new media institution is thus the occasion for a reassessment of the boundaries between the old and the new medium. The differences as well as the similarities between the two must be determined in order to assess the positions each will occupy in the marketplace. If a new institution emerges, offering the same or similar communication services as those offered by an existing media institution, that older institution might understandably be threatened. The very purpose of its existence is suddenly called into question. Its identity in relation to all other media institutions must be reconsidered.

This is why the arrival of a new communication technology can be so threatening to the identity of an established media institution. The capacity to radically alter the way in which the job gets done raises the possibility of fundamentally altering the nature of the job itself, and to redefine the job is to redefine the institution. As computer graphics and satellite technology transform the face of television news, the definition of broadcast journalism itself begins to change. As on-line services transform the newspaper, print journalism also changes. With these technological changes, new ways of gathering and disseminating the news become possible, and as the tools and techniques of journalism change, so does the institution itself.

One danger of this, for those working for the older media institution, is that their professional identity is threatened. The established codes and conventions, the familiar ways of doing things, are essential to the way they define themselves professionally. What it means to be a filmaker, a television producer or a journalist is to do a certain kind of job in a certain way. When a new technology comes along and allows people to do things in a new way, the professional identity of those still doing it the old way is threatened, and so they need to defend themselves.

When people feel threatened by the arrival of newcomers who do things in a new way, they often respond with hostility. They frequently claim some form of superiority over these outsiders, and thus dismiss them as lacking any value on the basis of their difference from the norm. Usually the standards of the majority are held up as an ideal to which the newcomers can't, or won't, aspire. Their failure to adhere to these ideal standards is then used to justify any attempts to deny them access to the mainstream. Attacking the newcomers becomes a way of protecting the identity of those who were there first.

Institutional self-defense seems to take much the same pattern. An examination of the Press-Radio War reveals the tactics that were employed by the institution of journalism in its attempts to defend its identity from the threat posed by radio. Faced with new competition from radio, the print journalists responded by invoking a set of ideal standards that defined the profession of journalism at that time. Broadcast news was compared against these ideal standards and found lacking. This failure of radio to live up to these standards was then used to justify the journalists' attempts to block the emergence of broadcast journalism.

The development of radio news posed a serious threat to the established institutional identity of journalism. With the arrival of radio came a new channel, a new set of messengers, and a new way to distribute news to the American people. For years, the institutional definition of journalism had been virtually synonymous with the codes and practices of the newspaper industry. These codes were the conventions and practices of accuracy and objectivity in reporting. By the time radio news emerged, these had become an integral element of the definition of journalism, and this definition of journalism was integral to the credibility and power of the institution itself.

Once radio arrived, there were suddenly a myriad of questions to be answered concerning the boundaries and definition of what it meant to be a journalist. Here were new messengers, speaking through a new channel in a new way. Should they be considered journalists? Were these radio newscasters engaged in a form of communication that could (or should) be considered journalism? Did the messages they were transmitting adhere to the established codes of news writing? Was the new technology they were using suitable for the job at hand? Was there a danger that using the new channel would somehow compromise the established industry standards of message creation? If the standards were compromised, how would this affect the credibility and authority of the institution?

At stake here were questions of what it means to be a journalist, who should deliver the news to the public, the manner in which this news should be presented, and the medium through which it should arrive. The same questions are heard today, as contemporary journalists grapple with the ways that new technologies are transforming their field. On-line services threaten to make the newspaper obsolete. Once-familiar editing and production codes of television news are also changing with the availability of live satellite feeds, computer graphic technology, and lightweight video cameras. Many journalists are concerned that the opportunities created by these new technologies may come with a price: the abandonment of the standards that govern and define the institution of journalism.

This chapter explores the concerns expressed by print journalists as they grappled with the threat posed by radio to their institutional identity. Using the codes and standards that defined journalism, they assessed their new broadcast competitors, and, as this chapter will show, their criticisms were not flattering. Revealed here are the self-defense tactics used by an established media industry as it struggled to protect its institutional identity in the face of threats posed by a new communication technology.

THE PROFESSIONALIZATION OF JOURNALISM

Radio arrived at a particularly interesting time in the history of journalism's institutional identity. Broadcast news emerged as American print journalists were in the midst of reassessing the definition and boundaries of their own field. Beginning in the early 1920s, just prior to the commencement of newscasting, journalists entered a period of institutional self-examination. During this time they grappled with questions of standards, ethics, training, and professional identity. This exercise in self-assessment continued well into the mid-1930s, spanning the period during which print journalism was grappling with the presence of new competition, in the form of radio.

The chronology of events rules out the argument that radio was the catalyst for this stage of professional self-assessment. It clearly began before the first newscasters took the air. It is quite possible, however, that the coincidence of radio's arrival, just as the nation's newsmen were in the midst of a collective conversation about what it meant to be a journalist, had the effect of heightening the urgency of this discussion. Not only were the print journalists in the process of redefining their professional identity, but now they also had competition, and this new competition came bearing news to the American public in a new and different manner. Thus, they found themselves in a position of needing to defend their professional boundaries precisely at a time when these boundaries were particularly ill-defined.

What brought on this period of self- reflection? It seems that there were a number of factors. During the period following World War I there was a new interest among print journalists in questions regarding objectivity and accuracy in reporting. This was not the first time in journalism history, of course, that reporters had stressed the importance of objectivity.[2] But this was a new wave of concern about the issue. It is likely that this was, at least in part, a response to the use of government propaganda during the war and the emergence of public relations as a new field of information dissemination.[3] Here were two forms of communication that had, as their express purpose, the aim of persuading the public, and neither was known for its fidelity to the truth.

It is not surprising that there were journalists at the time who began to wonder how their own work differed from these more explicit efforts in mass persuasion. Reflecting this new interest in the boundaries between truth and fiction, journalism critics of the day, such as Walter Lippman and Gilbert Seldes, began to ask tough questions about subjectivity and bias in the news.[4] Other events of the period may also have contributed to this new concern with objectivity in journalism. Journalism historian Michael Schudson suggests that the nation's journalists were responding to various changes in the intellectual climate at that time, such as the emergence of Freud's psychological theories and the dissemination of the writings of the existential philosophers. According to Schudson's argument, the print journalists of the day, faced with theories that challenged both the model of human beings as rational and logical, as well as the meaning of existence, retreated to the 'safety' of the ideals of objectivity. The model of objective reporting is one based on the assumption that there is an objectivity reality, external to and distinct from the subjective human experience. Ostensibly, observing and reporting upon this reality, to a world increasingly confused about the nature of truth, became the new focus for journalists of this period.[5]

For these or perhaps other reasons, by the early 1920s American print journalists were deeply engaged in a collective conversation about what it meant to be a journalist. This discussion took several forms. There was debate over the desired nature and extent of journalism education for young reporters. There was dialogue about whether journalism should be viewed as a craft or a profession. There was also extensive examination of whether there should be a set of standards or codes governing the dissemination of news and information.

In the process of exploring these issues, the institution of journalism underwent several important transformations. The first was the commencement of journalism education. Prior to this period, there was no formal education available to someone interested in becoming a journalist. Cub reporters simply learned on the job as apprentices. During the period between World War I and the Depression, however, universities around the country began to establish journalism programs. By the early 1930s, there were over 300 institutions offering training for young journalists. In keeping with the new interest in standards and quality, these programs placed a strong emphasis on objectivity and accuracy in reporting.[6]

The establishment of formal education programs marked another important change that occurred during this period. It was during this time that journalists began to redefine their work. Where they once had described journalism as a trade, they now began to define it as a profession. This is evident in the kind of language that they used in their debates about what should be taught in these new journalism programs. Articles in the trade press describing the ideal educational experience for the young journalist frequently made reference to the rigorous training processes required in the fields of law and medicine. In some cases, there were even comparisons of the duties of the press to those of the clergy. There was a clear attempt in these discussions to link journalism with some of the professions that are held in the highest esteem in our culture. These are fields that require rigorous training, professions upon whose members society bestows a great deal of prestige and power. The attempt to link the press with these professions marks a distinct shift in identity from a previous age in which journalists were known for their coarse language, their late hours, and their drinking habits. Clearly, the journalists of this new period were redefining themselves along new status lines.

In keeping with this new move toward professionalization, the print journalists of this period made yet another change in the established definition of their field. Up until this time there were no clear-cut guidelines to which journalists were supposed to adhere. There were no industry standards governing the performance of the press, and yet one of the distinguishing features of professions is that they hold their practitioners accountable to some set of ideals. Doctors can have their license to practice revoked, lawyers can be disbarred, and priests can be defrocked for violations of the standards of their professions. Indeed, one might argue that it is the very presence of these standards, and the vigilance with which they are upheld, that gives these professions much of their power. It is not surprising, therefore, that in their efforts to elevate themselves to professional status, the print journalists began to suggest adopting such standards.

Journalism differs from medicine, law, or the priesthood, however, in at least one important way. The terms of the First Amendment prohibit the government from imposing any formal limitations on the press. Thus, it is impossible to prevent journalists from practicing simply because they have violated some set of standards or guidelines. For this reason, journalism can never truly achieve professional status, because there is no legal way in which to enforce quality control.

Given this limitation on their professional aspirations, print journalists of this period did the next best thing. Various professional and trade associations during this decade issued codes of standards and practices that were to serve as informal guidelines for the field of news gathering. In 1923, the newly formed American Society of Newspaper Editors adopted what it called "The ASNE Canons of Journalism."[7] In 1928, the Associated Press offered its own set of standards that were codified and sent out to all staff writers.[8] In 1934, the American Newspaper Guild put forth a similar set of guidelines.[9] These codes all shared an emphasis on the importance of objectivity, accuracy and fairness, qualities that have come to be held as the sacred ideals of journalism. While toothless in their enforceability, these codes reflected the new identity of journalism emerging at this time.

It was just while the print journalists were in the midst of this phase of identity redefinition that radio arrived. At the very time in which journalists were especially concerned about the quality of their own work and the way in which their profession was viewed, they were suddenly being asked to make room for a new group of news messengers. These messengers delivered the news in a way that the print journalists perceived as violating the very standards that they were working so hard to establish. Even if broadcast technology had been introduced at another time, it still would have had the potential of posing a threat to the institutional identity of the press. The particular timing in this case, however, greatly increased the threat involved. For not only were the broadcasters potential competitors who could do the job of the print journalists in an innovative fashion, but they arrived just when the institutional identity of the press was especially vulnerable because it was in flux.

Some kind of institutional self-defense was clearly needed. The form it took was that of criticism. The print journalists were going to try to protect themselves by sitting in judgment of their new competition. Having recently constructed a set of standards to serve as their professional identity, they then used these standards as a cloak of professional legitimacy. The newsmen invoked the standards they had just adopted, claiming that these ideals were the true definition of what it meant to be a journalist. The new competition was then measured against this ideal model and found lacking.

This comparison of print and broadcast journalism took place on three levels: the messengers, the message, and the mode. The broadcasters were compared with print journalists, the radio news message was compared with the newspaper story, and the mode of communication used on radio, the spoken word, was compared with the printed word. On all three levels, at least according to the print journalists, the comparison was not favorable to radio. The newscasters were dismissed as unprofessional, their newscasts were denounced as sensational and lacking objectivity, and radio was rejected as an inappropriate medium for the transmission of news. Thus, the new competition was weighed against the newly codified ideals of the print journalists and found lacking. These imputed failings of radio were then used to justify the argument that the news dissemination process in America should remain in the hands of the print journalists.

CRITIQUE OF THE MESSENGERS

The trouble with the messengers of broadcast news, at least according to the print journalists, was that they lacked the training considered necessary to deliver accurate and reliable information. Since few print journalists at this time had attended journalism school, the "training" to which they referred was the "on-the-job" experience gained over time from working in the newsroom. In the eyes of the press, the broadcasters'lack of experience rendered these newcomers unqualified to occupy the role of journalist.

This issue of training and qualifications was raised, for example, by Roy Howard, the head of the Scripps-Howard newspaper chain. Howard addressed the problem of radio news by asking: "Is news a commodity which grocery clerks and filling station attendants are competent to gather and disseminate, or is there something to the idea that it takes *alert, trained journalists* to gather, transmit, edit and publish news?"[10] To perform the job of a grocery clerk or a gas station attendant requires neither great intellect nor extensive schooling. These are positions that tend to be held by people occupying the lower end of the socioeconomic scale. In comparing the radio news announcers to grocery clerks and filling station attendants, Howard invoked images of working class occupations, suggesting a level of "inferiority" on the part of the broadcasters.

Similar sentiments were expressed by Frank Parker Stockbridge, editor of the *American Press*. Commenting on the growing hostilities between radio and the press, he suggested that "the question about who is qualified to deliver the news goes to the root of the conflict" between the two industries. Stockbridge's own views regarding the qualifications of the broadcasters were quite clear. "Did you ever know a comic strip artist", he asked, "who was also a good reporter?"[11] This time, instead of grocery clerk and gas stations attendants, the broadcasters were being compared with artists who were producing some of the most popular mass entertainment of the day. It is evident that this was not intended as a compliment. In fact, it is a very telling comment. In it, we hear many of the ways in which the broadcasters were viewed as inadequate in the eyes of the print journalists.

As communicators, comic strip artists and journalists have very different professional images. They generally address different types of subject matter, aimed at different audiences, and they employ different symbol systems to deliver their message. Comic strip artists are primarily entertainers. One of the fundamental aims of their message is to amuse their audience, which is frequently composed of children. They provide this amusement by offering visual images that, by their nature as drawings, are a distortion of reality. Cartoons are not photographs. They lack accuracy as visual representations of the world. They also lack objectivity, for cartoon images are, by definition, the subjective expression of the artist. Indeed, it is precisely for their unique perspective on the world that we enjoy the work of cartoonists. Thus they are a group of communicators whose professional image is the direct inverse of that of the journalist.

If the cartoonist is linked with entertainment and subjectivity, the journalist, is usually associated with information and objectivity. The news message is seen as serving a very different function than the cartoon. News is generally written to educate or inform, and is aimed primarily at adults. We hold journalism to very different standards concerning accuracy than we do cartoons. This is reflected in the fact that journalists but not cartoon artists can be sued for libel. Clearly, we have very different expectations of these two groups of communicators regarding the degree of accuracy we expect from them in their representations of reality.

Attempting to describe the differences between journalists and cartoon artists is ultimately rather futile, however. Upon close examination of the boundaries between these two domains of communication, the distinctions between them begin to break down. There are, of course, political cartoonists, whose work could be described as being visual editorials. This essentially makes them journalists. Similarly, there are more than a few communicators who, while they call themselves journalists, seem to have far more in common with the stereotypical cartoonist. One need only look to the nearest tabloid newspaper to find messages that seem designed to entertain, rather than inform, and that are lacking in both accuracy and objectivity.

Despite the overlap of these categories, however, Frank Stockbridge apparently felt that comparing broadcasters with comic strip artists was a meaningful way to describe their ineligibility to serve as the nation's news bearers. In the context of the professionalization process in which American journalists were engaged at the time, the comic strip artist was the perfect symbol of the very qualities from which the press was trying to distance itself. At a time that journalists were attempting to establish a new image of themselves as trained professionals who could be relied upon to deliver news and information with accuracy and objectivity, the last thing they wanted to be associated with were news bearers who bore any resemblance, perceived or actual, to cartoonists.

Accuracy in Reporting

The pages of the journalism trade press during the initial years of radio news were filled with accusations that broadcasters lacked the skills necessary to serve as the nation's news gatherers. One area of weakness that received particular attention was their alleged failure to adhere to the journalistic ideals of accuracy in reporting. One editorial, for example criticized NBC for sending "men untrained in newsgathering" to cover a live boat race, complaining that "at no stage of the race were the radio reporters certain of the information they broadcast." The editorial notes that in contrast to this journalistic incompetence on the part of the broadcasters, the newspaper reporters who were on the scene "knew what they were seeing and how to describe it."[12] E. H. Wilder, manager of the California Newspaper Publishers' Association, told *Editor and Publisher* that "many of the details unnoticed by the radiomen would be noted almost unconsciously by the trained reporter."[13]

Another article expressed the view quite bluntly, stating that "the plain truth is that the radio newsmen are poor reporters."14

One incident in particular that drew heavy criticism of the broadcasters' level of accuracy was the Lindbergh baby kidnapping in March 1932. Because it was such a major news event of the day, and because its radio coverage proved to be such a sore point for so many print journalists, it warrants examination in some detail. As described in Chapter 2, the kidnapping of Charles Lindbergh Jr. received extensive coverage by the networks and local independent stations. At a time that newspapers were devoting hundreds of column inches and extensive resources to this story, many print journalists were unhappy about the competition on the airwaves.

One area of concern was that of circulation. There was a fear that the continual live updates available on air were drawing readers away from the papers. As one editorial put it, "Newspaper men are nearly unanimous that the extensive broadcast coverage has had an injurious effect upon circulation."15 Yet there is evidence to suggest that newsstand sales actually rose during this period. In the initial days following the kidnapping, *Editor and Publisher* ran a front-page story with a banner headline announcing: "Lindbergh Kidnapping Story Sweeps Nation's Front Pages, Circulations Leap Upward." The article described rising circulation in many large cities, including New York, Philadelphia, Chicago and Washington following the kidnapping, with "circulation managers reporting soaring sales," and the *New York Herald Tribune* selling out its entire edition on the day after the incident.16 It is possible, therefore, that complaints about radio's supposed impact on circulation were more a reflection of the journalists' fears than a measure of radio's actual impact on newspaper sales.

Circulation losses, however, potential or actual, were not the only thing about radio's coverage of the kidnapping that disturbed print journalists. Of far greater concern was the quality of the broadcast reporting itself. James Hasenack, circulation manager of the *New York Sun*, told *Editor and Publisher* that he did not feel radio had hampered newspaper sales because "people are beginning to doubt the veracity of news bulletins on the air." "So many inaccurate and fake announcements concerning developments in the Lindbergh story have been put out by radio," he said, "that people buy newspapers to find out the truth."17 The cause of the problem, according to a number of articles, was that the radio news men lacked the skills necessary to cover the kidnapping. One editorial, for example, accused radio stations of having sent men who had been "selected for voice quality and program skill," but lacked "trained news judgment" to handle the flood of information that confronted them at the height of the crisis.18 This particular charge is quite amusing, since in fact most of those sent by the stations to do the reporting were former print journalists who, during the Depression, had found jobs in the publicity branch of broadcasting.19

Nevertheless, the accusation of inaccurate radio reporting about the kidnapping was repeated by a number of critics, including Marlen Pew, editor of *Editor and Publisher*. Pew expressed the opinion that "during the Lindbergh case, the radio established its *novice rating in the dissemination of news,*" charging that "on three distinct occasions it flashed false reports that the child had been found."

Extending his criticism to a more general commentary on radio news technique, Pew observed that "far too often the radio has shown its lack of knowledge both of news editing and the ethics of journalism." As a solution, he advised that the broadcasters would benefit from a careful study of "the practices of the Associated Press and of the reputable newspapers served by that great news-gathering organization."[20] Note that it is the standards and practices of the wire services, from which most newspapers obtained their news reports, that were held up as the ideal to which the broadcasters should aspire. Clearly, the editorial perspective of *Editor and Publisher* was that the newscasters were often in violation of these canons.

Was there any truth to these accusations of false reports being broadcast over the air? Although it seems that there may have been some suspect bulletins, the little evidence that exists is inconclusive. On March 6, the *New York Times* reported that a complaint had been received by the Federal Radio Commission that "some radio station in or near Philadelphia" had been broadcasting a statement that the kidnapped child had been found. The matter was brought to the attention of the commission by the *Philadelphia Public Ledger*, which had received "hundreds of phone calls" from listeners who had apparently heard the statement. As the call letters of the station allegedly broadcasting the false information could not be determined, the Radio Commission expressed the belief that the misleading reports were being sent out by an amateur or unlicensed station.[21] Several months later, another article, in the *Times* told of further efforts to determine which station or stations were responsible for broadcasting erroneous reports of the suicide of Betty Gow, the Lindbergh child's nursemaid. The article noted that although radio stations received hundreds of calls from people who asked for information about the reports, no one "who had actually heard the bulletins could be found," and those who repeated them said they had heard the story from someone else.[22]

Even if there were false reports broadcast at this time, it seems that the radio announcers were not the only ones making reporting errors. Various sources of the period, describing the newspaper coverage of the kidnapping story, reveal that print reporters themselves also occasionally turned in stories that were not entirely accurate. For instance, addressing the Editor's Society in Washington, Marlen Pew observed that "a considerable volume of *reporter-faked news* has appeared in print, particularly in New York, on this case."[23] Similarly, an article summarizing various editor's views on newspaper coverage of the kidnapping, Henry Claus, editor-in-chief of the *Boston Evening Transcript*, noted that many papers had "things to answer for." He explained that they had "printed stories that they ought never to have printed", they had "listened to anyone who would talk and treated what was said as the gospel truth," and had "magnified backyard gossip into the status almost of official pronouncement."[24] Further evidence of accuracy problems in the newspaper accounts about the kidnapping are found in a master's thesis written at the time by a student at the Columbia University School of Journalism. The thesis reports that on the very day that one of the New York dailies ran an editorial severely criticizing the broadcasters for putting "vague rumors on the air" about the kidnapping, the same paper "was carrying a 'spread' on a Lindbergh story that was utterly baseless in fact."25

Thus, it would seem that despite their status as "trained" journalists, some newspaper reporters were capable of making the same kinds of errors as the untrained radio announcers. It is also interesting to note that several articles attempt to minimize or justify the errors made on the part of the print journalists. For instance, Fred Fuller Shed, editor of the *Philadelphia Bulletin* and president of the ASNE, took the position that while "undoubtedly there were some distortions of newspaper service, and perhaps some deliberate abuses" in the coverage of the Lindbergh kidnapping, he argued that for the most part they had done a good job. As he put it, "By and large the newspapers of the country exhibited creditable news enterprise, exercised sound news judgment and did their civic duty well."26 In another instance, the press was absolved of responsibility for the errors made in its handling of the case. *Editor and Publisher* noted that although "some unfortunate mistakes have been made in the search and there have been instances of blundering...newspapers have been led into errors by conditions beyond their control."27

Of importance here is the fact that when the broadcasters made mistakes in their coverage of news, it was held up by print journalists as evidence of the inability of the radio reporters to effectively perform the role of journalists. When newspaper men committed the same errors, however, it was dismissed as being "due to circumstances beyond their control." Apparently, occasional blunders by print journalists were excusable so long as the majority of press performance was found to conform "by and large" to industry standards. Errors committed by those already considered journalists were forgiven or excused far more easily than those committed by newcomers whose professional status and qualifications were viewed with suspicion.

Sensationalism

In addition to charging them with the professional crime of inaccuracy in reporting, print journalists also accused the newscasters of being sensational in their style of delivery. Here was yet another way in which the broadcasters were compared with the newly established standards of journalistic professionalism and found lacking. Sensationalism in reporting is the delivery of news in a way that is specifically designed to arouse strong emotional response. This is generally accomplished by exaggerating or emphasizing certain elements of a story, whether they be sexual, violent, or scandalous in some way. Through the use of images, headlines or writing style, newspapers have utilized sensationalism for centuries as a way of grabbing the attention of readers. 28

In the early twentieth century, however, this age-old journalistic tradition came under new scrutiny. As part of their growing concern with objectivity and professional standards, many of the nation's print journalists became increasingly critical of the use of sensational tactics. The tabloids of the 1920s, for example, were heavily attacked by the mainstream press for their attention-grabbing techniques.[29] Journalism critics called the tabloids "an unholy blot on the fourth estate," and accused them of bringing "discredit on the American press."[30]

Like the cartoon strip artists of the day, tabloid journalists were creating a message that was designed to entertain. The problem with entertainment, as opposed to information, is that it appeals not only to the intellect but also to the emotions. Emotions, by definition, are not rational, logical, or objective. Thus, the danger of mixing entertainment with information in the news delivery process is that the information may not be transmitted in the most objective manner possible. If one is trying to shock, amuse, or titillate the reader, it is quite likely that one is doing more than just presenting the facts. Or it may mean that the facts selected are chosen with the aim of arousing an emotional response rather than simply for the purpose of conveying information. Thus, the "crime" of those writing for the tabloids was that they were engaged in a form of journalism that blatantly violated the newly established codes of objectivity.

Just as they complained about the sensationalist tendencies of the tabloid journalists, and accused them of violating the standards of their profession, mainstream print journalists also accused the broadcasters of similar failings. Their complaints about sensationalism in newscasting focused on live coverage of disasters or crises. During such situations there is often a great deal occurring at once, and there may be high risk to the safety of people in the area. Such situations are not particularly conducive to the calm, detached style of reporting that is required to achieve anything even approximating objectivity.

While both newspaper and radio reporters might be on the scene of such a disaster, the print journalists had the benefit of being able to take notes and then write the story a bit later, away from the heat of the moment. The radio announcers, on the other hand, had to cover the event live from the scene, in the midst of the crisis. Thus, if they were observing something that was especially upsetting or frightening in some way, it was quite probable that these emotions would come through in their delivery on the air. This was particularly likely, the print journalists warned, given the broadcasters' lack of training in the skills of objective reporting. The danger was that radio announcers would provide inaccurate and sensationalist coverage of such crisis situations.

And so they did, at least according to the print journalists of the day. At the Chicago fire in May 1934, for example, newscasters were accused of delivering "hysterical reports" that exaggerated the extent of the danger and led the public to believe that the peril was greater than it actually was. Quoting an article in the *Chicago Daily News, Editor and Publisher* reported that:

> *Inexperienced* radio news broadcasters became *hysterical* with excitement and recited many *wild tales* from their point of view on tops of buildings close to the fire. . . . The radio boys, *untrained* in news gathering, *undisciplined* in the value of *accuracy*...hysterically broadcast every alarming rumor that reached their ears.

Meanwhile, the account continues, "the real facts were being gathered by *trained newspaper men*, whose technique it is to sift grain from chaff." [31] Here, the broadcasters are portrayed as "boys," whose lack of training and discipline render their news reports untrustworthy. The print journalists, on the other hand, are described as "men" with the professional skills required to deliver the true story to the public.

The word "hysterical" appears three times in the text of this article as well as in the headline ("Radio Reporting of Chicago Fire Called "Hysterical" by Press"). To become hysterical is to lose control over one's emotions, to enter into a state in which one's reactions and behavior are often irrational, controlled by the emotions rather than the intellect. Clearly, such a condition is far removed from the calm, detached state required for making objective observations. Thus, an accusation of hysteria is a grave one indeed, from print journalists whose professional ideals are based upon the code of objectivity. Someone who becomes hysterical would be unable to carry out the job of the journalist as it had been newly defined: to report, in as dispassionate and objective a manner as possible, the facts, uncolored by one's own emotions.

Similar criticism was offered of the way radio announcers handled the story of an earthquake in southern California in March 1933. "Quake Coverage Hampered by Radio," announced the headline of an *Editor and Publisher* article. The story told of "ugly, unfounded rumors spread by quavering radio announcers", who reportedly broadcast "terrorizing messages of tidal waves, vast death lists, famine, pestilence and horrors that could be conjured only in a *terror-stricken and uninformed mind.*" The article went on to report that newspapers and press associations were "deluged" with calls from citizens who had been frightened by the radio broadcasts, and that "much valuable time was wasted tracking down phantom disaster rumors." To prevent panic, newspapers issued extras to clarify the actual extent of the danger.[32] Once again, radio newscasters are depicted as being prone to extreme emotional states in which they are unable to distinguish fact from rumor, and are therefore dangerous to the public. In contrast, the print journalists are portrayed as stepping in with the objective facts to calm a public panicked by the radio newscasters' inaccuracy.

The Broadcasters' Defense

It is not surprising that the broadcasters were none too pleased about these constant attacks on their professional identity. In the pages of their own trade press, they voiced objections to the "sour attitude" [33] of the print journalists, the continual "radio baiting" [34] and "the persistent screeds against radio"[35] from the newspaper industry. A particularly bitter editorial in *Broadcasting* magazine complained that the press trade journals "never let slip an opportunity to slap radio," and boldly stated that:

(i)n the face of the askance with which our esteemed contemporary *Editor and Publisher* views broadcasting... we say unreservedly that the radio coverage of the recent political conventions proved with finality that radio has really arrived as a news reporting medium. [36]

Another editorial sarcastically asked its readers whether they had "heard of that big bad wolf, the 'Radio Menace'." Those who hadn't were directed to "ask *Editor and Publisher*, which professes to serve the newspaper industry."[37] Ultimately, in the eyes of the broadcasters, the attitude of print journalists toward radio was "comparable to the manner in which the livery stable operator derided the automobile."[38] As far as the broadcasters were concerned, print journalists were engaged in a futile attempt to block the inevitable tide of change.

The broadcasters also denied all charges made by the press concerning their lack of credentials and their unprofessional journalistic techniques. They made every effort to demonstrate the degree to which their news-gathering and disseminating procedures did in fact adhere to the journalists' standards of professionalism. Articles by broadcasters, describing radio coverage of various events, frequently compared their broadcast techniques with those of print journalism. These discussions included numerous references to vigilant monitoring of accuracy and objectivity. For example, when an attempt was made on the life of President-elect Franklin Roosevelt in February 1933, CBS news commentator Edwin Hill told *Broadcasting* that the "truth and accuracy" of the "essential facts" were carefully verified before he went on the air.[39] On another occasion, an article praised the newscasters at WSAZ for having provided 'round-the-clock coverage of a flood in the Ohio River Valley *"with the speed and precision of a metropolitan newspaper's city room."*[40]

This invocation of the standards of the newsroom was quite common. For example, Herbert Moore of Transradio Press, insisted that the radio newsmen on his staff were "being trained by press agencies and are using identical methods as regards gathering news."[41]

In his book on the story of the early years of the Yankee Network New Service, editor-in-chief Leland Bickford emphasized the Network's commitment to objective reporting. "[A]ccurary," he wrote, "is one of the prime requisites in our operation." Bickford explained that the "established policy of the Yankee newsroom was: 'Be fast, fair, and faithful to the facts.'"[42] The recurring message throughout these articles is that, contrary to the accusations of newsmen, radio broadcasters did apply the same news-gathering techniques as print journalists and were in fact conforming to the journalistic code of objectivity.

In addition to trying to prove that they adhered to journalists' standards, the broadcasters pointed out that many of their staff members were already trained journalists who had shifted from print to air. For instance, in 1933, *Broadcasting* predicted that despite the AP ban on providing radio with news bulletins, there would be little difficulty in "keeping on top of the news" because "networks and their stations--in fact, the whole radio industry--are manned so largely by former newspaper men."[43] Another article used virtually the same wording, observing that "radio is already very largely manned by ex-newspaper men."[44] The following year, when independent radio news-gathering agencies had begun to form, the Yankee Network News Service told *Broadcasting* that "most of the men engaged are experienced newspapermen."[45] This statement was echoed by Bickford who wrote that "all the men connected with the Yankee Network News Service are experienced newspaper workers," who bring to the radio "the same intelligence that gave them a rating in journalism."[46] Here the broadcasters are essentially arguing that they should not be considered outsiders because they are already insiders.

Exact figures are not available regarding the percentage of radio announcers who had backgrounds in print journalism. There is substantial evidence, however, to suggest that at least by the early 1930s, there were a number of former newspaper reporters working in radio news. When CBS began to establish its news division in the fall of 1933, the network directly solicited print journalists in its search for radio correspondents.[47] Many sources describing the resulting news department mention the fact that it was composed largely of former print journalists.[48] While it is harder to ascertain the backgrounds of radio announcers at smaller, independent radio stations, it does appear that at least at CBS, Transradio News, and the Yankee Network News Service, many of those who worked to gather news for radio did have experience in print journalism. This was also the case with at least some of those who brought this news to the microphone. Lowell Thomas, for instance, had been a reporter for the *Chicago Journal*, H. V. Kaltenborn was a columnist at the *Brooklyn Eagle*, and Floyd Gibbons served as a foreign correspondent for the *Chicago Tribune*. Elmer Davis, himself a former reporter for *The New York Times*, said that "radio lured many a veteran journalist away from his old vocation", and that "these men, captured by the broadcasting industry, formed the core of its news branch."[49]

It is therefore quite ironic that print journalists offered such harsh criticism of their colleagues in radio. As Leland Bickford of the Yankee News Network put it, "In thus seeking to dismiss radio news...the editors are casting reflection upon members of their own proud profession--men who possibly have worked under them."[50] If many of the radio newscasters did get their original experience working for newspapers, the claims of the print journalists about the broadcasters' lack of training was simply untrue.

It is difficult to know if the journalists who were making these accusations knew the backgrounds of the radio news personnel and were choosing to ignore the facts for the sake of their anti-radio arguments. It is possible that they were simply unaware of the kind of training that the broadcasters had had. In that case, they were simply making the assumption that anyone who was a radio news announcer could not possibly be experienced in news gathering and dissemination. There may have been an immediate or automatic assignment of outsider status to the broadcasters.

Regardless of whether they were aware of the backgrounds of these early radio newscasters, the tactic taken by the print journalists can be seen as one of self-defense. In an attempt to protect the boundaries of their profession, they argued that the broadcasters lacked the proper credentials to be granted membership. Invoking their own newly established ideal model of professional standards, a model to which many print journalists themselves could not truly adhere, they judged the broadcasters as ineligible for inclusion in the fourth estate. Thus they self-righteously took the stance that only they, the "trained" print journalists, were capable of properly carrying out the job of gathering and delivering the nation's news.

CRITIQUE OF THE MESSAGE

The print journalists did more than just attack the messengers of broadcast news. In addition to challenging credentials of radio announcers, print journalists also criticized the quality of the newscasts. At stake here were the established boundaries of the journalistic profession, and this profession was defined not only by who occupied the role of journalist, but also by how they carried out their duties. Just as print journalists had established a set of ideals about what it meant to be a journalist, so too did they have a set of codes and standards governing how the news should be delivered. And just as the broadcasters were accused of failing to live up to the idealized model of professional identity, so too were their newscasts found to fall short of the "ideal" news message. Indeed, the two forms of criticism are logically connected: If the broadcasters lacked the proper training to be considered real journalists, how could they produce news that lived up the standards of the profession?

Accuracy and Sensationalism

It is not surprising, therefore, that the faults that journalists found with the radio news message were a direct extension of the complaints they had about the broadcasters themselves. Just as news announcers were dismissed for lacking the training and experience necessary to report the news objectively, so were the newscasts denounced as inaccurate, sensational, or over-dramatized. In addition, print journalists pointed out, radio news gave only headline coverage, providing insufficient detail in its treatment of a story. In these many ways, therefore, the radio newscast was seen as failing to adhere to the conventions of the print news story, thereby falling outside the newspaper model of the proper news message. Thus, the newscasts, like the newscasters, were measured against the ideal standards of print journalism and found lacking. As radio commentator and former newspaper reporter Elmer Davis put it, "Day by day newspapers insisted, directly or by innuendo, that...you can't believe the news you get on the radio."[51]

For instance, an editorial in *Editor and Publisher* observed that as far as covering news is concerned, "the radio spirit is willing but the techniques are extremely weak," resulting in "newscasts that lack the hair-trigger speed and accuracy that newspapers must possess in superlative degree."[52] Similarly, the ANPA Radio Committee complained that radio newscasts frequently contained "news from unreliable sources."[53]

The issue of inaccuracy in newscasts was of such concern to print journalists that it was raised at several of their professional gatherings. At the annual convention of the ANPA in the spring of 1933, for example, the radio committee asserted:

Many false statements and exaggerated reports, which have been broadcast recently *by stations that do not have newspaper sources for news,* had demonstrated to the public that the unrestricted and unregulated broadcasting of news has resulted in the spreading of false rumors.

The committee's report went on to say that the "false statements and exaggerated reports" being broadcast had placed an added burden on newspapers to "reconstruct the true facts in the minds of the people."[54] Implicit in this statement is the belief that unless the radio news message is supplied by newspapers, it cannot be relied upon for accuracy. It is also suggested here that despite the presence of the new radio competition, there would still be a need for newspapers to provide the true story.

Similar concerns about the accuracy of radio news were expressed later that year, when numerous prominent publishers expressed their opposition to allowing CBS news reporters admission to the Congressional press galleries. James Stahlman, chairman of the Southern Newspaper Publishers' Association, argued that allowing radio newsmen into the galleries would be "inimical to the interests of accurate presentation of the news of Congress, as evidenced by numerous distorted and inaccurate news broadcasts." Stahlman explained that radio's record on spot news broadcasting was "wholly contrary to the public interest because of inaccurate reporting and willful misrepresentation of facts."[55]

So distressed were they about the problem of inaccuracy in radio news that some journalists sought legislation to address the matter. This proposal came from members of the fourth estate, who are theoretically dedicated to the protection of the First Amendment. Nonetheless, when the Minnesota Editorial Association met for its annual gathering in 1931, members adopted a resolution calling on radio to "cease the circulation of loose statements and rumors in news broadcasts."[56] The Association further resolved to pursue "the initiation of legislative action on a local or national level to prevent the circulation of loose rumors over the air." No attempt was made to offer an explanation of what standard of truth would be used by which to measure the veracity of radio news broadcasts. Fortunately, however, no such legislation was ever passed.

The accusation that radio was responsible for spreading rumors linked the news broadcasts with yet another form of news for which many print journalists had little regard--the tabloids. *Editor and Publisher* made this direct comparison in an editorial observing that radio, "as a news and advertising medium, appears to be developing along purely emotional lines, following lines that the 'tabs' have profitably exploited."[57] Coming from mainstream print journalists, this was hardly a compliment. It was also a fairly common description of radio news. Indeed, a number of articles in the early to mid-1930s emphasized this issue of radio's appeal to the emotions, complaining that the majority of newscasts were designed more to entertain than to inform the public.

For example, Karl Bickel told the *American Press* that he felt the technique of radio news broadcasting is quite different from that of newspaper production. "It is far more closely allied to the *theatre and the movies* than it is to journalism," he explained, adding that "successful broadcasting requires *showmanship* of a high order."[58] These sentiments were echoed by a reporter for the *Pasadena Star-News*, who commented that "the newspaper business is journalism" while "radio is a species of *show business*, with overtones of *peddling and soap-boxing*."[59]

Once again we find radio being compared to various forms of entertainment. This time it is not cartoon strips, but the theater, movies, and show business. While information may be conveyed in the course of a play or a film, the writers' primary focus is to provide amusement and diversion. The important thing in show business is to keep the audience entertained. Above all else, the primary goal of a performer is to please the audience, and in the realm of entertainment this often means creating some kind of illusion. The world of entertainment is by definition one of artifice and illusion. The actor, by definition, is attempting to create the illusion of reality. Indeed, the better the actor, the more "realistic" the performance. The magic of the stage is the art of artifice. Given the strong emphasis on the importance of truth and accuracy in journalism, then, this comparison of radio news with show business is not a flattering one.

It is the analogy to peddling and soap-boxing, however, that is particularly insidious. Here we have the picture of the unscrupulous salesman, barking his wares in a hyped-up manner, using an inflated and colorful sales pitch to draw the attention of the public. There is a distinct sense of untrustworthiness associated with this image. When we think of a speaker on a soap box, we think of someone delivering his or her message in an over-dramatized manner to draw a crowd. When we think of the peddler, we think of someone who will say just about anything to make a sale. Both the peddler and the soap-box orator are known for their use of exaggeration and dramatic speech as a way of winning over their audience. Both are associated not only with dramatic communication but with duplicity or dishonesty. Embedded in both images is the sense that beneath the sensationalized message is some degree of falsehood, and this is not an image that is compatible with the ideals of journalism.

The implications here, in terms of radio news, are quite clear. In comparing the newscasts with these various forms of show business, the print journalists implied that radio news was not only untrustworthy, but also that it had been deliberately exaggerated to make it more engaging. One editorial put it this way: "The technique of radio announcing is simply designed to get the listeners excited."[60] Another article voiced concern that news flashes were "polished" to "catch and hold attention."[61] On the occasion of the Chicago fire in May 1934, the radio announcers were described as having focused mainly on giving their listeners "a thrilling word picture," noting that this emphasis on "excitement and wild tales" leads to "highly colored reports."[62]

Marlen Pew, the editor of *Editor and Publisher*, wrote that for the radio broadcaster covering a political convention, the events at hand are simply "high tension interest for the passing moment, a colorful picture to be described in hot-fire talk."[63] The message here is quite clear: Radio news was not to be trusted on the grounds of its sensationalist delivery.

Here again is the tension between entertainment and information, between intellect and emotion. Blurring the boundaries between fact and fiction poses serious challenges to the credibility of journalists, and emotionally enhanced delivery, to some, implies subjectivity. The journalistic code of objectivity bases its claim to authority in part on presenting information in a detached manner, without apparent bias. This un-emotional stance was, and still is, considered a key component of the plausibility of news. Thus, print journalists who were critical of radio news during the 1930s were arguing that the emotionally enhanced delivery of the newscasts detracted from the accuracy and objectivity of the reports. This meant that, in their eyes, these newscasts violated the established codes regarding the form and content of the news message. Just as the broadcasters were judged as inadequate to be considered "real" journalists, so too were the newscasts deemed unworthy of being considered "real" journalism. The best it could hope for, at least from the print journalists, was the label of entertainment.

Brevity

Another feature of the radio news message that was harshly judged was its length. Radio news, according to the print journalists, was just too short. The brief bulletins, in their view, failed to provide the depth of coverage necessary to properly inform the public. Here was yet another way that radio news violated one of the established codes of journalism. While newspaper stories provided in-depth and detailed accounts of stories, radio news departed from that tradition, offering only a sort of "headline" service. This departure from established news codes was offered as yet another way in which radio violated the rules of journalism and thereby disqualified itself from serious consideration as a legitimate news medium.

Numerous articles compared radio news with newspapers on this issue and found the broadcasts to be inadequate. For example, an editorial in 1928 stated emphatically that "by no stretch of the imagination can we see radio doing a thorough job," and spoke of the disservice that would be done to the public "if radio *pretends* to cover the news field."[64] Several years later the *ANPA Bulletin* observed that because of the brevity of radio news bulletins, a man whose only source of information was "the smallest and poorest of our daily newspapers" would, by the end of the year, be better informed than someone who "had spent his entire time trying to get the daily news of the world through a radio set."[65] Such comments should sound quite familiar to the contemporary reader, for very similar things are often said about the paucity of information provided in a nightly television newscast.

In discussing the "insufficient" nature of radio news coverage, some articles argued that the brevity of the broadcast news message would ensure that Americans would never give up newspapers in favor of radio. Radio listeners, print journalists explained, would be compelled to buy a paper "to read the complete story,"[66] since the newscasts were not providing it for them. *Editor and Publisher* observed that while "the radio account merely calls attention to events of the day," the public can find a story's "full expression in a fully illustrated, carefully-worded article appearing in the newspaper."[67]

Several journalists used a gastronomic metaphor to address this issue. As Frank Stockbridge put it, the news bulletins "whet the appetite for the paper itself, with its fuller and more detailed account."[68] Similarly, at a conference in 1931 on the role of radio and the press in international relations, Victor Rosewater, editor of the *Omaha Bee*, likened radio to "a glorified megaphone" that merely "whets the appetite, and spurs the buying of the next edition of the paper carrying fuller details."[69] Just as food is essential for the proper nourishment of the body, so too is information necessary for the proper nourishment of the body politic. Without the right diet of news and information, the people will be unable to participate effectively in the democratic political process. In this information "menu" it is quite clear that radio news is merely the appetizer, with newspapers providing the more informationally sustaining main course. The similar concern today is that, in a nation that obtains most of its news from television, we have an informationally undernourished population.

Implicit in many of these comments is the assumption that radio's inability to properly nourish the public is somehow an inherent limitation of the medium itself. They suggest that the brevity of the broadcast is a given feature of radio. As *Editor and Publisher* put it, "Radio cannot do the news job *because of physical limitations that are obvious.*"[70] Exactly what these limitations were was never explained. It was simply implied that they were given, and that nothing could be done about them. They were, apparently, set in stone.

Attributing the brevity of the radio news message to some feature inherent in the technology served a very useful purpose for these anti-radio journalists. As long as these limitations were somehow built into broadcasting, radio could never be considered a serious threat to the newspaper. If, by its nature, radio news had to be brief, there would always be a need for the more extensive and in-depth coverage provided by newspapers. In addition, attributing the problems with the broadcast news message to the technology of radio meant, by definition, that it could never improve. If its faults lay not in its personnel but in its wiring nothing could ever be done about it. No matter how well trained the broadcasters were, or how accurate and objective the newscasts, the message would never be "good enough" because of the built-in shortcomings of the technology.

This was a technological determinist position, one that argued, that radio could never be an effective channel for the transmission of news because of the limitations of the medium itself. Radio   violated the established codes governing the shape and nature of the acceptable news message, but nothing could be done about it. The differences are never really explained; they are simply assumed as given. Thus, print journalists were taking the seemingly unassailable stance that newspapers were inherently superior as a news medium due to these 'given' problems with radio. Since radio could never do the job right, the job, by definition, should stay in the hands of the newspapers and the journalists who were trained to produce the news message correctly.

In making this argument, however, print journalists were making an error common to many technological determinists. They were confusing a socially constructed feature of the broadcast format with natural limitations of the technology. News by radio is *not* necessarily brief. It *can* be long-winded and detailed. Similarly, there is nothing in the technology of television that prohibits the nightly news from providing in-depth coverage. In actuality, if any limitations exist on radio or television news, they are much more institutional than technological in nature. The short amount of time allotted by radio and television for newscasts is a product of profit-oriented decision-making. Driven by the race for ratings and the competition for advertising revenue, the broadcasters have developed a format that is designed to grab and hold the attention of the public. This brings us to the complex question of whether it is harder to hold the attention of the audience when addressing them over the airways than through the printed page.

CRITIQUE OF THE MODE

In their argument that radio news is fundamentally different from newspapers, print journalists were right in at least one way: Radio is an aural medium. News by radio is conveyed primarily through the spoken, rather than the printed word. This difference prompted them to speculate about the inherent differences between these two modes of communication. This speculation about inherent modal differences was an essential element of the larger project in which the print journalists were engaged--defending the established definition of journalism.

Until the arrival of radio, newspapers were the primary means by which news was disseminated to the mass public. While word of mouth has always been a way that people spread information, the newspaper had been America's main news channel since the invention of the steam press in the 1830s. The printed word and the newspaper format were therefore essential components of the definition of journalism. Newspapers *were* the news. In the century since the Penny Press, the journalism industry had developed a very recognizable format though which to convey information to the American people, and newsprint itself was part of that format. The newspaper had become part of the definition of journalism itself. The way to spread the news was through this particular medium. Now, suddenly, there was a new medium. Not only were there new messengers, delivering the message in a new way, they were also using a new mode--the spoken word.

It is not surprising, given the perspective of institutional self-defense from which the journalists were assessing radio, that they took the position that the spoken word was an inherently inferior means by which to communicate news to the public. This was, perhaps, the most intriguing approach by which to defend the boundaries of their own professional identity. Here was a way in which radio could never compete with print. Print journalists argued that radio could never do a truly acceptable job of serving as the nation's primary news channel because of the fundamental limitations of the spoken word. Starting from the premise that there are intrinsic and predetermined differences between spoken and written communication, the print journalists attempted to build a case that their own mode, the printed word, is best suited for the transmission of news.

Reading and the Intellect

According to the print journalists, there were certain key ways in which the act of reading differed from that of listening. In their view, these differences made the printed word the superior means of transmitting news and information. One of these differences was the relative level of intellectual stimulus that is possible through the two modes of communication. Reading, the journalists argued, is a more intellectually engaging activity than listening. Radio, they claimed, appealed more to the emotions. This, by extension, made the printed word a more appropriate medium for the dissemination of news.

This position was argued, as early as 1924, when radio news first began to appear on the air. In what was one of the initial responses from print journalists to this new form of news, *Editor and Publisher* took the definitive position that "radio cannot possibly supplant the newspaper...because the sense of hearing does not satisfy the same *intellectual craving* as does the sense of reading."[71] A similar observation about this contrast between the two media was made several years later in an article that was appropriately titled "Radio vs. the Press." In it, Frank Stockbridge, the editor of *American Press*, predicted that people would continue to buy newspapers despite radio news, because they "want to *read* about the big events." The reason for this, he explained, was that "most folk are eye-minded. They get only *impressions* through their ears; they get *facts* through their eyes." [72]

Invoking a model linking emotions and subjectivity with the ear, and cognition and objectivity with the eye, Stockbridge suggested that the written mode is the best means by which to deliver the facts. This position, which might be deemed 'sensory determinism', claims that we naturally receive certain types of information better through particular senses, and therefore messages must be shaped in accordance with the built-in limitations of the human sense organs. It implies that the printed word is superior to the spoken as a mode for the delivery of news because facts can be better absorbed through the eyes than the ears, or that factual information is best trusted when it is seen rather than heard.

Given the emphasis that journalists of the day were placing on the importance of accuracy and objectivity, any medium that appealed to emotions instead of the intellect would naturally be viewed as suspect. The danger here was that if the spoken word appeals to the emotions of the listener, there is the risk that the radio audience might mistake a sensationalized speech or news report for actual fact. This concern was voiced in a particularly telling comment by print journalist Will Irwin, in his book *Propaganda and the News*. Irwin warned that "the radio, through the *magic* inherent in the human voice, has means of appealing to the *lower* nerve centers and of creating *emotions which the hearer mistakes for thoughts.*" [73]

There are several noteworthy points in Irwin's warnings about the dangers of radio as a propaganda tool. First, he describes the human voice as being magical in some way. Magical forces are by definition beyond logical, rational, explanation. They work in mysterious way, and unlike facts they are not easily understood or controlled. They have their own power, and we are vulnerable to their influence. Notice that this magical force is seen as *inherent* in the human voice. It is a given, and therefore inescapable. In addition, notice that this inherent magical force is described as appealing to nerve centers that are "lower." Irwin does not specify exactly what it is that these nerve centers are lower than, but his invocation of a vertical hierarchy makes it clear that this "lower" status is not to be viewed in a positive light.

Perhaps the ultimate danger of radio news, according to Irwin's model, is that the listener might mistake emotions for thoughts. For print journalists so concerned about preserving the boundary between objectivity and subjectivity, this is a matter of serious concern. If the line between ideas and emotions gets too blurry, there is the danger that we will no longer be able to tell the difference between reality and illusion. Once this line is dissolved, journalism is no different from fiction. In fact, it is worse. Since people expect to be able to rely on journalism as a source of factual information about the world, when they turn to the broadcast media for their news they believe that the information with which they are being presented is the truth. As Chapter 5 will show, print journalists of the day had grave concerns about the possible exploitation of radio by unscrupulous politicians for the manipulation of the masses.

The Convenience of the Printed Word

In comparing the inherent differences between the printed and spoken word, there were other matters to consider as well. In addition to the question of which one appealed more to the intellect, there was the question of which was the more convenient as an information source. Here, too, print journalists took the position that the newspaper was a superior form by which to receive news and information. In this case, the argument centered on the issue of consumer control over the reception process. Newspapers allow the reader to absorb information at their own pace, offering them greater convenience and control over the information consumption process. With radio, however, one cannot stop the announcer and hear a newscast again; neither is it possible to skip ahead to the portions of the news in which one is most interested.

As early as 1926 an editorial speculated that radio would never replace newspapers

> for the simple reason that a person will not sit patiently while a long list of market quotations are being read on the air to get the news concerning one or two stocks that he may be interested in when he may take his newspaper and turn to his particular interest without delay. [74]

Similarly, an article on new communication technologies in the *New York Times* made the following observations about the differences between reading and listening: "We read and reread papers selectively. In broadcasting there is no chance for selection, no chance for a rehearing." The article noted that reading the entire contents of a daily newspaper over the air would take hours, and that it was highly doubtful that anyone would "listen patiently until at last a news item of direct personal interest was reached."[75] This theme was echoed by the ANPA Radio Committee, which speculated that radio would ultimately serve as a stimulus to newspaper circulation rather than a deterrent, because with radio "the listener must catch the message on the fly, but the reader can study, assimilate and preserve if he desires things of interest which he finds in the newspaper."[76]

Here too, contemporary parallels can be found to the print journalists' arguments about the inherent superiority of the newspaper as a news medium. Today, faced once again with new technologies that seem to threaten the future of the newspaper, journalists are making very similar claims. It is predicted that someday soon we will receive personalized versions of the newspaper on-line either through handheld display devices that will serve as computers, fax machines, and telephones all rolled into one one, or perhaps through the more old-fashioned technology of our desk-top or lap-top computers. Either way, many warn, the days of the traditional newspaper are numbered. The counter argument to these information-age predictions is much the same as it was in the 1930s, namely, that the format of the newspaper is inherently preferable to these other means of receiving the news. Who will want to scroll through screens of unwanted information, people wonder, searching for the news they are looking for? Skeptical of the ultimate impact of these new technologies, many print journalists today continue to gamble that in the end, the public will prefer to continue getting its news the old-fashioned way.[77]

That was certainly a gamble that many journalists in the 1930s were willing to take. Some felt that what would keep the people loyal to newspapers was the fact that with radio, it was easy to be distracted or miss something in the process of listening. For instance, Edward Harris speculated that when the news is broadcast by radio, it may be possible "to get the real meaning of the news dispatch *if your mind and the surrounding environment are free from distractions.*" But what if you are thinking of other things, or there are distracting sounds to pull your attention away from the broadcast, or the signal is not entirely clear? In that case, Harris cautioned, "the listener may be sitting by his radio, reading or talking, and only half conscious of the radio message." The danger then, he warned, is that "a *false meaning is conveyed,*" and the audience is thus misinformed.[78] With newspapers, of course, there were no such dangers. If readers were distracted or needed to attend to something else, they could always come back and pick up the paper later.

The issue at stake here, however, was not only one of convenience for the listener. Like so many journalists who were concerned about radio, Harris suggested that if people listened to the radio, they would end up with an inaccurate picture of the truth, due to the alleged differences between reading and listening. Since the radio audience lacks control over the reception process, Harris argued, there is a greater danger that in the end the truth will be distorted. He compared listening to radio news with the game of "telephone" played by children, in which a sentence is passed from one person to another. The result of the game, he reminded his audience, was that the message "was always distorted so that the statement as it came out could hardly be recognized as the one made at the beginning." There is much less danger of this type of misunderstanding with newspapers, Harris explained, because "if the reader does not grasp the full meaning of the news item he can read it over and over until he finally grasps its true import."[79]

As evidence of the difficulties the listening public was having in understanding radio news, Harris reported that "on many occasions the telephone switchboard" at his newspaper had been "besieged with telephone calls as the result of a misunderstanding of a news item which the listeners heard over the radio." Here, as in so many other examples, the newspaper is held up as the authoritative source of truth in the face of radio's allegedly unreliable and inaccurate information. Given his firm belief that print was a far more effective medium for the transmission of information than the spoken word, Harris concluded that "the use of radio for the broadcasting of news and the interpretation of news *is a dangerous procedure*". As he put it, "the *inaccuracies of radio broadcasting* and the inability of the listening public to get the full meaning of a broadcast leads to many *misunderstandings and false reports*."[80] Once again, the message is clear: If radio and the spoken word are used to convey the news, the truth will get lost in the telling.

The Evanescence of the Spoken Word

Still another way in which the spoken word was seen as problematic as a means of information transmission was its lack of permanence. Even if the audience were paying full attention, and the broadcasters did a "proper" job of telling the news correctly, there was still the problem of the absence of a record. At this time, radio was live, and no recordings were made of daily news broadcasts. Thus, unlike the daily newspaper, there was no record of the precise nature of the news put out over the airwaves. In a culture that sets such a high stake on the importance of documentation as a method of truth assessment, this made some journalists nervous. If there were no record that something had been said, how could its accuracy be checked? The implications of this for journalists, who are ever concerned about the dangers of libel, were grave indeed.

Addressing this concern, an editorial titled "Libel Via Radio" described a hypothetical situation in which a news story might be read over the air, mistakenly charging a business with fraudulent practices. In such a situation, the writer asked, what course of action, is available to those wrongly accused? Once the newscast has been aired, "the spoken word has been sent forth to blacken their names, thousands hear it...but no permanent record remains to be challenged and corrected." [81] A *New York Times* editorial observed that there was greater motivation for the print journalist to tell the truth because "the news item in the newspaper is a permanent record" and if something in that item is "libelous or scandalous, there is a physical ownership and property from which to seek redress." The problem with radio, this editorial continued, is that "the radio news item is a vibration in the air, without record, without visible responsibility, *without that incentive to accuracy that comes with print*." [82]

The argument here is that since no evidence is left behind after speaking on the air, one person could speak in an abusive way about another without fear of being confronted with documentary proof of the slanderous statement. In other words, radio allows you to lie with impunity. The victim of such a verbal assault, in the absence of a written record of the attack, would be left without recourse. By contrast, the print journalists seemed to imply, it is the very presence of a written record that helps keep the newspaper honest. The *Times* editorial suggested that, people tend to trust the printed account more than the oral delivery, explaining that "it is the habit of man to be more certain of the fact he sets down in script or print than of the report he merely repeats."[83] Voicing this prejudice about the unreliability of the spoken word, this journalist spoke as a true member of print culture, seemingly unaware that for many centuries, in many parts of the world, people found ways to verify the spoken word before they were able to write things down.[84]

What can be heard in the print journalists' concerns about libel is a manifestation of even deeper fears. At issue here are questions about what happens to familiar standards of truth telling when new forms of communication technology become available.[85] In any communication environment, whether it be a culture dominated by oral, written or electronic communication, rules are established to determine which information counts as real and true. At various times in human history people have established different ways to establish the authority of information. Messengers have always been required to offer some form of proof that the message they carried was legitimate. They had to know the secret password, show the king's seal, or, in more recent times, be able to produce the mark of a notary public. All of these are ways of signifying that the information in question has in some way been validated. New communication technologies disrupt established conventions of information verification. They allow us to bypass the structures that have been established to prevent deceit. New media open the door to new forms of lying, because no rules exist yet to verify this new kind of information. But, gradually we do revise our rules regarding the different kinds of information that we will accept as true or real. For example, today's world is one in which major financial transactions take place each day via computer, over the phone lines. There are no signatures involved, no paper, no original copies, no witnesses, none of the older ways of ensuring the authority of these transactions. There are now new ways of verifying information. Today we have access codes and computer passwords. As information technologies change so do the means of assessing the veracity of information.

The arrival of new communication technologies can therefore be quite threatening to those who make their living by distributing information, particularly if their professional identity and reputation rests on the accuracy of that information. This is precisely the case with print journalists. Since the power of journalism rests on its credibility, a new medium was inherently threatening because it opened new doors for information distortion. Print journalism had established conventions that served as checks against lying in print. Libel laws were one of them. Radio, however, made it possible to lie and get away with it. While there are laws against slander, live broadcasts made it difficult to prove that the offending statement had ever been uttered. If news bearers can convey falsehoods without consequence, there is no longer any way to measure their credibility, and without credibility they can no longer be trusted. For print journalists, whose professional identity rested on their credibility, the prospect of news messengers bearing information that could not be verified was a grave danger indeed.

Because of the difficulties of verifying radio news, some journalists predicted that the public would continue to turn to newspapers when it wanted the truth. This view was expressed, for example, by Paul Williams, editor of *The Utica Daily Press*, in what was described as an "impromptu debate" took place with Merlin Aylesworth, president of NBC, at the American Society of Newspaper Editors Convention in April 1930. Williams argued that radio would never become a dominant medium of news and information because "precise information of any importance is best conveyed in print." Elaborating on this point, he explained:

You don't want contracts, orders, specifications or any other *significant statements* left to somebody's say-so. For that reason there will be a large publication field for important fact-information which will continue until doctors are willing to give their prescriptions verbally which I think is a long time in the future. [86]

Of course, today doctors *do* give prescriptions over the telephone, and "significant statements" *are* made over both radio and television. We have developed new conventions that help us assess the credibility of information conveyed through these new channels. But in the early 1930s, the idea of news delivered over the air was viewed, at least by some print journalists, as being as ridiculous as the idea of a verbal prescription. The message here was that for something to be true and believable it must be in print, which meant, by definition, that radio was an inherently unacceptable medium for the transmission of news and information.

Today there are also concerns about the impact of new technologies on the credibility of journalism. When it becomes possible to generate images by computer and create visual illusions that even trained professionals have difficulty recognizing as fabrications, the public is left to wonder which sources of information, if any, it can believe. The ease with which video technology allows the simulation of reality raises important questions about whether its use constitutes a compromise of journalistic ethics. Computer graphic technology, for example, makes it possible to transform a photograph and create visual illusions. Viewers can now be fooled into thinking they are seeing records of things that never existed. In a communication environment that makes it so easy to replicate reality, the public is increasingly faced with the question of whether what they are watching is real.

To journalists, whose institutional identity rests on the reliability and credibility of the information they provide to the public, these new technologies pose a serious danger, for once the news can no longer be trusted, the journalist can no longer be trusted. Since ultimately, the power of the institution of journalism rests on the credibility of the news message, any technological innovation that might pose a threat to this credibility is a threat to the identity of the institution itself. Not surprisingly, journalists faced with such a threat will respond by arguing that the technology in question, whether it be radio or computer-enhanced video editing, is inherently inappropriate, or at least dangerous, as a medium for the transmission of news.

In summary, print journalists who objected to radio news warned that in addition to lacking permanence, a message delivered orally was potentially subjective and inaccurate. In their view, these qualities rendered the aural

mode inherently unsuited for the purposes of news delivery, thereby
disqualifying radio as an acceptable medium for the transmission of news. For
these journalists, there was still only one mode that was appropriate for the job
at hand, and that was the written mode, the printed word, carried to the people
via the medium of the newspaper.

THE SOLUTION TO THE RADIO "PROBLEM"

Despite the various complaints print journalists had with radio news, by the
early 1930s it was clear that radio was here to stay. It was also clear, by the
fall of 1933, that if the newspapers and wire services were not willing to
supply radio with news, the broadcasters would do the job on their own. As
this chapter has described, the press was none too pleased with the way the job
was being done. In keeping with the saying that if you want something done
right you have to do it yourself, the print journalists' solution to the radio
news "problem" was to take over radio news. For the anti-radio publishers, the
approach to dealing with the situation was fairly clear: They were willing to
allow news broadcasting to take place, so long as they were at the helm.
"Radio," said Morris Atwood of the Gannett papers, "should be made a
handmaiden" to the press.[87] Indeed, the role of handmaiden was exactly what
was created for the broadcasters with the establishment of the Press Radio
Bureau in March 1934 (see Chapter 2).

The Biltmore Agreement stipulated that broadcasters would stop gathering
and disseminating their own news. Instead, under the new arrangement, the
wire services would provide the networks with two short news bulletins per
day to be aired at certain times of day, without commercial sponsorship. The
terms of this agreement brought network radio news under the complete
control of "trained" print journalists, who wrote and edited the bulletins for
the air. This meant that radio news would essentially consist of the oral
delivery of newspaper text, which would ensure that newscasts would conform
to the print journalists' standards.

In crafting this arrangement, newspapers managed to regain control over
two areas that greatly concerned them: the messenger and the message. Since
print journalists were going to be writing the newscasts, there would no longer
be the problem of proper credentials and training of the broadcasters. By
extension, this would insure that the form and content of the newscasts would
adhere to the established journalistic conventions of the "proper" news
message, which was essential to maintaining the credibility, and therefore the
power, of journalism as a profession.

Justifications for this newspaper control over radio news were offered in the
comments made as tensions between radio and the press were reaching their
peak. An editorial in *Editor and Publisher*, entitled "Radio Competition," for
example, took the position that "it is bad journalism to abdicate the news
function to an agency which has neither the *newspaper tradition* nor the
safeguards of a printed record assembled by trained and responsible newspaper

men."88 The established standards of the institution of journalism and the technological "superiority" of the printed word are invoked here to explain why the print journalists should control the news gathering and distribution process in America. Similarly, Roy Howard, president of the Scripps-Howard newspaper chain, noted that they were facing the development of a new medium, that, unlike newspapers, did not have "a century of journalistic ethics and tradition behind it." "What," he asked, "are we going to do about it?"89

The solution, it seemed, to the problem of radio's lack of experience, was for these "trained and responsible newspaper men" to take over and do things right. As Mr. Wilder, the San Francisco manager of the California Newspaper Publisher's Association put it, "If the public demands spot broadcasting of news events, there is no agency better fitted to provide this than the newspapers, *trained for generations* in the gathering of news."90 If the public had to have news via radio, he argued, it was best if it came through the reliable source of the newspapers. Similar sentiments were voiced by James Stahlman, chair of the Southern Newspapers Association. Just one week before the broadcasters and the publishers arrived at the Press-Radio Agreement, he asserted that "*the newspapers* of the country through their own trained representatives *are the only ones equipped to do an accurate, honest job of reporting.*"91

Particularly outspoken on this issue was Edward Harris, who, in his capacity as the chair of the ANPA Radio Committee, represented thousands of newspaper publishers in the country, the majority of whom were opposed to radio news. In a speech before the Inland Daily Press Association, he put the matter quite clearly, saying "*there is only one source of legitimate news, and that is the newspaper-owned news gathering organizations or the newspapers themselves.*"92 Within a year, of course, an arrangement to ensure this kind of newspaper control over radio news had been made, in the form of the Press-Radio Bureau. In a letter to Frank Mason, an NBC vice president, Harris discussed the importance of the new arrangement, explaining that the newspaper publishers of America had "a very definite obligation...to see that radio delivers the news to the public...*in a manner which is in keeping with the standards of our profession.*"93 On yet another occasion, Harris stressed that it was crucial that radio stations speak "with the authority of the regularly organized news agencies, which are *universally accepted sources of authentic news*", and had years of experience in "the collection, assembling and distribution of *accurate, reliable and unbiased news.*"94 Again and again he asserted that if the American people were to get accurate, reliable information through radio, it would have to originate from print journalists.

It was in precisely this way that print journalists presented and praised the terms of the Biltmore Agreement. Discussing the establishment of the Press-Radio Bureau, radio commentator Boake Carter remembered that the publishers had justified the arrangement on the grounds that this would provide the public with "real, *authentic*, proper news."95 A few months after the bureau went on the air, the ANPA Radio Committee issued a report praising the new service as lessening "the danger of *promiscuous* broadcasting of *unreliable* and *inaccurate* news."[96] The following year, the committee reiterated this point, asserting that "important news bulletins should be supplied to the broadcasters by the newspapers in order that the general public may enjoy complete protection on news obtained from *reliable* sources."[97]

Similarly, *The New York Times* described the Press-Radio Bureau as supplying "authenticated news gathered by the newspapers and press associations for broadcasting on the air."[98] The language throughout these comments consistently implies that accuracy and authenticity in radio news could be ensured only if the process of news dissemination remained in the hands of the nation's print journalists.

While there are no contemporary parallels to the Press-Radio Bureau, there are certainly many print journalists today who feel that newspapers offer more accurate, reliable, and comprehensive news coverage than television. Although television is no longer a new technology, there are still complaints about the inherent sensationalism and untrustworthiness of the video image. These print-broadcast comparisons are particularly prevalent at times of natural disasters, international crises, and national elections. On those occasions, when the nation's attention is particularly focused on the news media, print journalists can be relied upon to compare their coverage with that of their video-based colleagues, and their critique is rarely flattering. The complaints are almost the same as those issued sixty years ago: Television news anchors are accused of not being real journalists. They are dismissed as being mere talking heads who know nothing of the issues and have only been hired for their good looks and camera presence. We hear that the television news message lacks depth, objectivity, and credibility, and that the technology of television is fundamentally incompatible with the transmission of objective and accurate information. It would seem that the Press-Radio War never really ended, but just changed form.

Ultimately, in the Press-Radio War of the 1930s and contemporary tensions between newspapers and television, print journalists can be seen attempting to protect the boundaries of their institutional identity in the face of new competition brought on by new technologies. As new means to gather and transmit information become available, the established codes and conventions defining journalism are threatened. The messengers can change, the message can change, and the mode of communication can change. If all these things change, the very definition of journalism itself changes, for communication institutions are defined along these dimensions. Thus, when established media industries fight to protect traditional ways of doing things, they are fighting not only to preserve their profit margin, but also to preserve their identity, and thus their power in society.

NOTES

1. "Publishers Oppose Gallery Rights for Radio Reporters," *Editor and Publisher*, (December 2, 1933): 8.

2. For discussions about the development of objectivity in journalism, see Michael Schudson, *Discovering the News: A Social History of American Newspapers*, (New York: Basic Books, 1978), and Daniel Schiller, *Objectivity and the News: The Public and the Rise of Commercial Journalism*, (Philadelphia: University of Pennsylvania Press, 1981)

3. Schudson, *Discovering the News*, Chapter 3.

4. See for example, Walter Lippman, *Public Opinion* (New York: Harcourt, Brace and Howe, 1920); and George Seldes, *Freedom of the Press* (New York: Bobbs Merrill, 1935).

5. Schudson, Chapter 3.

6. Robert Desmond, *Professional Training of Journalists* (Paris: Unesco, 1949).

7. Alice Pitts, *Read All About It! 50 Years of ASNE* (New York: ASNE, 1974).

8. "AP Codifies Its General News Orders," *Editor and Publisher*, (March 3, 1928):5.

9. Norval Luxon and Philip Porter, *Reporter and the News* (New York: D. Appleton-Century Co., 1935), 112.

10. Frank Parker Stockbridge, "News Broadcasting and the Newspapers," *The American Press*, (October 1934), 1, (emphasis added).

11. Ibid.

12. "Reporters Needed," *Editor and Publisher*, (June 29, 1929).

13. "California Publishers Propose to Operate Radio Stations," *Editor and Publisher*, (July 11, 1931), 46.

14. "Crime on the Waves," *New Outlook*, (February 1935), 5.

15. "Spot News and Radio," *Editor and Publisher*, (March 26, 1932):6.

16 "Lindbergh Kidnaping Story Sweeps Nation's Front Pages--Circulations Leap Upward," *Editor and Publisher*, (March 5, 1932), 4.

17. John Roche, "Unparalleled Response by Press and Public Met Lindbergh Climax," *Editor and Publisher*, (May 21, 1932), 5.

18. "Spot News and Radio."

19. Arthur Wakelee, *News Broadcasting*, (M.A. Thesis, Columbia University, 1932), 24.

20. Marlen Pew, "Shop Talk at Thirty," *Editor and Publisher*, (May 28, 1932):44. (emphasis added).

21. "False Radio Report Charged," *New York Times*, (March 6 1932).

22. "False Radio Runors Bring Federal Action," *New York Times*, (May 18 1932): 16.

23. "The Press and Colonel Lindbergh," *Editor and Publisher*, (April 30, 1932): 29.

24. "Editors' Views on Lindbergh Coverage," *Editor and Publisher*, (April 16, 1932): 8.

25. Wakelee, *News Broadcasting*, 55.

26. Ibid.

27. "Press Co-operation with Lindbergh Family Unparalleled in Peace or War," *Editor and Publisher*, (April 16, 1932): 5.

28. Mitchell Stephens, *A History of News: From the Drum to the Satellite* (New York: Viking, 1988).

29. Gwenyth Jackaway, *The Press-Radio War, 1924-1937: A Battle to Defend the Professional, Institutional and Political Power of the Press*, (Ph.D. dissertation., University of Pennsylvania, 1992).

30. Ibid., p 221.

31. George Brandenburg, "Radio Reporting of Chicago Fire Called 'Hysterical' by Press," *Editor and Publisher*, (May 26, 1932): 30, (emphasis added).

32. "Quake Coverage Hampered by Radio," *Editor and Publisher*, (March 18, 1933): 7 (emphasis added).

33. "'Airing' the News," *Broadcasting*, (July 15, 1932): 16.

34. "Welcome Press Inquiry," *Broadcasting*, (December 1, 1932): 18.

35. "The Radio Menace," *Broadcasting*, (November 15, 1933): 22

36. "'Airing' the News," 16.

37. "The Radio Menace," 22.

38. "News Via Radio," *Broadcasting*, (February 1935): 30.

39. "Radio Journalism on the Job at Miami," *Broadcasting*, (March 1 1933): 12.

40. Vernon Bailey, "SAZ Stays on the Air Continuously Guide Huntington Through the Crisis," *Broadcasting*, (February 15, 1937): 67, (emphasis added).

41. "Rivals Form as Press-Radio Improves," *Broadcasting*, (Februrary 15, 1934): 11.

42. Leland Bickford, *News While It Is News* (Boston:Manthorne & Co., 1935), 95, 113.

43. "AP Fails to Hamper News Broadcasts," *Broadcasting*, (May 15, 1933), p 7.

44. "Network is Building Its News Service," *Editor and Publisher*, (June 9, 1934): 9.

45. Ibid.

46. Bickford, *News While It is News*, 67.

47. "Columbia Warns Against Pilfering News," *ANPA Bulletin*, (November 3, 1933): 609.

48. Mitchell Charnley, *News by Radio* (New York: MacMillan, 1948); Isabelle Keating, "Pirates of the Air," *Harper's*, (September 1934), 463.

49. Roger Burlingame, *Don't Let Them Scare You: The Life & Times of Elmer Davis* (Philadelphia: J.B. Lippincott, 1961), 167.

50. Bickford, *News While It Is News*, 67-68.

51. As quoted in Burlingham, *Don't Let Them Scare You*, 168.

52. "Spot News and Radio," *Editor and Publisher*, (March 26, 1932):6.

53. Report of Radio Committee, *ANPA Bulletin*, (May 3, 1934), 287.

54. "Five-Point Program Urged on Radio," *Editor and Publisher*, (April 29, 1933), 14. (emphasis added).

55. "Publishers Oppose Gallery Rights For Radio Reporters," *Editor and Publisher*, (December 2, 1933).

56. "Editors Warn Radio on News Broadcasts," *Editor and Publisher*, (January 31, 1931).

57. "Spot News And Radio," 6.

58. "Radio Needs Radio Men," *American Press*, (August 1936), (emphasis added).

59. "'Here, You Take the Mike!', Says Pasadena Star-News," *American Press*, (August 1931).

60. "Irresponsible Radio News," *Editor and Publisher*, (May 26, 1934): 22 (emphasis added).

61. Paul Spearman, "Press Held to Have No Air Priority," *Editor and Publisher*, (July 11, 1936).

62. Brandenburg, "Radio Reporting of Chicago Fire Called 'Hysterical' by Press."

63. Marlen Pew, "GOP Convention Machine Whirls in Open As Press Gives Unprecedented Coverage," *Editor and Publisher*, (June 16, 1928): 23.

64. "The Radio Question," *Editor and Publisher*, (December 22, 1928): 28, (emphasis added).

65. "95 Stations Owned by Newspapers," *ANPA Bulletin*, (January 6, 1933): 7.

66. "Says Radio and Press Have Own Fields to Serve," *Editor and Publisher*, (August 10, 1940): 27.

67. Frank Arnold, "Radio and Newspapers."

68. Stockbridge, "News Broadcasting and The Newspapers," *The American Press*, (October 1934): 1.

69. "Says we Are linked in Latin America," *New York Times*, (June 28, 1931): 2.

70. "Radio 'News Service'," *Editor and Publisher*, (September 30, 1933): 32, (emphasis added).

71. "Returns by Radio," *Editor and Publisher*, (November 8, 1924): 22, (emphasis added).

72. F. Parker Stockbridge, "Radio vs. the Press: Will the Newspapers Control Broadcasting?" *Outlook and Independent*, (December 31, 1930): 692, (emphasis added).

73. Will Irwin, *Propaganda and the News*, (New York: McGraw Hill 1936): 252, (emphasis added).

74. "Radio and Circulation," *Editor and Publisher*, (October 23, 1926): 32.

75. "From Telegraph to Television - and Beyond," *New York Times*, (September 13, 1931) 4:8.

76. Report of the Committee on Radio, *Editor and Publisher*, (April 25, 1925).

77. See, for example, Roger Fidler, "Mediamorphosis, or the Transformation of Newspapers into a New Medium," *Media Studies Journal*,

Fall 1992.

78. Edward Harris, "The Attitude of Publishers on Radio Broadcasting," Report made at the annual meeting of the Inland Daily Press Association, Chicago, February 22, 1933, NBC MSS p 6, Box 15, folder 17A, (emphasis added).

79. Ibid.

80. Ibid., (emphasis added), p 5.

81. "Libel Via Radio," *Editor and Publisher*, (June 16, 1928).

82. "News by Radio", *New York Times*, (April 19, 1929), 24:3, (emphasis added).

83. Ibid.

84. See, for example, Michael Clanchy, *From Memory to Written Record: England, 1066-1307*, (Cambridge, Mass: Harvard University Press, 1979).

85. Carolyn Marvin, *When Old Technologies Were New*, (New York: Oxford University Press, 1988).

86. "Editor and NBC Chief Discuss Radio," *Editor and Publisher*, (April 26, 1930): 31, (emphasis added).

87. Idib., 31.

88. "Radio Competition," *Editor and Publisher*, (January 17, 1931), (emphasis added).

89. Gilbert Cant, "Publishers Liberalize Press-Radio Plan," *Broadcasting*, (May 1, 1935), p 7.

90. "California Publishers Propose to Operate Radio Stations," *Editor and Publisher*, (July 11, 1931):46, (emphasis added).

91. "Publishers Oppose Gallery Rights for Radio Reporters," *Editor and Publisher*, (December 2, 1933): 8. (emphasis added).

92. Harris, "The Attitude of Publishers," 5, (emphasis added).

93. Edward Harris to Frank Mason, June 14, 1934, NBC MSS, Box 27, Folder 61, (emphasis added).

94. "Radio and the Press," *Annals of the American Academy*, (January 1935):164, (emphasis added).

95. "Hits Newspaper Control of Radio," *Editor and Publisher*, (October 3, 1936) 9, (emphasis added).

96. Report of Radio Committee, *ANPA Bulletin*, May 3, 1934: 283 (emphasis added).

97. "Radio and the Press," (emphasis added).

98. "Press Fight Urged to Keep Radio Free from Censorship," *New York Times*, April 24, 1936.

4

Radio's Threat to the Institutional Structure of the Press

We feel that the newspapers alone should have the privilege of broadcasting news or sponsoring the broadcast of news.[1]

C.C. Jenkins
Editor, *Toronto Globe,* 1931

We must see that the dissemination of news does not get out of the hands of the newspapers.[2]

S. Thomason
Publisher, *Chicago Times*, 1935

Institutions are not monolithic entities. They are, rather, multifaceted and conglomerate entities, complex structures comprised of various components. Like parts of a machine, each component has its job to play for the entire mechanism to work. Like players on a team, each has its own role in the game. The various parts are all interconnected, and each serves an essential function in the overall operation. Indeed, the relationship among these parts is a crucial component of the structure of an institution. On a baseball team, for example, the structure is defined not only by the nature of each position but also the relationship of the various positions to one another. Each player's job is defined not only by what they do, but also by what they do not do. The pitcher does not have to function as the shortstop. There is a division of labor, with each person free to do their job because the others are doing theirs. The positions are interdependent.

Thus, the structure of a media institution is made up of a system of relationships. In order for the work of the institution to be executed, there are certain tasks that must be performed, certain roles that must be filled. Media institutions that disseminate messages, for example, must divide the duties of the creation, production, and distribution of the message. Different aspects of the job of getting the message to the public are handled by different segments of the institution.[3] The way in which these responsibilities are distributed, and the relationship among the component parts, helps to shape the institutional structure.

This established pattern of relationships can be disturbed by the introduction of a new communication technology. Just as new media can disrupt the established identity of media institutions, so too can they disrupt their structure. Since the tools available to do the work shape the way in which the work is done, communication technologies define, at least in part, the various roles to be filled. A different set of skills is required to work with film than with video. As the technology changes, so do the job descriptions. In other words, then, the division of labor within a media institution is effected by the available technology.

Technology shapes not only the roles in the division of labor in a media institution, but also the relationship among these roles. Since each job is interconnected, the various roles are interdependent. The news director, for example, can only produce the evening newscast if the reporters have gathered their stories. But what happens to these relationships when new communication technologies make possible new ways of gathering, storing and distributing information? Suddenly, there are new ways of doing things. This has the potential to be quite disruptive to the long standing division of labor. Thus, *the introduction of new communication technologies is potentially quite threatening to established institutional structures, for they have the capacity to render long standing procedures and organizational relationships obsolete.*

For example, with the advent of affordable hand held video cameras, almost anyone can now be a reporter. This makes it possible for the news flow to bypass established institutional structures governing the collection of news, thereby robbing journalists of their exclusive role as the nation's news gatherers. Similarly, the advent of video and audiotape technology allowed people to tape material directly off the air, and also to duplicate commercially produced tapes. These technologies made it possible to bypass established institutional structures governing the distribution of such tapes, thereby robbing the purveyors of this material of their monopoly over the distribution process. As this chapter will show, the advent of radio made it possible to bypass the newspapers in the distribution of news, disrupting the established division of labor and thereby threatening the institutional structure of the journalism industry.

Division of labor is not the sole determinant of institutional structure, however. Legal and regulatory restrictions often place limitations on the way in which media institutions are permitted to function. In America, a commitment to free enterprise has produced a complex set of laws designed to limit monopoly and promote competition. Media institutions, for example, must   function within the constraints of antitrust and copyright laws. In addition to such legal restrictions, certain communication institutions are also subject to government regulation. As the regulatory body with jurisdiction over communication technologies in the United States, the Federal Communication Commission has the power to issue regulations governing the daily operation of various media institutions, including those of radio, broadcast and cable television, and telecommunications. These regulations, designed to operationalize the laws governing business and communication practices in this country, have the power to significantly shape the structure of these institutions.

Just as changes in communication technology can disrupt the internal division of labor of a media institution, new technologies can also alter the existing institutional structure, by rendering old laws and regulations obsolete. When information can be gathered, stored and transmitted in new ways, the old rules governing its flow may no longer be applicable. Old rules must be revised or entirely new ones devised to address the realities of the new communication environment. Laws and regulations tend to support the existing institutional structures of the period. However, new technologies call for new rules and new relationships. When the media environment changes, the regulatory environment must change with it. This leads to changes in the ways of doing business, which in turn alters the structure of the institution that is doing the business. By necessitating regulatory changes, therefore, new communication technologies may catalyze changes in the institutional structure of established media.

Recent media history offers numerous examples of this phenomenon. For instance, changes in television technology have lead to amendments in the regulatory restrictions on broadcasting. With the rapid expansion of cable television in the 1980s and the sudden proliferation of channels that came with it, old arguments justifying regulation of broadcast television in the name of 'spectrum scarcity' were challenged. As a result, networks can now own more of their own stations, and can enjoy the syndication profits from their own programming.[4] These regulatory changes had a structural impact, altering previously existing relationships between the networks and both the affiliates and the independent production houses. Similarly, the 1992 Cable Act fundamentally realigned the relationship between cable companies and broadcasters. The broadcasters are now required to offer some sort of compensation to cable operators in exchange for carriage of their signals on local cable systems. Technological innovation led to regulatory changes, which in turn resulted in changes in institutional structure.

Similarly, new media necessitate changes in the legal arena. For example, new communication technologies render existing rules governing intellectual property rights obsolete. By offering communication options not previously available, new technologies might greatly increase the speed or efficiency of the transmission, duplication or distribution of information. This makes it quite easy to violate established copyright laws. Intellectual property laws are designed to protect the rights of an author or creator of a work to profit from its sale or use. Written at an earlier time, such laws could not anticipate the new forms of copyright violation that would be made possible by technological innovation.

By limiting who can profit from the production and distribution of information, copyright laws directly effect the division of labor within an institution and thereby change its structure. Companies that profit from selling ideas are threatened by new media that can bypass established patterns of information distribution and violate rules originally formulated to protect these patterns. When such rules are no longer be enforceable, the stability of the established institutional structure may be disturbed. In recent years, concerns over this issue have been expressed regarding the private reproduction of commercial computer software, the academic use of xerography, and the home use of digital audiotape. In each case, the established structure of a media institution is threatened by the ease with which information can be reproduced by these technologies.

New communications technologies, then, threaten the institutional structure of existing media industries in several ways. They disrupt established division of labor patterns, and they render obsolete both the laws and regulations that were designed to preserve the original structure. In other words, *new technologies threaten media institutions on the economic, regulatory and legal levels*. Changes in any of these three areas can lead to fundamental changes in the structure of the media institution itself. Thus, when old media wage 'war' on new media, part of what they are fighting to protect is the established structure of their institution. They are fighting to defend and preserve the familiar institutional relationships, as well as the established legal and regulatory boundaries designed to maintain those relationships.

Defending institutional structure is not the same as defending institutional identity. Institutional identity is a fairly abstract construct, shaped by ideals and standards. Its defense, therefore, is likely to involve the invocation of rhetoric appealing to those ideals. In contrast, institutional structure is a far more practical realm, governed less by ideals than by economic expedience. At stake is something more tangible than identity. What is being defended at this level are existing roles, rules and relationships. Defending institutional structure means attempting to preserve the ways in which business is done, the division of labor, the relationships between the various players in the institution, and the patterns of profit distribution. These are matters of procedure and practice. They are ways of doing things that have been developed over time, as the most efficient and effective means of doing business. As practical matters, they must be defended in a practical, rather than a philosophical manner. This calls for some form of action.

This chapter examines the ways a new medium threatened the established institutional structure of old medium, and explores the actions taken by established institution to defend the status quo. The story of the Press-Radio War suggests that this action can be economic, political or legal in nature. Since these are the three ways in which new media threaten the established structure of existing media, it only makes sense that defensive action must be taken on all three levels. Pressure against the emergent industry can be exerted on an economic level through an industry boycott of some kind, on a political level through regulatory lobbying, or on a legal level through litigation. These different forms of action are all means to the same end: the preservation of the established rules, roles and relationships that shape the structure of the already established institution.

As this chapter will show, all three of these defense tactics were used in the Press-Radio War as the print journalists fought to protect the established structure of their industry. The advent of broadcasting fundamentally threatened the division of labor patterns that had long governed the institution of journalism. There was a new way of disseminating information through the culture. Roles and relationships long ago established within the journalism industry were no longer 'given'. This disruption of the familiar patterns of information flow also raised new questions about the rules and regulations that had been established to control the channels of communication. So the print journalists fought back, using economic, political and legal tactics to preserve their institution.

The chapter begins by discussing the economic actions taken by the print journalists as they established an industry-wide boycott to preserve familiar division of labor patterns in the gathering and distribution of news. Next their political actions are explored, revealing the ways in which the journalists used the threat of regulatory lobbying to pressure the broadcasters into agreeing to an arrangement that put the control over radio news in the hands of the press. Finally, the chapter closes with an examination of the legal action brought by print journalists to prevent broadcasters from violating established rules governing news flow.

THE THREAT OF RADIO

The advent of radio news posed two key threats to the established institutional structure of journalism. One was that radio would replace newspapers as the nation's primary news source. The other was that radio would disrupt the long-standing relationship between the wire services and the newspapers. Both of these dangers were by-products of the fact that radio opened a new pathway for the flow of information through the culture. This made it possible for news to reach the public without ever passing through the newspapers. It also provided a new channel for the distribution of news by the wire services. In both cases the fear was that news would now bypass the newspapers, and the danger was that radio news would fundamentally alter structure of journalism.

The Threat to Circulation

With the coming of radio news the newspapers faced an entirely new form of competition. While they had long been competing with each other and with magazines for the attention of the American public, here was a competitor that could provide the news much faster than print sources. By the early 1930s over

20 million American homes had a radio receiver.[5] Even when news events were not covered live, radio could deliver information to the people with a speed that simply could not be approximated by the newspapers. Radio news meant that by the time papers hit the news stands, chances were that most people already knew the lead stories of the day, having already heard them on the air. For journalists who for decades had struggled to 'scoop' rival papers and be the first to get the news to the public, this new medium posed a daunting challenge. Many articles in the professional trade journals asked whether the emergence of radio news signaled the death of the newspaper. For instance, Frank Stockbridge, editor of the *American Press*, wondered whether "the newspaper will be supplanted by the radio, as dreamers from Edward Bellamy to H.G. Wells have imagined?" Stockbridge suggested that perhaps "the time will come when receiving sets will be placed in every commuter's train, street car, subway and elevated train and bus, so that the worker on his way to toil can hear the news and not have to bother to read the paper." [6]

Journalists were particularly fearful that the public would no longer have any desire to buy the newspaper once they had heard the news on the radio. As early as 1926, an editorial in *Editor and Publisher* predicted that "if the radio satisfies the natural interest of the public in major news events...the motive to buy newspapers (will be) retarded."[7] Another editorial cautioned that "if news is known by the public through radio broadcasts there is no logical incentive to buy a newspaper to get the news."[8] The Pennsylvania Publishers Association took the position that news broadcast on radio "has a tendency to destroy the surprise value of the news, divert the attention of readers and induce less public interest in the news content of newspapers."[9]

In these predictions of the death of the newspaper is a theme that has reappeared with the introduction of almost every new medium in this century: namely, that the new channel of communication will cause the demise of a previously dominant medium. With the commencement of television, for example, many speculated that the days of cinema were numbered. These warnings were repeated with the arrival of cable, home video and direct broadcast satellite (DBS). The death of network television was forecast in the boom days of cable in the early 1980s, and recently, with the widespread adoption of home computers and the new availability of on-line services, there have been numerous predictions, once again, that the newspaper will soon become obsolete.

History tells us that such predictions have been consistently inaccurate. Clearly, newspapers were not made obsolete by the advent of radio, nor did cinema disappear with the arrival of television, cable or home video. And while network television no longer holds the exclusive position of power it once enjoyed, it remains a powerful force in the broadcast industry. It would appear, then, that the arrival of a new medium is not necessarily the death knell for existing media. While older media may be forced to change in order to adapt to the new communication environment, that does not mean that they will cease to exist. Based on this pattern, it seems safe to speculate that despite the changes taking place in the media environment with the explosion of on-line services, it is highly probable that the newspaper will continue to play an important role in the dissemination of news and information in this country.

The journalists at the time of the Press-Radio War, however, did not have the advantage of history to teach them that established media can survive the arrival of new, competing communication technologies. They could only look to the evidence of circulation and advertising revenue to gauge the extent of the threat posed by broadcasting, and at the time, the numbers did not look promising. Tables 1 and 2 offer a portrait of the financial state of affairs in the journalism industry precisely when the conflict between radio and the press became heated. These figures show a steady decline in both circulation and advertising revenue for the nation's newspapers during this period. Between 1929 and 1933, newspaper sales were down by more than 10 percent, and advertising decreased by nearly 50 percent. While the drop in ad revenue was far greater than the loss in circulation, clearly neither of these numbers were good news for journalists worried about being replaced by radio. However these were also the worst years of the Depression. By the mid 'thirties, circulation and advertising were back up. This strongly suggests that the losses experienced by newspapers during this period were due, at least in large part, to the state of the national economy at the time, and not to radio.

For the journalists of the day, however, radio appeared to be an easy scapegoat for the hardships they were facing. Certainly, there was a Depression going on, and no journalist was unaware of it. Yet it was quite tempting to lay some of the blame for their own hard times on the new competition, for despite the national hard times, radio was having a boom period. During the years that print journalists were watching their own advertising revenue plummet, the broadcasters were enjoying a rapid rise in sponsorship. Table 3 shows the nearly steady increase in radio advertising revenue that took place at this time. Indeed, while newspaper advertising was cut in half during this period, radio ad revenue doubled. It is not surprising, then, that many journalists of the day felt that some of the advertising that could have been theirs was being siphoned off by the new competition.

When the California Newspaper Publishers' Association gathered for its annual meeting in January 1931, the organization president, Harold Judas spoke with concern about the issue of "the radio advertising menace." He described the increases in radio advertising revenue during the previous year, compared them with the considerable loses suffered by newspapers during the same period and suggested that there was "plenty of evidence to indicate the loss in part, if not in whole, of many of the old major advertising schedules from newspapers to radio."[10] Addressing the same matter, an editorial in *Editor and Publisher* titled "Radio Competition" speculated that "considerable money formerly devoted to printed space was not withdrawn because of the business depression, but was diverted to the new and fascinating channel of the air."[11]

An ANPA report on radio competition argued that the significant advertising losses suffered by newspapers during 1930 were "undeniably due in part to the switching of advertising accounts from newspapers to the air."[12]

Table 1
Combined Annual Circulation Figures for Morning and Evening
Newspapers in the U.S., 1929-1937

YEAR	NUMBER OF PAPERS	NET PAID CIRCULATION
1929	1,944	39,425,615
1930	1,942	39,589,172
1931	1,923	38,761,187
1932	1,913	36,407,679
1933	1,911	35,175,238
1934	1,929	36,709,010
1935	1,950	38,155,540
1936	1,989	40,292,266
1937	1,993	41,418,730

Table 2
Estimated Newspaper Advertising Revenue for the U.S., 1929-1937 (in millions of dollars)

YEAR	REVENUE
1929	800
1930	700
1931	620
1932	490
1933	450
1934	500
1935	530
1936	580
1937	600

SOURCE:
Table 1: *Editor and Publisher* Annual Yearbooks, 1927-1937.
Table 2: McCann-Erickson, Inc, for *Printer's Ink*, March 1, 1940.

Note: Figures have been rounded to nearest 5 million.
Totals include national, local retail and classified advertising revenue.

As it turned out, the report was probably right, at least to some degree. As Table 2 indicates, although newspaper advertising revenue recovered with the nation's economy at the end of the 1930s, it did not return to its pre-Depression levels. This makes sense, for despite the fact that the hard times were over, there was now a new channel through which the advertisers could reach the public, and they were diverting a portion of their advertising budgets to the new medium.

Table 3
Estimated Radio Advertising Revenue for the U.S., 1929-1937 (in millions)

YEAR	REVENUE
1929	40
1930	60
1931	80
1932	80
1933	65
1934	90
1935	105
1936	120
1937	145

Source: McCann-Erickson, Inc, for *Printer's Ink*, March 1, 1940.

Note: Figures have been rounded to nearest 5 million.
   Totals include national, local retail and classified advertising revenue.

The timing of all of this suggests that conflicts between old and new media may be intensified by the economic context in which they occur. In what turns out to have been an interesting accident of history, radio arrived in the American home just before the nation plunged into a Depression. Suddenly, people across the nation found themselves out of work and unable to afford entertainment. For those lucky enough to have bought a receiver before they lost their jobs, radio was the answer to the question of what to do in the evening. Radio came along at the perfect time, offering the public free news and entertainment just when they needed it the most. And wherever the public goes, advertisers are sure to follow.

This particular combination of circumstances meant that the emergence of radio posed an especially grave threat to newspapers. Far greater, it would seem, then if radio had arrived during a time of economic stability and prosperity. Suddenly, the newspapers were being bypassed. The audience was turning to a new source, and the advertisers were happy to support this new medium. Several longstanding relationships were being disrupted: the relationship between the newspapers and the public, and the relationship between the newspapers and the advertisers. Roles were shifting. The radio was becoming a viable way for advertisers to reach consumers. It was also becoming an effective channel for the delivery of news to the public. The monopoly that newspapers had held for so long in these areas was crumbling, and as roles and relationships within an institution change, so too must its structure.

The Threat to the Newspaper-Wireservice Link

In addition to threatening the relationships of the newspapers to both the advertisers and the public, radio posed a threat to yet another relationship: that between the newspapers and the wire services. This relationship was one in which the tasks of gathering and distributing the news to the nation were divided between various segments of the journalism industry. It was a relationship that had developed with the advent of another communication technology, the telegraph. The arrival of telegraphy in the 1840s had made possible the instantaneous, long-distance transmission of text. With this new technology came new possibilities in the distribution of information. There were new jobs to be done, new roles to be filled, and new relationships between these roles to be established. The means of distributing information had changed, and with this change came fundamental changes in the institutional structure of journalism.

During the mid-to-late nineteenth century, with the establishment of the Associated Press and its competitors, a network-like arrangement developed. Much like the broadcasting networks that would be established in the twentieth century, these were networks of newspapers linked by telegraph wire. Just as television or radio stations gain access to network programing when they become network affiliates, so too did newspapers gain access to wire service "programming" when they became members or clients of a wire service. By becoming a "node" on one of these networks, a newspaper gained access to news from around the country.

There were, in fact, two different versions of this network-like structure: the Associated Press model, and the United Press/INS model. As explained in Chapter 2, the Associated Press was a cooperative news-gathering organization, with all member papers contributing their own news into the system, and paying membership fees to gain access to the news collected by AP reporters and other member papers. The United Press and International News Service, on the other hand, had their own staff of reporters that gathered the news and made it available to clients in exchange for payment. Under this system, client papers had no obligations to provide UP or INS with their own news. Both arrangements created networks of papers linked together by wire, dependent either upon each other or on a central source for much of their news.

This network-like structure became even more powerful between 1910 and 1940. During this time the institution of journalism transformed, marked by the consolidation and collapse of a great many newspapers across the country. Faced with a number of challenges, including economic pressure resulting from wartime inflation, the Depression, and competition for advertising and circulation revenue, over 250 newspapers went out of business or merged with other papers.[13] During the same period there was a growth in newspaper groups or chains. In 1900 there were only eight groups of dailies, and by 1935 there were sixty-three such groups, controlling over 300 papers. Some of the largest included the Hearst papers and the Scripps-Howard group.[14] Since the various papers in such chains often share news, or all obtain their news from one of the larger papers in the chain, chain publishing, like the newspaper-wire service arrangement, is one in which the individual papers are heavily dependent upon others for much of their news.

The advent of radio news was quite threatening to these well-established news distribution structures. Prior to the advent of broadcasting, news moved from the wire services through the newspapers to the people. In the early days of radio, before broadcasters began to gather their own news, they, like the newspapers, looked to the wire services for their news bulletins. If the press associations provided the broadcasters with the news needed for radio, it would be aired before the newspapers could go to press. The flow of news would now be from the press associations through the radio to the public. This meant that the very papers that had paid for the gathering of this news would be bypassed, thereby fundamentally altering the institutional structure of the newspaper industry. Radio news threatened to undermine the relationship between the wire services and the newspapers, effectively cutting newspapers out of the information flow. The role of distributing the news gathered by the wire services, so long occupied by the newspapers, could now be filled by radio instead.

As described in Chapter 2, press-radio relations during the mid-to-late 1920s were characterized by considerable conflict over the issue of whether the wire services should provide radio with news bulletins. While the majority of journalists objected, those associated with papers that owned or were affiliated with radio stations supported the practice. It was not until the spring of 1933 that a consensus was reached within the newspaper publishing community, and all wire services agreed to stop making their services available to the competition. In the years before this agreement was reached, the trade press was filled with articles protesting the provision of radio with news. Their comments reveal the concern that supplying the broadcasters with news was a fundamental threat to the stability of the established institutional structure of the newspaper industry.

For example, Justus Craemar, president of the National Editorial Association, complained that "news agencies which lend themselves to the use of the broadcasters are literally giving away that which belongs to their members and customers." "This condition," he explained, "is intolerable and must be stopped."[15] Craemer was not alone in this view. An article in *Editor and Publisher*, titled "Giving News to Radio Viewed as Menace to Newspapers by Many Editors" revealed that many prominent journalists of the day had similar misgivings. One editor stated that he did not think that the wire services, "which are created and operated for the main purpose of disseminating news to newspapers, should distribute news through radio" before newspapers have a chance to publish such news. Speaking of the press associations, he said that "their main customers, their original customers and the customers they are created to serve are the newspapers, and their first duty is to the newspapers." He concluded that wire service news "properly and rightfully" belonged "exclusively to the newspapers."[16]

In the same article Joseph Pulitzer said that "*the news associations exist for the purpose of disseminating news to the public through the newspapers*," and therefore "only on rare occasions such as Presidential elections should the news be released for dissemination by radio prior to publication."[17] In both of these comments there is an assertion of a "natural order" to the flow of news in the culture. Clearly this "natural order" did not involve the airwaves.

Some felt that even election returns should be withheld from radio. Just after the elections of 1928, for example, an editorial complained that "the whole country heard the broadcasters read the news of the three press services," despite the fact "that expensive service [election coverage] has been built up through the years at huge expense by the newspaper interests of the country." The editorial observed that by engaging in this practice the wire services were "making a most stupendous and wholly gratuitous contribution to a competing medium," and that "it was nothing short of amazing that the broadcasters were even permitted to read the 'news leads' written for publication in newspapers."[18] Four years later, following the 1932 election, the publisher of the *Tulsa Tribune* asked incredulously, "[h]as the Associated Press decided to kill the newspaper business in the United States?"[19]

A particularly eloquent expression of frustration over the Associated Press policy of supplying election returns to radio came from Walter Humphreys of the *Temple Telegram* in Texas. "We fight the growing encroachment on our field by the radio," he complained, "only to have the news organization to which we belong turn around and help the radio thumb its nose at our honest efforts. Every bulletin we printed in our extra was second hand." In the end, Humphrey concluded, "radio *with the assistance of the Associated Press* scooped us miserably."[20] Similar sentiments were expressed at the annual meeting of the Associated Press in April 1929, during a discussion on whether AP member papers owning stations should be allowed to broadcast AP news. In the words of one disgruntled publisher, "It is not fair for several hundred publishers to gather news and then have it given to the public before they are able to publish it themselves."[21] And another observed with anger that the newspaper "apparently, is only a queer kind of business which gives its product away to a competitor, and stands idly by to see a natural and rightful function supplanted."[22]

The provision of radio with news bulletins was viewed as having serious ramifications for the newspapers of the nation. Numerous articles warned that it was a policy that should be abandoned. Some even suggested that the continuation of this practice threatened the very stability of the industry itself. *Editor and Publisher* warned that "it is a major error for the press to build up the radio as a news instrument by sharing its news reports with that medium of public communication."[23] At its annual convention in 1933, the California Newspaper Publishers' Association issued a resolution that the broadcasting of news gathered and developed by wire services and newspaper staffs was to be viewed as not only harmful to the sale and promotion of newspapers, but also as *"detrimental to the development of the entire newspaper business individually and collectively."*[24]

Elezy Roberts, the first chair of the ANPA radio committee and a staunch opponent of providing radio with news, told *Editor and Publisher* in the spring of 1932 that "we cannot keep on selling news if we permit and encourage others to give it away."[25] Roberts implied that the very role of newspapers as the news vendors of the nation was at stake if they continued providing radio with news bulletins. He felt so strongly about this matter that when he was unable to unite the nation's newspapers on the issue, he resigned his post as Radio Committee Chair. Within a year of his resignation the nation's print journalists finally agreed to put aside their differences on the issue of radio to form an alliance to preserve the established structure of their business.

THE PRESS TAKES ACTION

In their efforts to protect the structure of their institution, print journalists took action on economic, political and legal fronts. On the economic front they formed an alliance with each other to create several economic blockades. On the political front they lobbied in Washington to put regulatory pressure on the broadcasters, and on the legal front they filed charges. In each of these realms their goal was ultimately to preserve the institutional status quo. This three-pronged approach allowed the press to pressure the broadcasters from several directions, all with the aim of preventing radio from disrupting the longstanding patterns of news flow.

ECONOMIC ACTION

One of the ways in which established institutions can attempt to block the development or emergence of competition is through economic action. While political and legal action may cause economic harm as well, they are a less direct way to block the economic development of the competition, and they require the assistance of legal or regulatory bodies to implement decisions. Economic action is more direct. It can be carried out by the established industry itself, without the help of government officials. Economic action generally takes the form of some sort of industry-wide alliance among the various groups or players within the existing industry. Indeed, unless such an alliance takes place, it is usually impossible for any effective economic action to occur.

Once the different players within an industry band together, they can stage a boycott or form a blockade designed to stop the flow of resources to or from the new, competing industry. This might mean refusing to do business with the enemy, refusing to do business with anyone who does business with them, or refusing to hire anyone who also works for the competition. It might mean refusing to run advertising for any company that also advertises with the competing medium, or pressuring the distribution outlets to carry only products from the older medium. Whatever form it takes, economic action is, in essence, a form of institutional blackmail, designed to make the marketplace environment financially uncomfortable for the competition.

In the case of the Press-Radio War, there were two forms of economic action with which the print journalists pressured the broadcasters. The first was the formation of an alliance among the wire services in which they agreed to withhold their news from radio. The second was an action the print journalists never truly took, but merely threatened: a complete, industry-wide ban on the publication of radio program logs. By banding together and refusing to supply radio with news, the wire services and newspapers ensured that their established division of labor would remain undisturbed. By threatening to cease publication of the program logs, the newspapers pressured the networks to agree to an arrangement putting print journalists in charge of gathering and distributing the nation's news.

The Wire Service Blockade

Print journalists were divided over the issue of whether the wire services should provide radio with news. One key factor determining a paper's position was whether it had any financial ties with a local radio station. For those papers involved in some way with broadcasting, their radio stations could be used as promotional devices for their own newspapers. The stations could air wire service bulletins and then direct the listeners to the pages of their newspaper for further details on a story. Papers without ties to radio lacked this option. Thus, if local stations aired wire service stories, the other papers in the area found themselves scooped by radio with no recourse. By the time their own papers hit the news stands, the news would be outdated. For non-broadcasting papers, wire service provision of news bulletins to radio was not in their best interest.

The other factor determining a paper's position on the issue was the wire service to which it subscribed. The wire services of the day were divided the issue of radio, and so, by extension, were papers that used their services. As described in Chapter 2, structural differences between Associated Press and its rivals, the United Press and the International News Service, separated these press associations on the question of providing radio with news. Associated Press, the larger and more powerful of the wire services, opposed the practice, while its smaller competitors supported it.

Thus, in the early stages of press-radio relations, there were two camps on this issue, two groups of print journalists clearly divided on the issue of wire service provision of news bulletins to radio. On the side favoring provision were those journalists who worked for a paper that was affiliated in some way with a radio station, and those whose papers were clients of UP or INS. On the side opposed to provision were those whose paper had no ties with a radio station, and those who were AP members. The two groups differed significantly in their size and composition. Because the Associated Press was much larger than the other two wires services, and the expenses involved with broadcasting were well beyond the reach of most newspapers, the majority of the nation's newspapers fell into the anti-radio camp. The pro-radio camp, while much smaller, included some of the nation's largest and most powerful papers, such as the *Chicago Tribune*, the *Los Angeles Times*, the *New York Sun*, and the *Boston Post*. Thus there were two groups of newspapers and wire services, deeply divided over the issue of radio due to the differences in their positioning in the larger institutional structure of journalism.

These differences translated into nearly ten years of internal conflict between the two camps of journalists on the radio question. The clashes between these two groups on this issue were particularly heated at the annual meetings of the AP and ANPA, and in the years of national political elections. At those times, the pro-radio journalists would campaign for the right to air Associated Press bulletins freely. Following the 1924 elections, in which a number of AP member papers defied Associated Press regulations and broadcast AP election returns, the AP modified its policy to allow news of "transcendent national and international importance" to be aired. 26

While this solved the problem for a short time, the bigger question of what to do about radio remained unsolved until circumstances converged to shift the balance of interests. It was not until the early 1930s that a coalition of forces was formed. By then, the stock market had crashed and the national economic situation had transformed radio from a minor annoyance into a considerable threat in terms of the potential competition it posed in circulation and advertising revenue. In addition, several events had occurred that served to underscore to many of the nation's journalists the serious threat radio posed to the stability of their institutional structure. The 1932 presidential election was fraught with difficulties over the issue of wire service provision of election returns, and the kidnapping of the Lindbergh baby served as a lesson to many journalists regarding the competition they would increasingly be facing with radio over the coverage of high-profile events.

It seems that the lessons learned from these pivotal events, coming as they did in the midst of the Depression, finally tipped the scales in the conflict over news bulletins. The different groups of journalists were finally ready to put aside their differences in the name of their common interest--the preservation of journalism as an institution. Internal division is a luxury that nations and institutions (as well as other social groups) can afford only when they are not also at war with an outside force. During the prosperous years of the 1920s, print journalists could afford to bicker among themselves about radio. But once the hard times of the early 1930s hit, it was time to close ranks and form an alliance against a common enemy.

By the spring of 1933, enough journalists had been convinced of the dangers of radio that an agreement could be reached between the various factions of the industry on the wire service issue. Linked by their losses in advertising and circulation, the nation's journalists decided to put aside their differences and adopt a common policy on the issue of providing radio with news bulletins. At their annual conventions that year, all three wire services agreed to cease providing radio with news bulletins.[27] For the Associated Press, this meant that election returns and other items of transcendent importance would no longer be supplied. For the United Press and the International News Service, this meant a compete cessation of their long practice of giving news to radio for free.

By joining forces, they had formed a blockade designed to control the flow of information by preventing news gathered by print journalists from being disseminated by broadcasters. It was a blockade designed to preserve established patterns of information movement. The longstanding relationship among the various segments of the industry was reaffirmed by this action. The blockade was a statement on the part of the wire services that their role was to supply the newspapers with news. By preventing the flow of news from the wire services to the broadcasters, the print journalism industry had, at least momentarily, protected itself economically. By forming an internal alliance the various players within the journalism industry forced the broadcasters to look elsewhere for their news. By ensuring that the established relationship between the newspapers and the wire services was maintained, the blockade served to preserve, for at least a time, the longstanding institutional structure of journalism.

The Program Log Blockade

Blocking the flow of news to radio was not the only form of economic action available to the print journalists in their fight against radio. Another arena in which they had leverage was that of the publication of radio program logs. In the mid-1920s, when radio programming was in its infancy, many newspapers had developed the practice of publishing radio program logs free of charge. In those days, radio posed little threat to newspapers. Radio was the novelty of the day, and the publication of these logs was seen as a circulation booster.[28] Furthermore, these early logs took up very little space in the newspaper, since the initial offerings of the early stations were so limited. As program line-ups started to expand broadcasting took on more and more advertising. Thus, not only were the logs taking up more room in the paper, but the programs listed in them began bearing the name of their sponsor, such as the "A&P Gypsies" or the "Maxwell House Orchestra."[29] The publication of the program logs therefore meant the provision of free advertising to the sponsors of these programs, much to the distress of many journalists.

Like the debate over supplying radio with wire service bulletins, the program log issue was one over which the press had a difficult time reaching consensus. From the mid-1920s through the early 1930s, numerous resolutions were adopted by newspapers and publishers associations either to cease the publication of radio program logs entirely, or to modify the listings so that the sponsor names were eliminated. Such modifications would mean, for example, listing a program as "orchestral music" rather than as the "Maxwell House Orchestra." These resolutions never held for long however. Invariably, after a time, the practice would resume.

The issue was first raised for formal consideration at the 1925 annual convention of the ANPA. What emerged from that meeting was the first of many announcements that newspapers should or would stop printing the names of sponsors in program logs. On this occasion, the Radio Committee of the ANPA recommended that its members "refuse to publish free publicity in their news columns concerning programs consisting of direct advertising" and further suggested that they "eliminate from program announcements the name of trade-marked merchandise or known products obviously used for advertising."[30] This was the first such pronouncement, but it would not be the last. From 1925 through 1933, the logs were an issue of contention. As with the question of providing radio with news, the program log issue was one over which the print journalists could not seem to agree. Again and again, publishers associations or newspapers would declare their intention to stop printing radio program logs, or to modify the logs in some way so as to eliminate the trade names. But inevitably, the logs would eventually reappear.

Most publishers supported the idea of banning the logs in principle. *Editor and Publisher* reported that when "scores of newspapers" were questioned, "general sympathy" with banning the trade names was expressed. The *Chicago Tribune,* for instance, took the position that "radio programs are news columns and that advertising has no more place in them than in other news columns of the paper."[31] The view of many publishers seemed to be "that to print free advertising in the radio columns is bad newspaper practice."[32] Despite widespread support for the boycott in principle, the newspapers had great difficulty upholding the practice. The problem was that while the newspapers resented the logs, the public loved them. Each time the papers tried to eliminate the listings, they were inundated with letters and phone calls from their readers.

For instance, in November 1926, the *New York Telegram* announced it was resuming publication of the program logs, after having dropped them only a few months earlier. In justifying the *Telegram's* decision, G. B. Parker explained that the paper had received "literally thousands of letters and telephone calls" from radio listeners, "people representing the rank and file of newspaper readers, who simply wanted their radio news and information presented to them in an understandable manner."[33]

Several years later, when the Southern Newspaper Publisher's Association polled its members about how they were handling radio logs, many responded that they had attempted to omit or modify them, but had returned to providing them in full after receiving complaints from readers. "We omitted programs for a few days," said one publisher, "but protests caused us to resume publication." Another reported, "We discontinued radio programs about a month ago, and have received a fair number of complaints."[34] When the complaints grew loud enough, most newspapers abandoned the blockade.

While some papers were willing to hold out and resist the temptation of printing the logs, it was difficult to maintain this stance when other newspapers were giving in to public pressure. Boycotts only work effectively if everyone participates in them. When papers participating in the boycott reversed their position, it became difficult for others to uphold the blockade. When the *New York Telegram* reversed its position for example, within a week the *New York Evening World* and the *New York Sun* had made similar announcements. *Editor and Publisher* explained that "the consensus of opinion was that since the *Telegram* had broken the pact there was nothing to do but to follow."[35] Some papers said that they would be willing to eliminate radio listings if other papers would do so as well. *Editor and Publisher* reported that "nearly every publisher polled answered affirmatively" when asked if they would be willing to co-operate with their competitors in adopting a universal policy on handling radio logs.[36] Achieving such a consensus was quite difficult, however. Speaking before a gathering of the American Society of Newspaper Editors, Mr. W. G. Vorpe, editor of the *Cleveland Plain Dealer*, suggested, "If you can find any group of editors who will agree on this we ought to get a photograph of them."[37]

It is appropriate to ask whether publishers' opinions on the program log issue were determined by whether their paper owned a radio station since this was very much the case with whether or not to provide radio with news. On this issue however it does not seem to have been so clear cut. Many non-broadcasting newspapers chose to publish program logs simply to avoid alienating their readers. However there is at least one piece of evidence that those papers owning stations may have been more favorably inclined to publish radio logs than their non-broadcasting colleagues. In his address before the ASNE, Vorpe noted that the opinions of publishers whose newspapers also operated radio stations "naturally differ from those of the newspapers publishers who so far have had no direct action in connection with broadcasting."[38]

By the spring of 1931, however, with the Depression well under way and many newspapers feeling the pinch of lost advertising dollars, the membership of the ANPA was able to come to some agreement on the matter of program logs. After what was reported as a "spirited attack on radio competition" delivered by the ANPA Radio Committee, members adopted a resolution stating that radio programs, if published, "should be handled as paid advertising." This resolution seems to have had a bit more impact than previous ones. A survey the following year showed that only twenty-four members were publishing the radio logs in full, with 320 eliminating the trade names and sixty-six publishing them only as paid advertising.[39] Ultimately, however, this ANPA resolution did not have a strong effect on the practice of printing program logs, because two years later, in 1933, when all of the publishers put aside their differences to take more formal action against radio, they found it necessary once again to issue *another* recommendation that newspapers publish radio listings only as paid advertising.

The challenge here, as in the case of the wire service issue, was reaching a true industry-wide consensus on the matter of program logs. As long as some papers felt it was in their best interest to print the listings, there was no possibility of taking any real action on the matter. Such an industry-wide alliance was not possible until the wire service issue had been settled. As it turned out, the program log issue was a card that the print journalists would not play until they were deep in negotiations with the broadcasters over the Press-Radio Bureau. At that point, threatening the networks with the elimination of the program logs became a useful way in to pressure them to acquiesce to the terms of the Biltmore Agreement. But before telling that piece of the story, however, it is first necessary to explore how the press managed to get the broadcasters to the negotiating table.

POLITICAL ACTION

Having united to take economic action in the form of the wire service boycott, print journalists had taken the first step in protecting the structure of their industry. The formation of a news blockade served to protect the newspaper-wire service relationship, and thus preserved that portion of the news stream. News would continue to flow from the wire services through the newspapers to the people. Still, at this stage, there was nothing to prevent the broadcasters from gathering news on their own and transmitting it directly to the public, which is precisely what began to happen. Since the blockade left the broadcasters without a news source, they were driven to form their own news divisions. This meant that the economic action of refusing to provide radio with news bulletins was only the first step. If the press was to retain control over the gathering and dissemination of news, further action was needed to pressure broadcasters into surrendering to an arrangement that would return the reigns to print journalists. This time, the action was political.

The political stage of the Press-Radio War involved lobbying to bring about changes in the regulatory environment that would support the existing institutional structure. As part of their battle to block the emergence of new media, the press attempted to enlist the help of the government against the new competition. They were looking for assistance in creating an environment that would prove inhospitable to the development of a new communication institution and that would assist in preserving the existing structure. Print journalists attempted to do this by trying to persuade the government to limit or eliminate advertising from the airwaves.

Calls for Government Regulation

Print journalists of the early 1930s had good reason to be hostile to commercial broadcasting. As mentioned earlier, radio enjoyed considerable gains in advertising revenue in the years that the newspapers were suffering severe losses. Although most of these losses were due to the national financial crisis, many journalists felt that radio was stealing advertisers from newspapers. This made radio a particularly good target upon which print journalists could vent their frustrations about the dire economic straits in which they found themselves. It was about this time that the calls began to be heard, from the journalists, for the government either to curtail or eliminate advertising from the airwaves.

In calling for government regulation of radio advertising, these print journalists were joining a small, growing movement to bring about regulatory reform in broadcasting. In the period between the passage of the 1927 Radio Act and the 1934 Communication Act, a vocal group of lobbyists emerged to wage a campaign against commercial broadcasting. Consisting mainly of educators, religious leaders, and labor organizers, the broadcast reform movement fought hard to bring about changes in spectrum allocation and to rid the airwaves of commercials.[40] These activists argued that the airwaves belonged to the people and that this resource should not be given wholesale to commercial broadcasters for the purpose of making a profit. While their efforts were ultimately unsuccessful, they were able for a brief time to put the issue of broadcast reform on the national political agenda, and they received assistance in this project from some of the nation's print journalists.

One of the first and most outspoken journalists on the issue of broadcast reform was Harold Davis, the publisher of the *Ventura Free Press*, a daily newspaper in a small town north of Los Angeles. In 1931 Davis launched a national campaign to unite the newspaper publishers of America against the growing threat of radio. His specific complaint was with radio as a direct competitor for advertising revenue. Davis dedicated himself to trying to bring about legislative reform that would eliminate direct advertising from the air. Using his own publication as a forum for his views, Davis filled the pages of the *Ventura Free Press* with articles calling for a change in the laws governing radio advertising. He also attempted to form an alliance with various other lobby organizations in the country, such as the National Committee on Education by Radio (NCER), the American Civil Liberties Union (ACLU), and the National Congress of Parents and Teachers (NCPT), which were engaged in their own efforts to fight the increasing commercialization of the airwaves. Finally, Davis directed a tremendous amount of energy toward enlisting the support of the publishers of small newspapers around the country. For several years he inundated some 900 daily papers with press releases, articles, and letters, urging them to join him in the effort to "arouse public sentiment for the support of legislation that will defeat the purpose of the radio monopoly and drive direct advertising from the air."[41]

That Davis targeted his campaign at *small* publishers, i.e, without ties to radio is quite clear. It can be seen immediately from a glance at the names of some of the newspapers that were the recipients of his missives. Those on his mailing list included the *The Niles Center Press* in Niles Center, Illinois, *The Citizen* in Asheville, North Carolina, *The Norfolk Daily News* in Norfolk, Nebraska, and *The Zepyrillis News* in Zepyrillis, Florida. These were not papers of major stature, nor were they likely to be heavily invested in radio stations of their own. In describing his objectives, Davis acknowledged that one of his aims was to unite those publishers who were not involved with broadcasting. In one of his letters soliciting support, he pointed out that "very few of the present publishers' associations would be able to make the kind of aggressive fight that is needed to win the battle," because "too many of the influential members have radio stations or are connected by contract with such stations." He went on to explain that "unity of action" was needed, and that the route to achieving that goal was to create "an organization of interested publishers."[42] Clearly, Davis saw himself as attempting to forge such an alliance.

Just how much support Davis found among his fellow publishers is hard to say. According to him, newspapers all across the country were enthusiastically backing his efforts. The *Ventura Free Press* reported, for example, that in the first six months of the campaign, "more than a thousand newspapers promised their cooperation."[43] Another *Free Press* article claimed that these papers were regularly publishing the articles and press releases about the dangers of radio advertising sent to them by Davis. The article went on to offer quotes from letters of support from various journalists around the country. One, for example, was sent by G. L. Caswell, of the Iowa Press Association, who wrote: "Your efforts to stop the unfairness of the present national radio set-up are appreciated. We are ready to encourage and back your efforts."[44] Another letter came from a Mr. Holford, the managing editor of the *Zephyrillis News*, who stated that he was "deeply interested in your campaign to hold the air free for ourselves and posterity," and asserted that the campaign "should enlist newspaper support all over the nation."[45]

That Davis was not alone in his views is evident from the fact that other print journalists of the period issued their own calls for tighter government control over radio advertising. Some argued for government control specifically in the area of news sponsorship. At the spring meeting of the ANPA in 1930, for example, Morris Atwood, associate editor of Gannett Newspapers, took the position that the government should not allow advertisers to sponsor news. Addressing his fellow publishers, he asserted that "just as the government has said that the packers shall not sell groceries, so it would not be unreasonable for the government to say that lipstick factories, orange juice stands, iron foundries and microscope manufacturers shall not broadcast news."[46]

Others questioned the legality of using the public airwaves for commercial purposes at all. At its annual spring meeting in 1931, the ANPA adopted a resolution calling for an investigation of "the legality of radio broadcasting of direct advertising under exclusive government franchise of wave lengths in competition with other advertising media not enjoying similar governmental protection."[47] Several years later, the ANPA Radio Committee issued a similar statement, suggesting that efforts be directed toward an inquiry "into the question of vested rights in these valuable [radio] channels to determine just what right the Federal Government has to hand them out to private capital for the purposes of profit."[48]

Similarly, Frank Rogers, editor of the *Leader-Republican* of Gloversville, New York, speculated that "ten years from now," people will wonder "why the government of the United States took upon itself the parcelling for commercial purposes of something which belongs to the people of the country."[49]

In addition to questioning the legality of commercial broadcasting, some print journalists also complained that radio was receiving preferential treatment from the government. The broadcasters, they complained, were being granted monopolistic control over the airwaves and were thus essentially protected from competition. Since none of the other media had the benefit of such government protection, some journalists felt that this arrangement was unfair. In an article titled "Radio Reform Imperative," *Editor and Publisher* called radio a "monopolistic monster...maintained against competition by so-called regulation of the air by our government for which and to which it makes no return."[50] What is not mentioned here is that newspapers had long enjoyed their own version of special treatment from the government, in the form of reduced postal rates.

Many of the calls by print journalists for stricter government control over radio contained references to the "European system," with praise for a model in which the governments controlled the airwaves and there was little or no advertising. The California Press Association, for instance, brought forth a resolution favoring "government supervision of all radio programs along the lines followed in continental Europe and a stricter control of the air in the interests...of the people."[51] A similar resolution was adopted by the California Newspaper Publisher's Association, asking that "by Federal enactment a start be made to return to the people the air channels now used by commercial interests, similar to the plan now in effect in England."[52]

Similarly, when the ANPA Radio Committee issued its annual report in April 1933, it suggested that the United States follow the example of Europe, where most "foreign countries have placed radio broadcasting under government ownership or have definitely restricted the amount of advertising." The report went on to suggest that "what has been done in foreign countries does lend material for serious thought and consideration," and took the position that "the only way in which to control the broadcasting of news is through government ownership, in cooperation with the newspapers, or by strict government regulation on what can and cannot be broadcast."[53] Note that in this proposal, newspapers are offered as an institution that would work with the government to help "control" radio.

A few months later, Edward Harris delivered a speech before the National

Editorial Association in which he raised many questions about who should control and finance radio. Noting that there were only a limited number of radio frequencies available, and that Congress had given these channels over to private interests for the sole purposes of making a profit, Harris asked his audience: "How can we have freedom of speech over radio so long as the holders of these exclusive privileges are the sole judges of what can and cannot be broadcast?" The answer to this dilemma, he suggested, lay in following the example of the European model. "Foreign governments," he explained, "have found the solution in government ownership or government control, and it is possible that we also may be compelled to adopt this policy if radio is actually to be used in the 'public interest, convenience and necessity.'" [54] The irony is that here we have the American press, a longstanding symbol of freedom from government control over the channels of communication, suggesting that in the name of free speech, the government should take over radio.

Public Interest Rhetoric

The justification that print journalists offered for this rather un-American proposal was quite clever. Borrowing from the language of the 1927 Radio Act, those print journalists who called for government restriction of broadcast advertising invoked the rhetoric of "serving the public interest." They claimed that the use of the airwaves for commercial purposes failed to serve the public interest. On these grounds, they argued that the government was justified in limiting or entirely eliminating commercials from the airwaves. Chapter 3 described the print journalists' invocation of the rhetoric of objectivity in their argument that radio was unable to provide news that met the professional standards of journalism. Here again, sacred rhetoric was invoked, but this time the language comes not from the unofficial codes of professional journalism, but from existing broadcast legislation. This was a brilliant tactical move on the part of the print journalists, who argued that no new legislation was needed. They suggested that the current institutional structure of broadcasting was in violation of existing regulations, and should thus be brought into compliance with the rules. The use of the term "public interest" was also a marvelous smokescreen, for it allowed print journalists to campaign for regulatory changes that would ultimate serve their own interests while appearing to be working for the common good.

Harold Davis, for example, relied heavily on public interest rhetoric as a part of his campaign against commercial radio. In one of the many letters he sent to editors of small town papers, he asked his fellow journalists to consider the question: "Are radio-broadcasting stations really serving the 'public interest and necessity,' or have they degenerated into strictly commercial enterprises...forcing insolent ballyhoo into millions of American homes?"[55] Similarly, in one of his many anti-radio articles, he attacked the broadcasters for "crowding more and more advertising on the air for the selfish purpose of piling up more and more private profits for themselves," and for doing so "without proper consideration of the public interest".[56] Another missive, entitled "Exploiting the Public," accused the "radio monopoly" of "using the ether for the promotion of private business enterprise," and went on to complain that "owners of receiving sets are not consulted as to their wishes, but the broadcasters presume to use them in a scheme to get more revenue for selfish profit." The article concluded with a prediction that the day would come when the American people would "decide that they have had enough of radio advertising and will sweep it into the discard, where it belongs," and that "the days of broadcasting for private profit at the expense of the people are numbered."[57]

Davis was not the only one to frame the issue in public interest terms however. Several years later, when the independent radio stations chose not to go along with the networks in participating in the Press Radio Bureau, the ANPA Radio Committee interpreted this move as an abdication on the part of these broadcasters of their responsibility to serve the public. The year after the Press Radio Bureau began operations, the Radio Committee praised the two networks for cooperating in the arrangement and thus "performing a public service to radio listeners." That the independent stations had chosen not to cooperate, the Committee explained, could be attributed to the fact that "the sound of the cash register means more to them than the preservation of principles which affect the welfare of the general public."[58]

Public interest rhetoric showed up in many other places as well. In November 1933, soon after the Columbia Broadcasting System established its own news division, *Editor and Publisher* ran an editorial titled "The Radio Menace," written in reaction to CBS's request that its reporters be admitted to the Press Gallery in Congress. *Editor and Publisher* took a strong stand against this proposal, partly on the grounds that "radio's primary news objective *is not public interest*, but the profitable sale of advertising to sponsors of its *alleged news service*."[59] This statement challenges both the quality of radio news coverage and the commitment of the broadcasters to serving the public. The implications here are that radio news reporters should not have access to the proceedings of Congress because the networks for which they work are too profit hungry. (Given that line of reasoning, of course, no newspaper reporters should have been allowed into the gallery either.)

As part of their general argument that radio was failing in its responsibility to serve the public, some print journalists attempted to draw an analogy between the institution of broadcasting and those of learning and religion. They took the position that advertising on the radio is as inappropriate as placing ads on the walls of schools or churches. For example, in a debate with NBC President Merlin Aylesworth over a luncheon at the St. Regis Hotel, Charles Russell, a former newspaper editor, took a strong position on this matter, asserting that "to have this force [radio] used for purposes of private greed is as disastrous as it would be to make similar use of public school education." He went on to say, "[w]e should no more give over the function of radio to advertising than we should use our high schools to increase the sales of somebody's cure for warts."[60]

This view was also voiced by Bruce Bliven, editor of the *New Republic*. In October 1934, at a meeting of the National Advisory Council on Radio in Education, Bliven spoke against the use of radio for commercial purposes, saying that it is just as reasonable to turn the airwaves over to advertisers as it is to "put a showcase full of placards extoling laxatives into the anteroom of every church and public library" or to "turn over half of the blackboard in every school room to signs which sing the praises of chewing gum or bunion cures."[61]

Others speculated on the many ways that radio could be used to serve the public, and lamented the highly commercial orientation that dominated American broadcasting. One article observed that while in other countries radio "is rapidly becoming a tool of popular education, a means of promoting national unity," in the United States "its most spectacular victory so far has been the sale of toothpaste, cigarettes and patent medicines."[62] And Harold Davis noted that if "properly and wisely handled, radio "could be a remarkable instrument for the common good," but predicted that "its 100 percent advertising exploitation for private profit will turn out to be a real American tragedy."[63]

It was, ostensibly, to the goal of preventing this dire outcome that Davis' campaign was dedicated. "Newspapers have the patriotic duty," he wrote in 1931, "to assist Congress in recovering full public control over this national asset (radio)." He explained that this could be achieved, by "removing the profit motive, by barring from the air all advertising except the bare announcement of program sponsorship."[64] Similarly, in another mailing, he later portrayed the campaign against commercial radio as a public duty of the newspapers. As he put it, "the newspapers of America must undertake the destruction of the radio monopoly as a duty they owe the public. The newspapers are the guardians of democracy, of American institutions. It is up to them to defend freedom of the air..." [65] Here again public interest rhetoric is invoked as a justification for attempting to bring about broadcast regulation reform. In the end, however, the efforts of the journalists were dedicated not to protecting the public's interest, but to protecting their own.

Lobbying and The Biltmore Conference

By late autumn in 1933, the print journalists had locked radio out of the newspaper-wire service relationship by forming their alliance and staging an economic boycott against the broadcasters. In response, the networks had established their own news divisions. The problem facing print journalists was how to regain control over the process of disseminating news to the American people. The solution they turned to was the use of political pressure to frighten the broadcasters into accepting the terms of a rather one-sided agreement.

In early December 1933, a crucial meeting was held between representatives from the print journalism and broadcasting industries at the Biltmore Hotel in New York City. That meeting produced an arrangement that came to be known as the Biltmore Agreement. Under this plan, it was agreed that the networks would dismantle their news divisions and would henceforth receive two brief news bulletins a day, to be supplied by the Press-Radio Bureau. This Bureau, which was to be established following the Biltmore Conference, would have the job of taking wire service news bulletins from the three press associations and turning them into copy to be read over the air. These bulletins could only be aired at certain times of the day, to avoid competition with the morning and evening additions of the newspapers. They were also to be aired without sponsorship.66 (See Chapter 2 for further details on the Biltmore Conference.)

Why were the networks willing to participate in an arrangement that forced them to stop their own news gathering, limited them to two brief bulletins a day, and prevented them from earning advertising revenue from these newscasts? The answer, it seems, is that they were pressured into cooperating by the threat of increased political lobbying on the part of the print journalists. The timing could not have been better, for it was precisely at this point that plans were in the works for an important new piece of broadcast legislation, the 1934 Communications Act. The NCER was hard at work in Washington trying to win support for their cause. If ever the publishers had an opportune moment to frighten broadcasters into cooperating with them by threatening to join the fight against commercial broadcasting, this was it.

The evidence for this comes primarily from various comments made at the time about the Biltmore Agreement. Following the conference, for example, *Broadcasting* magazine observed that the networks had agreed to cooperate with the press "with the thought in mind that a friendly and cooperative attitude would preclude *newspaper agitation against radio during the coming session of Congress.*"67 Another editorial noted that in consenting to the Biltmore Agreement the networks had secured from the press "*a plainly implied acceptance of the fact that sponsor-support is the proper American way of broadcast operation.*"68

Isabelle Keating, a journalist writing for *Harper's* at the time, described the kind of "agitation" in which the newspapers had been engaging. Publicly, she wrote, the press "could and did challenge radio's methods of serving the public interest convenience and necessity."

> Privately, the press inquired, in quarters where radio's representatives could not fail to hear, whether there might not have been some irregular allocation of wave bands from time to time; whether radio was not in fact subservient to the reigning political party because of its governmental license; whether as a result it was not qualified to purvey disinterested news.

With the press raising such uncomfortable questions in "strategic quarters," Keating notes, it came as no surprise when the ANPA Radio Committee announced that the networks had made "an urgent appeal" to meet with them in December 1933.69 Not long after the agreement, the *New Republic* observed that the broadcasters had capitulated to the publishers' demands primarily out of "fear of newspaper agitation against monopoly."[70]

Political pressure was not the only form of incentive print journalists gave broadcasters to surrender, however. They combined the threat of political action with economic action, by once again bringing up the issue of the program   logs. Although it was never explicitly mentioned as part of the agreement, it was apparently understood that in exchange for acquiescing to the Biltmore plan, the networks were assured that newspapers would continue to publish radio program logs in full. As NBC President Merlin Aylesworth explained, "There was a general feeling on the part of the part of radio broadcasters that this cooperative experiment would result in all of the newspapers of the country rendering a program service...to the vast number of readers who listen to radio."[71]

Similarly, an article in *Broadcasting* reported that the networks were "virtually forced" into an agreement with the publishers in order to avoid seeing the majority of the nations' papers "eliminate all program listings and *wage a bitter war on radio generally.*"[72] Another article reported that several weeks before the Biltmore meeting, the National Radio Committee of the ANPA, representing "the majority of the 1,800 daily papers in the United States," had approached the networks, saying that it was ready to "*ban together not only to eliminate radio program listings but to carry on a fight in Congress and in their columns against radio.*"[73]

In the words of H. V. Kaltenborn, "If you ask why the broadcasters accepted such an unsatisfactory and humiliating arrangement, the answer is simple. They feared the power of the press. That power was ready to swing against them."[74] Just how real this threat was is hard to know. Robert McChesney presents convincing evidence to suggest that in actuality the majority of the nation's press was relatively inactive when it came to offering any real support to the broadcast reform movement.[75] While very little action may have been taken, there are enough statements about lobbying to strongly suggest that at least the threat of political action played some role in getting the broadcasters to acquiesce to the journalists' demands.

Another reason that the publishers were so successful in getting what they wanted out of the Biltmore conference was that they went into the meeting with something that the broadcasters lacked--a united front. The networks were divided. NBC had no real news-gathering organization to speak of, and had very little to lose by agreeing to the plan. Given the climate of political pressure at the time, NBC was quite ready to capitulate to the publishers' demands. CBS was more willing to fight, but it could not do so alone. If it did so, newspaper publishers across the country were threatening to boycott CBS, publishing only NBC's program listings. The danger here was that since advertisers preferred backing programs that were mentioned in the newspapers, a press boycott of CBS programs could have resulted in an exodus of sponsors from CBS to NBC. Thus, CBS had little choice but to cooperate.[76]

While the networks may have lost this round in their battle with the press, they ultimately won on the political front. Not long after the formation of the Press-Radio Bureau, Congress essentially abandoned all discussion of the structure of the broadcast industry. The Wagner-Hatfield Amendment, a proposal to set aside twenty-five percent of the airwaves for noncommercial use, was defeated. The 1934 Communication Act was passed, with no significant reallocation of frequencies. Advertising-supported, commercial broadcasting had won and the initial stages of the social construction of broadcasting were complete.

The press also abandoned the subject of government control over radio at this time. Once they obtained agreement from the networks to participate in the Press-Radio Bureau, the matter was dropped from the print journalists' discussions about radio. Despite the fact that tensions between the two industries were not yet fully resolved, once the networks agreed to stop broadcasting sponsored news, the press suddenly lost interest in agitating for legislative reform. As Robert McChesney puts it in his discussion of "Press-Radio Relations and the Emergence of Network, Commercial Broadcasting in the United States" during this period, "after December 1933 [the Biltmore Conference], the [print journalism] industry never again threatened to use its influence to challenge the legitimacy of commercial broadcasting."[77] Thus it would seem that all of the talk about public interest was purely rhetoric. As soon as the real problem of losing advertising dollars to radio looked as if it were settled, journalists were no longer so concerned about the public interest, for their own interests were no longer so threatened. [78]

LEGAL ACTION

At the Biltmore Conference the press had achieved an important victory. Through a combination of economic and political pressure they had succeeded in persuading the networks to agree to their terms and had regained some degree of control over the process of news gathering and dissemination. Winning a battle, however, does not necessarily mean winning the war. Despite the apparent success of the Conference, the independent broadcasters left the meeting without consenting to the terms of the agreement. This left the press with a serious problem, for only about 150 of the nation's 600 radio stations were network owned or affiliated.[79] Thus, the independent stations were the majority. While they lacked the financial clout enjoyed by the network affiliates, they had strength in numbers. This strength, in the end, would be a key factor in the failure of the Biltmore Agreement, and in the press' loss of their war with radio.

When the Press-Radio Bureau began operations on March 1st, therefore, it was without the participation of the independent broadcasters. No longer able to turn to the newspapers or wire services for news bulletins, the independent stations were in need of a new source for their news. A vacuum had been created, and it was not long before several news-gathering agencies emerged to fill it.[80] As described in Chapter 2, these were essentially wire services for radio, consisting of teams of reporters who gathered their own news and provided bulletins to the broadcasters by telegraph and teletype. Unlike the

Press-Radio Bureau, however, these services placed no limitations on the time of day the newscasts could be aired, neither did they prohibit the stations from airing the news with commercials. Because they provided a service for which there was a great need, these news services were well received and soon posed serious competition for the Press-Radio Bureau.

There was nothing that the press could do to block these new services. Supplying radio with news was a legitimate business, and there was no justification for the press to take any kind of legal action against them. What the journalists could do, however, was closely monitor the broadcasters for any violations of rules governing the flow of news. Specifically, they were concerned with the unauthorized use of "their" news by the broadcasters. The press was suspicious that the independent broadcasters might be "stealing" news from either the wire services or the newspapers. This would have constituted a violation of intellectual property rights laws governing news and would be grounds for legal action.

In the period following the Biltmore Conference, the press shifted its attack strategy from a political and economic approach to a legal one. Having pressured the networks into an agreement that would preserve the existing institutional structure of journalism, print journalists then took legal action to prevent the independent broadcasters from disrupting that structure. On the lookout for rule violations, they placed broadcasters under close surveillance and filed charges when they found what they felt were infractions of the laws governing information use.

The invocation of property rights over the news assumes that news is a commodity or an article of trade, a product over which one can claim ownership. This concept is borrowed from the domain of copyright, in which commodity status is conferred upon ideas. Copyright is designed to protect the creator of an original artistic, literary, or scientific work from the unauthorized use of that work for a certain period of time.[81] The laws of copyright are based on the premise that ideas belong to someone, and that their authors are therefore entitled to protection from the theft of those ideas.

Intellectual property laws define and maintain control over the flow of ideas. They assist in the establishment of boundaries in the communication process. Just as national borders delineate geographic territory, copyright laws define territorial boundaries in the realm of communication. They establish ownership over ideas, which places restrictions on the ways ideas can be used, by whom and for what purposes. They are part of the larger, ongoing process in which society is constantly engaged--the management of social discourse. By helping to establish and maintain patterns of communication in society, rules of this kind help preserve the communication status quo, for they control who gets to speak to whom, and in what ways.

When new communication technologies are developed, they often facilitate the violation of established rules. New technologies make it possible to send and receive information in ways that old copyright laws never anticipated. Such laws, written to protect the authors of ideas from the theft of their work through unauthorized duplication, are greatly challenged by the invention of new communication technologies. These technologies often allow people to gain access to, reproduce, and/or disseminate the work of another without the author's knowledge or permission. In recent years there have been numerous examples of this phenomenon as various communication institutions have grappled with questions of copyright pertaining to home use of videotape technology, reprographics, and digital audiotaping. Current debates rage over how intellectual property rights can be protected in the transmission of information on-line.[82]

Because they make it so easy to break the old rules governing copyright, new media are potentially disruptive to established patterns of control over the flow of information in society. The intellectual property issue is therefore deeply linked with the question of stability of existing media institutions. If an institution can no longer protect its ownership of information, it can easily lose its position of power in the cultural communication process. Thus, battles over the issue of intellectual property rights are ultimately battles for control over the flow of information in society. At stake in fights of this nature is the stability of the established information order.

But do the laws of copyright apply to journalism? After all, one might argue, news is public information that is available to anyone. How can anyone claim ownership over it? By the time radio came along, the question of whether one can in fact have property rights over news had already been settled. In a precedent-setting case in 1918, *International News Service v. Associated Press*, the AP accused the International News Service of stealing AP news. At that time, the Supreme Court ruled that while a news-gathering agency had no property rights over its news with relation to the public, it did have such rights with respect to its competition. The ruling stated that news theft between competing industries in the business of selling news was prohibited on the grounds of unfair competition in business.[83] The case was thus settled along the lines of fairness in business rather than intellectual property rights. Nonetheless, a precedent had been established. News was found to have commercial value and unauthorized use of this property for commercial purposes was considered unfair competition. Thus, according to this ruling, those who gathered the news had the exclusive rights to sell that information to the public.

With the *INS v. AP* case, rules governing the relationship between competing news agencies were established. Such rules provided order and control over the way in which news and information flows through the society. But the stability achieved with the 1918 ruling did not last for long. These rules were established when the institution of journalism was defined by two primary media of communications, the newspaper and the telegraph. The arrival of radio brought the capacity to transmit information in new ways that disrupted the established patterns governing news flow. The new medium created a new situation not covered under the old rules. Previously, if one wire service stole news from another, the stolen news could not be printed any faster by the thief than by the original owner. But radio could take news off the wires and print it long before the newspapers had a chance to publish the news for which they had paid. This was a new kind of news theft, one not anticipated by previous rules governing intellectual property rights over news. Thus, once again the issue of news theft was brought before the courts.

In pursuing legal action, just as they had when taking economic and political action, the print journalists invoked a "sacred" rhetoric to justify their stance against radio. Earlier we heard of their invocation of the ideals of objectivity and public service. In this case the sacred value being called upon was that of private property. The concept of private ownership and property rights is a key principle in our economic system. Capitalism is fundamentally linked with the belief in private ownership and private property. There is something essentially American about the federal protection of property rights. The Fourth Amendment to the U. S. Constitution protects citizens from unlawful entry of their homes or unlawful seizure of their material property. Copyright laws are an extension of the basic principles of property rights. They are laws that embody the concept of private ownership. In claiming that radio was violating their intellectual property rights, the journalists were therefore invoking a national ideal to justify legal action on behalf of their own interests.

Accusations of Radio Piracy

The invocation of private property rhetoric came in the form of accusations of news theft. Again and again, articles in the professional trade journals portrayed radio as a thief. In *Editor and Publisher*, for instance, the broadcasters were described as "filching" and "lifting" the news from newspapers.[84] Similarly, *American Press* wrote of attempts by a radio station to "chisel" news from a local paper for broadcasting purposes.[85] The ANPA complained that broadcasters were "appropriating" the news without the consent of the publishers, and stated emphatically that "we should not tolerate a situation in which there is a general pilfering of our news." [86]

Ultimately, the most common image in these articles was that of "piracy." For example, an article in *Broadcasting* magazine in 1935 presented the views of a number of editors on the subject of radio as a medium for the dissemination of news. Noel Macy of the *Statesman* in Yonkers, New York, encouraged his fellow journalists to "condemn the piracy of news by radio."[87] When legal action was taken against various stations on charges of news theft, the trades generally referred to these as "news piracy" cases. Headlines reading "Radio Piracy Hearing Set for Monday,"[88] "AP Pushes Fight Over 'News Piracy,'"[89] or "Radio 'News Piracy' Case Continued"[90] were quite common.

The term "piracy" is an interesting one. Pirates are a particular type of criminal. The broadcasters were not called burglars or thieves or robbers. They were called pirates. Historically, pirates were often small groups of men who would attack and over-power big cargo vessels, plundering their holds and killing their crews. Despite the fact that the ships of their victims were often considerably larger and far better supplied with men and arms, the pirates were frequently triumphant. It is in this light, apparently, that print journalists viewed the radio newsmen. Clearly the broadcasters were traveling in a much smaller "ship" (a newly formed industry), with a much smaller "crew", and far fewer resources to call upon. Yet the newspaper industry, in its large, well-stocked vessel, apparently felt quite vulnerable to marauding attacks from its small competition on the "seas" of news dissemination.

Convinced that radio was stealing the news that wire service and newspaper staffs had worked hard to gather, newspapers and press associations began placing stations under close surveillance, trying to catch them in the act of using stolen news. With the start of the Yankee News Service, one of the first independent radio news associations formed after the Biltmore Agreement, *Editor and Publisher* reported that several Boston newspapers were "keeping close check on the radio news service to determine its character of bulletins and also if there is any duplication of their own contents." In addition, the article noted, the *Boston Evening American* "appears on the street with a warning that all contents are copyrighted daily."[91] Given the prevailing concerns about news theft by radio, there seems little question about the intended recipients of this message about copyrights.

Whether the broadcasters were actually stealing news from the newspapers, and if they were, how extensive and frequent the news theft was, is difficult to ascertain. The charges were often denied. Herbert Moore, head of the TransRadio News Service, one of the independent, radio news-gathering organizations formed after the establishment of the Press-Radio Bureau in the spring of 1934, stressed that "every news story which TransRadio delivers to its clients is an authenticated news item, *gathered or confirmed by its own correspondents.*"[92]

Similar denials of the news piracy charges came from the Yankee Network News Service in Boston. In a book on the history of the Yankee Network, Leland Bickford, editor-in-chief of the service, stated that Yankee was "not in any way dependent upon the papers for its continued existence" and insisted that his Network did "all its own fishing without borrowing tackle."[93] This account was corroborated by *Broadcasting* magazine, which reported that "the independents all deny that they are getting their news in any way except through their own staffs" and asserted that "they are prepared to meet any litigation brought against them on such charges."[94]

Despite these protestations of innocence, some broadcasters were forced to defend themselves in a formal manner. During the period in which print journalists were exerting economic and political pressure against radio, they also took legal action in the form of lawsuits charging stations with violation of intellectual property rights. In the spring of 1933, for example, the Associated Press brought suit against station KSOO in Sioux Falls, South Dakota (*AP v. KSOO*). That year four New Orleans newspapers filed similar charges against the Uhalt Broadcasting Company. In both cases the charges were the same: The radio station in question was accused of "news pilfering," or unauthorized broadcasting of either newspaper or press association news. In both cases the ruling was the same. Following the INS precedent, the judges ruled in favor of the print journalists, arguing that the broadcasters had engaged in "unfair competition in business practices." 95

One of these news piracy cases went all the way to the Supreme Court. In the fall of 1934, the AP filed suit against KVOS, a station in Bellingham, Washington, accusing the broadcasters of appropriating news items from three member papers in that area, (the Bellingham *Herald*, the Seattle *Post-Intelligencer* and the Seattle *Daily Times*) and broadcasting it before these newspapers could reach their subscribers. Again, the complaint was of unfair competition and violation of property rights in the news. Since the Associated Press had its headquarters in New York and KVOS was located in the state of Washington, the case met the interstate qualifications necessary to ensure it a hearing in a federal court. 96

The initial ruling, from the Federal District Court, was in favor of the radio station instead of the press association, a clear departure from the INS precedent. The judge held that there was no violation of property rights because there can be no absolute property rights in the news. On the matter of unfair competition, the court took the position that since newspapers are in the business of selling news while radio stations do not charge their listeners for news broadcasts, the two media cannot be considered to be in competition, and where there is no competition, there can be no *unfair* competition. The judge acknowledged that radio and newspapers do compete for advertising revenue, but, departing from the precedent set in the INS case, held that this does not make them "competitors for business profits in the dissemination of news." He went on to explain that such competition could only be said to exist if the case involved "the pirating by one news gathering and distributing agency of news of another such agency."97 The initial ruling in this case stated that competition could only exist between two rival news agencies, and because the radio station was not a news agency, there was no competition, and therefore no unfair competition. The old rules did not appear to apply to this situation, because the new technology disrupted the established patterns of information flow and division of labor in news distribution. The implications of this were that, in theory, radio was now free to "pirate" news from newspapers at will.

The Associated Press quickly filed an appeal, protesting that the piracy of news by a radio station was in fact no different than similar piracy on the part of the INS in 1918, and that the initial precedent should apply in this case as well. The lawyers for the AP argued before the Circuit Court of Appeals that KVOS was a competitor on the grounds that both radio and newspapers "disseminate news for the purpose of rendering their respective mediums more effective as advertising carriers, and respectively charge their advertisers for radio time and newspaper space." On this basis, their argument continued, "It is manifest that the parties are competing with respect to the dissemination of news." 98 The Associated Press was trying to argue that the rules should remain the same despite the fact that the communication environment had been transformed by the introduction of new technology.

One of the ways they tried to justify this was by invoking, once again, the ideals of public service. This time they made the claim that unless the press associations were protected by law from news theft by radio, they might ultimately be forced to go out of business. The outcome, they claimed, would be contrary to the public interest. As the AP lawyer put it, "It is clear that *public policy* agrees with the established law in according legal and equitable protection to news gathering agencies." He warned that if these agencies were "subjected to pilfering under the guise of a *short-sighted public interest, they might sooner or later be forced to limit or abandon their highly useful service.*"[99] In attempting to protect its own economic interest, the Associated Press did just what many other print journalists were doing at the time: it used public interest rhetoric to claim that its own survival was in some way essential to the nation.

It seems that this warning about radio's potential threat to the economic survival of the press associations was not lost on the Court. Ruling in favor of the Associated Press, Judge Denman of the Circuit Court of Appeals took the position that since the gathering and disseminating of news is essential to a democracy, it is in the public interest to protect the profitability of the press, to ensure that the press will continue to serve its function in the society. He explained that when the Framers of the Constitution were considering the role of the press as the fourth estate, the founding fathers had envisioned newspapers as being controlled by *private* interests. As Denman put it, "[w]hen the Constitution speaks of the freedom of the press it refers to the freedom of *private and non-governmental persons or bodies,* engaged in news gathering and dissemination, from interference by governmental agencies." What this meant, he explained, was that "the public function in the gathering and dissemination is *presumed by the Constitution to be in private hands.*"[100]

The judge went on to point out that only if newspapers can make a profit will they stay in business, stating that "under our capitalistic system...news distribution as a public function will be in large part carried out by businessmen acting under the inducement of the profit motive."[101] The implications of this, according to the judge, were that *"the public therefore has an interest in protecting the business of news gathering and disseminating agencies* against the impairment of their efficiency" that would result from the "misappropriation" of their news.[102] The Appeals Court agreed with the argument of the Associated Press, concluding that radio "news piracy" is contrary to the public interest because it might put the news associations out of business.

In overturning the ruling of the lower court, Judge Denman also challenged the concept that radio is not a competitor of the press associations, explaining that radio and newspapers both compete for advertising revenue. Since the broadcasting of news prior to the delivery of papers tends to decrease the value of the printed news, which therefore decreases the value of the paper to advertisers, radio can legitimately be considered a competitor in the news business. He concluded that "we are unable to see any theory under which such a diversion of advertising income from the Associated papers to KVOS...can be called anything but 'unfair competition.'"[103] This meant that KVOS was bound to the same rules of unfair competition that guide newspapers, as determined in the INS case.

The final decision of the Appeals Court was that KVOS was to refrain from using any Associated Press news items for its newscasts for the period "during which the broadcasting of the pirated news to KVOS' most remote auditors may damage the complainant's papers' business of procuring or maintaining their subscriptions and advertising."[104] This meant that so long as the airing of AP news might cost the newspapers advertising or circulation revenue, KVOS (or, for that matter, any other station) was not to include it in their newscasts. Having appealed to the law for protection, the print journalists had found it. The Court determined that broadcasters had no legal right to engage in the unauthorized use of newspaper or press association news. A decision had been made that despite the change in technology, the rules developed to govern the flow of news prior to the advent of radio still applied.[105] For at least a little longer, the established relationship between the wire services and the newspapers was safe.

Print journalists are not the last to have appealed to the law for protection from the threats posed by a new communication technology to established patterns of information distribution. Legal action has been a consistent defense tactic in various Media Wars as old media have battled new ones. Questions about intellectual property rights have been raised in response to the development of audio tape, video tape, reprographics, and digital tape. Similar concerns are now being voiced about the transmission of on-line information. Again and again, established media have sought legal protection from the threat posed by new technologies to the structure of their institutions. They can only seek such shelter for so long, for as the technology of communication changes, so must the laws governing the communication process. As the laws of communication change, so too does the structure of media institutions. When the laws of doing business change, the ways of doing business must change, and institutions must reshape themselves to accommodate the new laws governing their activities.

In summary, the story of the Press-Radio War suggests that new communication technologies threaten the established structure of media institutions in several ways. They disrupt established patterns of the division of labor within the institution itself, and they render old rules obsolete. By changing the way we communicate, they change the job of the institutions that help us to communicate with each other. This means that battles waged by old new media against new media are fought, in part, to try to preserve the old way of doing things. They are an effort to stem the tide of progress. They are an attempt to maintain the familiar roles, rules and relationships that define the structure of established media institutions. They are battles fought by taking economic, political, and legal action against the disrupting force--the new competition.

NOTES

1. "Free Publicity Being Eliminated From Radio Programs, Editors Say," *Editor and Publisher*, (June 13, 1931).

2. "Publishers Liberalize Press-Radio Plan," *Broadcasting*, (May 1, 1935): p 7.

3. For a more detailed discussion of the division of labor within media institutions, see Joseph Turow, *Media Industries: The Production of News and Entertainment* (New York: Longman, 1984).

4. In 1992, the longstanding Financial Interest and Syndication Rules were significantly altered to permit the networks to profit from more of their own programming.

5. U.S. Department of Commerce, *Historical Statistics of the United States: Colonial Times to 1970* (Washington, D.C.: Bureau of the Census, 1975).

6. Frank Parker Stockbridge, "Radio vs. The Press: Will the Newspapers Control Broadcasting?" *Outlook and Independent*, (December 31, 1930): 692.

7. "Radio and Circulation," *Editor and Publisher*, (October 23, 1926): 32.

8. "A Radio Dream," *Editor and Publisher*, (October 8, 1927): 44.

9. "Radio 'Lifting' of News Attacked," *Editor and Publisher*, (January 17, 1931): 9.

10. "California Publishers Will Unite In Opposing Radio, Magazines," *Editor and Publisher*, (January 24, 1931): 52.

11. "Radio Competition," *Editor and Publisher*, (January 17, 1931).

12. "Publishers Warned of Radio Dangers," *Editor and Publisher*, (April 25, 1931): 19.

13. Michael and Edwin Emery, *The Press and America* (Englewood Cliffs, NJ: Prentice Hall, 1988), 334-35.

14. Ibid., p. 627

15. "'Ignore Radio,' Says N.E.A. President," *Editor and Publisher*, (February 18, 1933).

16. "Giving News to Radio Viewed As Menace to Newspapers by Many Editors," *Editor and Publisher*, (December 22, 1928): 4, (emphasis added).

17. Ibid., (emphasis added).

18. "Radio and Elections," *Editor and Publisher*, (November 10, 1928).

19. "ANPA Acts to Frame Radio Policy," *Editor and Publisher*, (November 19, 1932): 7

20. Ibid.(emph added)

21. "AP to Continue News Broadcasting," *Editor and Publisher*, (April 27, 1929): 11.

22. "Radio and Elections."

23. "Quake Coverage Hampered by Radio", *Editor and Publisher*, (March 18, 1933): 7.

24. "News Broadcasting Hit by Coast Group," *Editor and Publisher*, (February 4, 1933), (emphasis added).

25. "Press Service Policies Differ On Giving News to Radio," *Editor and*

Publisher, (March 26, 1932): 15.

26. "AP Modified Rules on Radio Broadcasting," *Editor and Publisher*, (April 25, 1925): 11.

27. "AP and ANPA Declare War on Radio," *Broadcasting*, (May 1 1933): 5.

28. Eric Barnouw, *The Golden Web*, p 18.

29. At this time radio programs were generally sponsored by a single company, and it was common practice for the name of the sponsor to be incorporated into the name of the program.

30. "ANPA Band Radio Free Publicity, Raises Agency Requirements," *Editor and Publisher*, (May 2, 1925): 14.

31. Arthur Robb, "Cutting Free Publicity From Radio Programs," *Editor and Publisher*, (October 2, 1926): 5.

32. Ibid., 5.

33. Ibid., 5.

34. "Competing Dailies Most Generous With Radio Space, Survey Shows," *Editor and Publisher*, (March 7, 1931): 31.

35. Ibid., 31.

36. Ibid., 31.

37. *Proceedings of the 9th Annual Convention of the American Society of Newspaper Editors*, Washington, D.C., (April 16-18, 1931): 147.

38. Ibid., 147.

39. Emery, *The History of the ANPA*, p 202.

40. Robert McChesney, *Telecommunications, Mass Media and Democracy: The Battle for the Control of US Broadcsting, 1928-1935*, (New York: Oxford, 1993).

41. H.O. Davis to W.A. Dealey, December 9, 1931, Box 5, folder 65, *Ventura Free Press*, National Broadcasting Company Manuscripts, Wisconsin State Historical Society, Madison, WI. [hereafter NBC MSS].

42. H.O. Davis to Thomas Clark, January 21, 1932, Box 5, folder 65, *Ventura Free Press*, NBC MSS.

43. H.O. Davis to A. R. Williamson, March 1932, Box 15, Folder 5, *Ventura Free Press*, NBC MSS.

44. "Free Press Radio Campaign Backed by 726 Newspapers," *Ventura Free Press*, October 15, 1931, Box 15, Folder 5, *Ventura Free Press*, 1932, NBC MSS.

45. Ibid.

46. "Report of the Radio Committee," *Editor and Publisher*, (April 26, 1930): 68.

47. "Publishers Attack Radio Evils," *Editor and Publisher*, (April 25, 1931): 9.

48. "New Radio Control System Needed," *Editor and Publisher*, (June 10, 1933): 15.

49. "A Keen Analysis," *Ventura Free Press*, (March 23, 1932).

50. "Radio Reform Imperative, Says Seitz," *Editor and Publisher*, (December 19, 1931): 9.

51. "ANPA Fails to Renew Radio Attack, California Body Urges European System," *Broadcasting*, (December 1, 1931).

52. Rudolph Michael, "History and Criticism of Press-Radio Relationships," *Journalism Quarterly*, (1938): 180.

53. "Five Point Program Urged on Radio," *Editor and Publisher*, (April 29, 1933): 14.

54. "New Radio Control System Needed."

55. H.O. Davis to the Editor of the *Asheville Citizen*, (December 1932), Box 15, folder 5.

56 "Tax Broadcasting," *Ventura Free Press*, (June 9 1932).

57. "Exploiting the Public," *Ventura Free Press*, (July 18, 1932).

58. Gilbert Cant, "Publishers Liberalize Press-Radio Plan," *Broadcasting*, (May 1, 1935): 7.

59. "The Radio Menace," *Editor and Publisher*, (November 4, 1933): 6 (emphasis added).

60. "Public Control of Radio is Argued by Author, Aylesworth Disagrees," *Editor and Publisher*, (November 29, 1930): 36.

61. "Radio is 'Pure News' Channel," *Editor and Publisher*, (October 13, 1934): 5.

62. "Anti-Radio Organ Urges New Set-Up," *Broadcasting*, (April 15, 1932): 10.

63. H.O. Davis to A.R. Williamson, November 10, 1931, Box 5, folder 65, NBC MSS.

64. H.O. Davis to Marcy Darnell, July 31, 1931, Box 5, Folder 65, NBC MSS.

65. H.O. Davis to H.L. Williamson, September 25, 1931, Box 5, Folder 65, NBC MSS

66. Martin Codel, "News Plan to End Radio-Press War," *Broadcasting*, (January 1, 1934): 10

67. "News Plan to End Radio-Press War," *Broadcasting*, (January 1, 1934):10 (emphasis added).

68. "Peace with the Press," *Broadcasting*, (January 1, 1934): 22 (emphasis added).

69. Isabelle Keating, "Pirates of the Air," *Harpers*, Vol. 169, (September 1934): 463.

70. T.R. Carskadon, "The Press-Radio War," *The New Republic*, (March 11, 1936): 133.

71. "Radio News Plan Arouses Opposition," *Broadcasting*, (January 15, 1934): 11.

72. "Radio-News Program in Final Stage," *Broadcasting*, (February 1, 1934): 7.

73. Ibid., 7 (emphasis added).

74. H. V. Kaltenborn, as quoted in Robert McChesney, "Press-Radio Relations and the Emergence of Network, Commercial Broadcasting in the United States, 1930-1935," *Historical Journal of Film, Radio and Television*, 11 (1) 1991, p. 46.

75. Ibid., p. 46.

76. Keating, "Pirates of the Air," p. 468.

77. McChesney, "Press-Radio Relations," p. 47.

78. This discussion of the broadcast opposition movement, and the role played by the press in the efforts towards regulatory reform is drawn largely by Robert W. McChesney, *Telecommunications*. Readers interested in a more detailed exploration of these themes are directed there.

79. "Radio-Press Arrangement Stirs Dissension," *Broadcasting*, (March 1, 1934): 9.

80. Among the independent radio news services that were started at this time were the Yankee Network in Boston, the Continental Radio News Service in Washington and the Radio News Association in Los Angeles.

81. U.S. Government Printing Office, *What Copyright Is: Copyright Basics*, Circular No.1, (1992): 2.

82. Citations and further examples will be added here providing updated information on current debates over intellectual property rights.

83. For a detailed discussion of *AP INS*, see Paul Sullivan, "News Piracy: Unfair Competition and the Misappropriation Doctrine," *Journalism Monographs*, (May 1978).

84. "Radio 'Lifting' of News Attacked," *Editor and Publisher*, (January 17, 1931): 9.

85. "Refused Radio News," *The American Press*, (February 1934).

86. "Newspapers End Antagonism to Radio," *Broadcasting*, (May 1, 1937): 15.

87. "Editors Becoming Reconciled to Radio as Medium for Dissemination of News," *Broadcasting*, (May 1 1935): 46.

88. "Radio Piracy Hearing Set for Monday," *Editor and Publisher*, (June 17, 1933).

89. "AP Pushes FIght Over 'News Piracy,'" *New York Times*, (May 4 1936).

90. "Radio 'News Piracy' Case Continued," *ANPA Bulletin*, (March 10, 1933): 125.

91. "125 Stations Using News Report," *Editor and Publisher*, (March 10, 1934): 7.

92. Herbert Moore, "News War in the Air," *Journalism Quarterly*, 1935, 51, (emphasis added)

93. Leland Bickford, *News While it Is News: The Real Story of the Radio News*, (Boston: Manthorne & Co., 1935), 76.

94. "Rivals Form as Press-Radio Improves," *Broadcasting*, (April 1, 1934): 11.

95. "AP Victory Over KSOO Stirs Interest in Radio News Group," *Broadcasting* (April 15, 1933):8, "New Orleans Papers Win Radio Injunction," *New York Times*, (June 30, 1933): 15.

96. Sullivan, "News Piracy," p. 8.

97. Associated Press v. KVOS, Inc. (9th Cir. 1935), *Brief for Appellant*, 5.

98. Ibid., 17.

99. Ibid., 42 (emphasis added).

100. Ibid., 11 (emphasis added).

101. Ibid.

102. Ibid., (emphasis added).

103. Ibid.

104. Ibid., 20.

105. It should be noted here that while *AP v. KVOS* was heard by the Supreme Court in 1936, the case "was remanded to the District Court for retrial on the basis of technical errors in both the lower court and the Circuit Court of Appeals" (Sullivan, "News Piracy," 9). Thus the Supreme Court never actually ruled on whether or not the INS precedent was applicable in this case.

5

Radio's Threat to the Institutional Function of the Press

Oddly enough, it is not advertising revenue they [radio and the press] are going to fight over... They are coming to blows over the privilege of telling you and me what happened today in Tokyo and Timbuctoo and New York City; over the right to recount what the President plans to tell Congress... *They are going to fight, in brief, over the privilege of purveying the news.*

Isabelle Keating
Harper's, September 1934[1]

Communication institutions serve certain functions in society. These institutions, like those of finance, education, or medicine, play key roles in the life of a nation. Just as there is a division of labor within institutions, so too is there a division of labor within society as a whole. We turn to various institutions to meet our different needs. Banks serve very different functions from hospitals. Communication institutions serve communication-related functions--the surveillance of the social and physical environment, the interpretation of events and phenomena in these environments, and the provision of entertainment.[2] Thus, to find out what has happened today, to learn what it means, or to simply be amused, one need only turn to any number of media institutions whose function is the gratification of such needs. Similarly, to communicate with another person or send a message to many people simultaneously, one can chose from a variety of communication institutions whose function is the provision of a suitable channel.

To fully understand the concept of institutional function, it is necessary to differentiate it from institutional identity. Institutional identity, as described in

Chapter 3, is largely defined by a set of formal or informal standards, generally set within the institution itself, governing quality and performance. Some institutions have legal requirements controlling the use of certain identifying nomenclature, such as "doctor," "lawyer," "bank," or "hospital." Only individuals and organizations meeting certain requirements can claim membership in these institutions. In the case of these fields, the name is an essential element of institutional identity, and it conveys a particular meaning about the minimum standards that must be met by that organization or individual. Even among those banks, hospitals, doctors, and lawyers that do meet the institutional requirements of their field, and there are variations in the quality of service available. But the consumer can assume that any organization or individual bearing the formal institutional name has met the basic minimum requirements of the field.

In some cases, membership in an institution is determined not by the possession of a degree or by meeting certain legal requirements governing performance and quality, but by some other standard. Only certain companies, for example, can be listed on the New York Stock Exchange. Some country clubs permit only members who earn over a certain level of income. Some creative fields do not really consider people members until they have had their first public showing or performance of their work. Whatever the institution, there are always boundaries, either formal or informal, that define and distinguish it and its membership from other institutions.

Even if an individual or organization is for some reason disqualified from membership in a particular institution, however, it is still quite possible for them to serve the same or a similar function as those in the established institution. *This is because institutional identity is quite distinct from institutional function.* While someone who practices acupuncture or herbal medicine might be denied membership in the institution of Western medicine, he or she can still serve the same function of providing health care as those who are legally allowed to call themselves doctors. An accredited University and a home school can both serve the function of educating young people. A newspaper and a radio station can both serve the function of supplying the public with news and information. In each of these cases there may be significant differences in the quality of the service provided, and in how well the job gets done. It is this achievement of quality that often determines, at least in part, whether or not a group or individual can claim institutional membership.

But even if the criteria of institutional identity have not been met, it is still possible for a group or individual to serve the same *function* as the established institution. For whether or not the institution of medicine recognizes the legitimacy of acupuncture or herbal medicine, these modalities can be effective forms of health care. And whether or not print journalists acknowledge the professional legitimacy of tabloid television news programs, these shows can provide the public with information about their environment.

Institutional function, like institutional identity, is neither monolithic nor static. Institutions can serve a variety of functions, and these functions can evolve over time. The Church, for example, plays a number of roles in people's lives, and these roles have continued to transform over the centuries. Changes in institutional functions may be brought on by a variety of factors, such as changes in the political, economic or religious climate of a society. They also may be the result of changes in technology.

New communication technologies are threatening to the established functions of existing media institutions, because they redefine the communication environment. In taking over the old functions of established media, new media may render the original institution functionally obsolete. For example, the social function of the telegraph (instantaneous interpersonal communication) was essentially taken over by the telephone, leaving the telegraph virtually extinct. Of course, the basic function of the telegraph (instantaneous *written* communication) has now been revived in both the form of the fax machine and electronic mail. Another option is that instead of becoming extinct, the older medium adapts and transforms, taking on a new role. Radio, for example, was not eliminated with the arrival of television; it simply changed. As television took on the job of providing narrative entertainment, radio took on a new role as the nation's disk jockey.

A third option is mutual coexistence, with two or more institutions serving similar but distinct functions. This can be seen, for example, in the case of cinema and its adaptive response to the introduction of television, cable and home video. Cinema was not rendered obsolete with the arrival of any of these new media, neither did it begin to serve a dramatically different function. Instead, television, home video, and cinema all serve similar entertainment functions, each offering the consumer variations on the amount of control available over content and viewing environment.

Communication functions, like so many other aspects of our lives, are socially constructed. The roles these media play in our lives are roles that we create for them. The functions they serve in our lives are functions that we have devised. The needs they fill are largely needs we have developed. Many of the communication functions that we now consider essential are needs we didn't even know we had not long ago. Consider the fax machine, or voice mail, or cellular phones. These technologies are now considered essential in many people's lives, and their absence is experienced as a loss of one of life's basic necessities. What was once a technological luxury has become an essential service.

If a communication institution serves a function in people's lives that is considered essential, and if it serves that function effectively, then that institution is likely to be quite successful. Economic success translates into power. Functionally essential institutions tend to be powerful not only economically, but also politically, socially, and culturally. By providing an essential service, such an institution has the opportunity to touch many lives, which gives it great power. A good example of this is the institution of telephony. By providing a service that has become essential, point-to-point voice communication, the telephone fundamentally redefined the way in which business, friendship, romance, and politics are conducted. This technology, and the institution that supports it, is at the center of so many aspects of life that it has acquired the power to alter the shape of our social reality.

The power to affect the shape and nature of social reality extends far beyond the concerns of the bottom line. Those who control such socially essential communication institutions have an opportunity to profoundly affect the way people perceive and interact with the world around them. Those who hold the reins of this kind of power become key players in our society. Not only do they earn a great deal of money, but they also earn the attention and respect of others in positions of power. When they talk, people listen. They have true lobbying power in Washington. Politicians take their calls and heed their demands. By providing an essential communication function, they have rendered themselves indispensable, and therefore quite powerful.

It is not surprising that they are interested in retaining this power. Established communication institutions have a vested interest in preserving their role in the communication process. When new media threaten to replace them, they tend to respond defensively. As earlier chapters have shown, one common tactic employed in institutional self-defense is the invocation of "sacred" rhetoric. This is a process in which claims are made that one of the revered values of the culture will be threatened in some way if the new technology takes over a particular aspect of the social communication process. The rhetorical strategy here involves constructing an argument that claims the ontological centrality of the existing media institution. In other words, the old medium makes claims that unless it continues to play its established role, serving its particular communication function, one of the culture's most treasured ideals will be compromised in some way. Thus, for example, when defending their institutional identity, print journalists invoked the rhetoric of objectivity; when defending their institutional structure, they invoked the rhetoric of public interest and private property.

When it comes to defense of institutional function, this "sacred rhetoric" defense is particularly appropriate. If a media institution has been serving an essential communication function, the obvious way to defend its position is to argue that this function will not be properly served by the new competition. Since communication-related functions are so crucial to so many key areas of life, it is not hard to find a "sacred" value or ideal that might be effected by a disruption in the established patterns of social communication. For example, the stability of the family, the church, and the community all rest on preserving established communication patterns, and it is easy to invoke these sacred values as a way of defending the communication status quo. One might argue that if the new medium is allowed to take over the function of entertaining or informing American citizens, the stability of one of these areas of life might be compromised.

Another "sacred" American value that might be imperiled by changes in the communication environment is democracy. America's constitutional commitment to the principles of freedom of expression fundamentally links all media institutions with one of the values we hold most dear in this nation. The arrival of a new channel of communication often raises questions about access, censorship and government regulation, all of which pertain in some way to questions of freedom of expression and its centrality to democracy. Most common are warnings that with changes in the patterns of information flow in the society could come the loss of freedoms we hold dear, and ultimately the collapse of our political system.

Recent examples of this can be found in contemporary media wars, such as the struggle between the ANPA and the Regional Bell Operating Companies (RBOCs) (also known as the Baby Bells) during the late 1980s. After the breakup of ATT, under the terms of the 1984 Consent Decree (the agreement between the Justice Department and AT&T), the Baby Bells were limited to serving as "common carriers". This meant that the only function they could serve was that of carrying the signals sent by others. In other words, they were restricted from using the phone lines for the transmission of anything but phone calls. Interested in cashing in on the emerging phenomenon of on-line information services, the Baby Bells began to lobby for the right to use their lines to provide news and information to subscribers. It should come as little surprise that the newspapers of the nation were unenthusiastic about this development. What followed was a heated battle in Washington, as the ANPA fought to block the entry of the telephone companies into the news business. And in the end, just as they had lost the battle against radio thirty years earlier, the journalists of the 1980s were similarly unsuccesful in their attempt to protect their territory, for eventually the RBOCs were given the green light to go on-line.

In that case, as the older media institution struggled to make room for the new competition, the rhetoric of the First Amendment was invoked. The ANPA warned that the monopoly enjoyed by local phone companies would compromise the democratic ideal of a free and open marketplace of ideas. The print journalists predicted that on-line news provided by the phone companies would lack diversity, which would have the net result of silencing voices. These journalists painted an Orwellian picture of a Big Brother world, in which Ma Bell's Babies would control the information flow in our lives.[3] Monopolistic control over the distribution of information, they warned, will lead to a loss of the freedoms we hold so dear.

The rhetoric of democracy and freedom of expression was also invoked by print journalists in the Press-Radio War. The introduction of broadcasting greatly disrupted long-standing patterns of political communication in this country. For nearly a century and a half, newspapers had been the primary channel through which politicians communicated with the people. Because they occupied this key position in the stream of political information, newspapers were able to serve several communication functions that are essential for the survival of a democracy. They were the primary channel through which news and information reached the people. They were able to provide a forum in which a variety of voices could be heard on public matters of the day. Finally, because of the freedom they had been guaranteed by the First Amendment, they also were in the unique position of being able to filter and comment upon the words of politicians. Serving these functions gave the newspapers tremendous amount of power in the political communication process. Until the advent of radio, the newspapers enjoyed a monopoly over that position of power.

All that changed in the late 1920s. Suddenly there was new medium available. Radio made it possible for politicians to speak directly to many more people, allowing them to bypass the press and address a mass audience. The function of informing the people about political issues could now be served by another media institution. By challenging the monopoly of newspapers over the news dissemination process, radio threatened to rob the press of the tremendous power it had long enjoyed in its key position in the political communication process. Now the people had a new source of information, and as Franklin Roosevelt quickly learned, this could be used to combat newspaper opposition.

As this chapter will show, many print journalists at the time expressed great concern about the threat radio posed to their established role in the democratic political process. Journalists of the day argued that for various reasons, ranging from the fact that radio is federally regulated to the fact that broadcasters use the spoken and not the written word, radio was incapable of doing an effective job serving the communication functions of the press in a democracy. Using the doomsday approach that so often accompanies the invocation of "sacred" values, they warned that the values of democracy and the survival of our political system would be endangered if radio attempted to serve these functions. They predicted that with radio news would come demagogic politicians who would sway the passions of the masses with skilled radio oratory. They warned that the airwaves would simply become tools of government propaganda, as they had in Europe, and they cautioned that radio was incapable of effectively serving one of the most important functions of the press in a democracy, that of the watchdog of the government.

Radio provided the listening audience with something they had never before had available to them: direct access to the news event while it was happening. The sounds of a parade or a speech could be brought to listeners live. It was this direct access that had the print journalists of the day worried. Today we have new communication technologies that provide even greater access at even farther distances. With satellite and cable technologies, people can sit in their living rooms and watch a war unfold. Like their colleagues of the 1930s, contemporary journalists have expressed reservations about the wisdom of providing the average citizen with that level of uninterpreted, direct access. Such reservations were expressed, for example, during the Gulf War, when twenty-four hour news coverage by CNN brought home viewers constant live-action video imagery, but offered little in the way of in-depth, contextual analysis. Many argued that the great emphasis on live footage turned the war coverage into little more than a video game or action-adventure movie. Such coverage, they warned, denied the American people the full understanding of the events in the Gulf.

An uninformed public is a vulnerable public, which is a dangerous thing in a democracy. For if the people do not have a good understanding of public issues, they are vulnerable to manipulation or abuse of power by their elected representatives. The fact that the imagery beamed out of the Gulf was officially sanctioned and censored by the government was cited as perfect evidence that live broadcast coverage during wartime was a threat to democratic values. If the government is feeding the people a partial picture of the world, the public cannot make informed choices at election time. Having found its own role as witnesses and interpreters of events usurped during the Gulf War, the established press (both print and broadcast) responded by arguing that this disruption of the established patterns of communication was potentially quite dangerous for the American people. Invoking the ideal model of the press in a democracy, they warned that the public needed not only facts, but some assistance in interpreting the meaning of those facts. Without such assistance, they warned, the public might be left vulnerable to abuse of power by those in power.[4]

Just as these new technologies bring the public greater access to news events, they also provide politicians with greater access to the voters during a campaign. This was evident in the 1992 presidential campaign, for example, when candidates used new channels to reach voters in ways they had never done before, appearing on cable talk shows and music video channels to bring their message to the people. Ross Perot bought his own series of half-hour time blocks to explain his platform in uninterupted "infomercials." These new venues disrupted the established flow of political communication in much the same way as radio did when it first arrived. Politicians could now bypass the traditional press and speak directly to the people. Like the print journalists of the 1930s, contemporary journalists were dismayed by this change. This time they voiced concerns about the dangers of allowing politicians such direct access to the voters. Some cautioned that the "infomercial" was no more than unfiltered political propaganda. Much was made of the new "electronic democracy," and concerns were expressed about whether the public was being provided with enough information to assess the campaign rhetoric of the candidates.

In both of these examples, contemporary journalists can be heard invoking democratic rhetoric to justify their objections to changes in the familiar patterns of news and information flow in our society. The arguments made by print journalists sixty years ago were virtually identical. This chapter explores the rhetoric invoked by journalists in the 1930s as they argued for their own irreplaceability in the face of technological innovation. Examined here are the kinds of claims made when existing media fight to retain their institutional function. The fight to preserve institutional function can ultimately be seen as a fight to retain the tremendous power that comes from filling an essential role in society. If another media institution takes over that job, the original institution may find itself stripped of its social, cultural, and/or political authority. With so much at stake, it is not surprising that they are willing to fight to preserve their position.

RADIO'S THREAT TO THE FUNCTIONS OF THE PRESS

For a democratic system of government to operate effectively, certain communication functions must be served. These functions are so essential that if they are not served, the survival of our system of government could be seriously endangered. Participatory democracy presumes a populace that is familiar enough with the issues and candidates to make an informed decision in the voting booth. To function properly, a democracy needs a well-informed electorate. Thus, one of the key communication functions in our form of government is that of providing the people with the information they need to participate in the process of creating and maintaining their own government.[5]

To fully participate in their own self government, however, the voters need more than just information, facts and figures. They also need to be exposed to a broad range of perspectives about that information so they can form their own opinions about important public issues. To that end, what they need, is "an open market place of ideas." This open marketplace, as envisioned by some of the earliest libertarian political philosophers, is a place in which the full range of opinions can be expressed. It is a place where anyone can speak without fear of government censorship. Such theorists as Milton, Locke, and Mill argued that since people are capable of exercising reason to distinguish right from wrong, they are also capable of weighing all the options and making rational and logical choices. According to this perspective, therefore, there is no reason to limit the expression of any particular viewpoint. The libertarian theorists argued that only when the people are exposed to all ideas and information do they have the resources necessary for making sound voting decisions. [6]

There is, of course, always the danger that some of the information or opinions voiced in the marketplace are wrong, deceptive or manipulative. Yet, according to the "self-righting principle," libertarian philosophy posits that in the end, the truth will prevail. This position argues that while people may make temporary errors, they will eventually recognize the best and most logical course of action. This is why they are to be trusted to govern themselves. What they need, to finally arrive at the best course of action, is full access to all perspectives in an open marketplace of ideas.[7] A second communication function that must be filled in a democracy, then, is the creation and maintenance of a forum in which open dialogue can take place between a diversity of voices.

Finally, someone must keep an eye on the government, to make sure that our elected officials are doing their job in an ethical, legal, and effective manner. Should any abuse of power or incompetence take place, the public must be informed. Then the people, armed with the information they have been given by the press, can act accordingly at election time. When the press is functioning in this capacity it is sometimes referred to as the "fourth estate."[8] According to this model, the press acts as an unofficial fourth branch of government, whose job it is to serve as a check on the three official branches. Libertarian theorists speculated that having the press serve in this capacity would also help to keep government officials on their toes. The idea was that politicians would be more likely to act in the best interests of the people if they knew that their every move might be reported and criticized in the newspapers. Indeed, without the press serving in the capacity of watchdog, there would be no way for the citizens of a democracy to keep an eye on the people they elected to represent them.[9]

Thus, there are at least three key communication functions that the press theoretically serves in a democracy: creating an informed electorate, providing an open marketplace for the free exchange of all ideas and opinions, and acting as the fourth estate. The only way any of these functions can truly be served is if the press is free to operate without fear of government sanction, and that is precisely what the Framers of the Constitution had in mind when they wrote the First Amendment. They were attempting to create a new form of government in which citizens would no longer be subject to the kinds of oppression of individual liberties that they had experienced under the British monarchy. To protect the people, they gave them a weapon that could be used to fight governmental abuse of power--a free press.

Clearly, the simple creation of a free press does not ensure that all of these functions will be fully served. The press has no legal requirements binding it to fulfill any of these roles. In fact, a quick glance at journalism history shows that much of the time the press has failed to serve these functions effectively. In a way, the functions of a free press in a democracy are idealized goals, much like the ideal of objectivity in reporting. Like most ideals, these functions of the press have thus far remained more ellusive than attainable. Even when unattainable, however, professional ideals can be used to serve the important institutional function of self-protection.

As discussed in Chapter 3, print journalists invoked the ideals of objectivity as a way of protecting their professional identity. They claimed that radio newscasters were not journalists because they were incapable of delivering news that lived up to the standards of the profession. They also claimed that the very nature of the medium of radio itself, the fact that it involved the use of the spoken as opposed to the written word, eliminated any possibility of objective reporting. The fact that very little print journalism lived up to these professional standards never seemed to enter the conversation.

When it came to protecting the function of the press, print journalists took a similar approach. They invoked the ideal functions of the press in a democracy and claimed that radio was incapable of effectively serving them. This was an argument that warned of great dangers to democracy itself if radio were to attempt to assume the various roles of the press. It was an argument that linked the survival of our political system with the preservation of the communication status quo. It was also an argument that implied that the press was immune from any criticism of its own performance in serving our democracy.

One of the problems with the news on the radio, according to its journalistic critics, was that it lacked depth. Since broadcast news tended to offer only brief bulletins, the print journalists argued that people relying solely on radio for news would not be sufficiently well-informed to make sound voting decisions. Thus, according to the journalists, radio was incapable of serving the vital communication function of assisting in the creation of an informed electorate. One editorial, for example, warned that since radio can do no more than "superficially cover the legitimate news field, the evil effect would be obvious." The danger, according to this editorial was that "...*it would strike at the heart of the system of popular government.*" The gravity of the situation was underscored with a serious appeal to the readers, who were told that "there is no greater demand upon the editorship of the day than to see that this does not happen."10

Several years later, when radio once again provided election returns in the fall of 1932, *Editor and Publisher* explained that "one of the most menacing conditions in this country today is the apathy, superficiality and plain ignorance of the voting masses," and predicted that if a large number of people came to depend on "the bulletin services of radio ...the problems which now confront our form of government would be increased in direct ratio to the number of people so affected."11 Another editorial on campaign coverage put it simply: "By no stretch of the imagination can we see radio doing a thorough job" in airing and interpreting public matters.12

The following year, when the Columbia Broadcasting Company started its own news service, CBS was criticized for "toying irresponsibly with public opinion," and the prediction was made that "if the American people...were to depend upon scraps of information picked up from air reporting, the problems of a workable democracy would be multiplied incalculably."13 Similarly, an editorial criticizing the radio coverage of the Chicago stockyard fire in May 1934 described radio as being "physically incapable of supplying more than headline material," and concluded that it was "inconceivable that a medium which is *incapable of functioning in the public interest* will be allowed to interfere with the *established system of news reporting in a democracy.*"14 The implication here is that only the established system of news delivery, the press, is capable of protecting democracy.

If journalists found radio incapable of informing the electorate, they found it equally inadequate to serve the function of the fourth estate. In their attempts to preserve their role in the nation's political process, radio's journalistic critics invoked this ideal quite frequently. Their argument was that because radio is licensed to operate by the Federal Communications Commission, this opens the door to government control over the use of the airwaves, and could make it possible for the party in power to censor the news or use radio for the purposes of political propaganda. Because the FCC has the power to revoke a station's license, thereby making broadcasters dependent upon the government's approval for their right to operate, the press claimed that radio therefore lacks the independence necessary for it to serve as a watchdog of the government.

References to the crucial role played by the press in a democracy appear frequently in the print journalists' attacks on radio. For example Carl Ackerman, dean of the Columbia School of Journalism, observed that "journalism is a profession *upon which rests today the destiny of representative governments.*"15 In contrast, discussing broadcasting, he drew an analogy between the control of radio by government license in the twentieth century and the control of the press by printer's licenses issued by European monarchs during the sixteenth and seventeenth centuries. The danger, he explained, was that the government might use radio to impose its views on the people, just as the authoritarian rulers of Europe had used the press to further their own interests. Since the FCC has final control over the airwaves, Ackerman warned, "any government in Washington may, if it wishes, use the radio...to build a backfire in American homes against any individual, business or institution." 16

A similar approach was used in protesting the admission of radio reporters into the Congressional press galleries in the fall of 1933. Print journalists from around the country sent hundreds of telegrams to the Senate Rules Committee expressing their opposition to sharing the gallery with radio reporters. One argued, for example, that radio should be denied access because "it operates under a Federal license and its utterances can be directly controlled," whereas *"the press cannot be controlled and therefore operates as a stabilizer of government,"* concluding that "there is no place in the press galleries for both."17 Another publisher wrote that allowing radio reporters into the galleries would constitute an "official recognition of radio broadcasting as a medium of disseminating news," which, since radio is licensed by the FCC, would be "an official sanction of the censorship of news" by the government.18

One of the obvious dangers of government control of radio, according to print journalists, was that broadcasting could become a powerful propaganda tool for the administration of whatever president occupied the White House. Were this to occur, it would be a direct violation of the principles underlying the concept of the fourth estate. Rather than serving as a check on the government, the news medium would become a tool for the government to promote its own policies. This would leave the people completely vulnerable to those in power, and there would be no opportunity for opposing or critical views to be voiced. One group that was particularly vocal on this matter was the ANPA Radio Committee. It warned that "no matter what party happens to be in power, this system offers to that party a temptation to use this medium of communication for propaganda purposes."19 The irony here is that few newspapers operate completely free from political influence themselves.

In addition to the government use of the airwaves for propaganda purposes, print journalists warned that there was the further risk that the administration would use its license-granting power to favor certain stations. The danger here was that this might create a chilling effect, in which stations critical of the administration might avoid airing such views for fear of losing their license. As the ANPA Radio Committee put it, under our system of regulation, "where the licenses to broadcast are granted by a political body, a station is not likely to jeopardize its license by offending this political body." "It is for these reasons," the Committee explained, "that radio offers *a convenient vehicle for control by a political party.*"20 In his book *Propaganda and the News*, Will Irwin, a foreign correspondent for the *New York Tribune*, observed that "the very existence of the licensing power makes radio corporations, and especially the larger ones, chary of refusing favors to a party in power," noting that "after all, the commission might hold over them the threat of instant death." [21]

In the eyes of many print journalists, the fact that radio is regulated by the government disqualified it as an effective medium for serving the communication needs of a democratic political system. "Any attempts of radio to function in the field of journalism," the Committee warned, "must fail because *a government license destroys the freedom on which any journalistic endeavor rests.*" In the view of its members, only the press, which enjoyed independence from federal licensing, could effectively serve the functions of the fourth estate.[22]

Committee Chair Edward Harris had similar views. As he put it, "the fundamental problem at hand" was "whether radio as a free agency *can exist in a democratic form of government*, or whether the control which must be applied by the government will destroy or impair it as a medium for the presentation of facts and the free expression of thought."[23] In his view the answer was clearly "No." Like so many others, Harris warned that federal powers over the airwaves posed the danger that "radio could be used for the dissemination of deceitful government propaganda," a situation in which the government could eventually exercise an effective censorship over every word spoken into microphone."[24]

Harris used this reasoning to justify the argument that the nation's newspapers should retain a monopoly over the role of gathering and disseminating news in this country. Addressing the Pennsylvania Newspaper Publishers Association in January 1936, he emphasized that "the press should not surrender its trusteeship to an agency which is under a government license." [25] With the use of the word "trusteeship" here, Harris invoked the ideal of the press as the fourth estate, holding a privileged place in the democracy, having certain obligations to the public that the radio simply cannot fulfill. He went on to say that "if the broadcasters are encouraged to form their own newsgathering organization for general broadcasts," they would inevitably be subject to "governmental supervision over their output." He predicted that this could lead to complete censorship of the news, which would be *"a retrogression from American ideals and the principles of government through an enlightened citizenry."* [26]

As it turned out, the print journalists' predictions did not materialize. The government did not take over the airwaves for propaganda purposes, free speech was not lost, and radio did not bring about the fall of democracy. It seems that broadcasting was not as dangerous to our political system as the journalists had warned. What they were right about, though, was the threat posed by radio to the established functions of the institution of journalism in this country. Radio broadcasting provided politicians with a direct link to the public, allowing them to address the citizens of the nation without having their words edited and interpreted by the press. This, of course, disrupted the long established arrangement in which newspapers acted as the main channel of communication between the government and the people.

Suddenly politicians could address the public directly. No longer were their speeches edited or cut to fit a particular space in the newspaper. In this way, radio was a true threat to the long established and powerful role of the press as the primary channel of communication between the American people and their elected representatives, and as the primary disseminators of news and public information. The press was in danger of having its institutional functions usurped by radio, and print journalists were quite unhappy about it.

In their attempts to protect their position, the print journalists constructed a line of defense in which the very stability of democracy was dependent upon the preservation of their established role in the political communication process. They warned that without the protection of the press, the people of this nation were in danger, constructing an argument that linked the survival of our political system with the preservation of their familiar role as intermediary between the public and the politicians. The press warned that certain communication functions essential in a democracy can be properly served only by newspapers. Left in the hands of radio, they predicted, these functions would not be served effectively, which would place democracy itself in jeopardy.

This argument rests on certain key assumptions. One is that without the watchful eye of the press, politicians cannot be trusted to act in the best interests of the nation. The second is that print journalists *can* be so trusted. The third is that the public is helpless and in dire need of protection. These three assumptions form a worldview in which the press is seen as the benign and altruistic intermediary between the evil politicians and the vulnerable public. According to this perspective, displacement of the press from its established role as go-betweeen would result in dire consequences.

Evidence from Abroad

In their warnings about the dangers of radio, print journalists had only to look across the ocean for evidence to support their argument. At this time, government-controlled radio in Italy, Germany, and the Soviet Union was being used quite effectively by Mussolini, Hitler, and Stalin. While propaganda and censorship were hardly new in the history of political communication, these leaders took the practice of shaping public opinion to new extremes. Unlike the dictators and authoritarian rulers of centuries before, the Fascist, Nazi and Communist governments had at their disposal a mass press and the radio. With these they could attempt to control the flow of ideas and wage an active campaign to shape and control public opinion.

In crafting their argument that radio was incapable of effectively serving the political communication needs of a democracy, American print journalists made frequent reference to "European dictatorships," citing them as proof of the dangers inherent in government-control of the airwaves. In many ways it was the perfect rhetorical strategy, for here was tangible evidence for their claims that radio could be used as a tool of totalitarianism. Here was real support for their argument that in the hands of political leaders with dictatorial goals, radio was a weapon that could contribute to the destruction of liberty.

An editorial on the dangers of government controlled radio, for example, observed that "it is one of the manifestations of centralization of power in many countries in recent years, that autocracy everywhere has striven, first of all to control the mediums of communication."[27] Karl Bickel warned that governments were always looking for a means to control for their own purposes "all possible channels of contact with the public mind," and pointed out that "in Europe, radio has been either frankly or openly taken over by the government and forced to become a governmental creature."[28] Edward Harris noted with concern that "all European countries exercise strict government control or censorship over radio broadcasting" because they are aware that this medium of communication is a powerful tool "for enlightenment or *deception* of the citizenry."[29]

Oscar Riegel, the director of journalism at Washington & Lee University, explored the topic of government propaganda in his book, *Mobilizing for Chaos*. Published in 1934, this book looked at the growth of nationalism and intolerance at that time, examining the ways that "the physical equipment of rapid communications, including telegraph, cable and radio has been made service to the demands of nationalism." He also explored the ways that the news was being manipulated by various governments to influence public opinion in support of national interests.[30] Riegel opened his first chapter with a reference to "the docile journalists of Berlin" who had by then capitulated to the demands of Joseph Goebbels. He went on to mention Russia and Italy, other countries that had shown how "not only the press but every other instrument of communication...could be brought under the centralized control of the state and made to build a national mass psychology favorable to the interests and ambitions of the national government."[31]

After discussing the ways that radio was being used by foreign governments to further their own ends, Riegel warned that "even in the United States" there are tendencies in this direction. He pointed out that the U.S. Postal Service was a government monopoly, the telegraph and telephone were regulated to some extent by the Interstate Commerce Commission, and radio was under the control of the Federal Radio Commission. Arguing against the newly proposed 1934 Communications Act, which would have given the new FCC power over the regulation of both telecommunications and broadcasting, he observed that "the strongly urged proposals to...merge the communications systems of the country under government supervision, indicate a *marked tendency in the direction of the European system*." [32] The danger of this, Riegel explained, "is that radio is the most important single factor in domestic and political social control, because no other modern invention has opened up such limitless possibilities for influencing public morale." In his conclusion he warned that while the United States had "thus far resisted the tendencies of certain European countries, the signs of danger have already appeared."[33]

Reigel was not the only one predicting that the European trend of government-controlled radio might spread to the United States. Frank

Stockbridge, the publisher of *American Press*, cautioned that government censorship of radio "may be the entering wedge to censorship of the press itself." [34] The ANPA Radio Committee put it this way: "Seeing that in other countries, radio has been used as a weapon to destroy liberty, we must solemnly undertake to see that it does not happen here." "Eternal vigilance," it observed, "is the price of liberty." Committee members pointed out that under the new Communications Act of 1934, the president of the United States had been empowered to take full control of radio facilities in the event of war or any other national emergency, which could lead to the dictatorial use of radio in our own country. Commenting on this, the committee warned, "we cannot come to grips with the radio propaganda problem merely by thinking, 'It can't happen here'. We said the same thing about the Spanish influenza when it broke out in Europe in 1918, but it did happen here."[35] Here radio propaganda in Europe is portrayed as analogous to a foreign virus, highly contagious and dangerous.

In the event that America 'caught' the propaganda disease, some journalists predicted that radio would not be the only medium infected. They warned that government control over broadcasting could lead to the death of press freedom in this country, and that once radio became the medium of official propaganda, it would only be a matter of time before such control was extended to newspapers. Evidence for their argument could be found in Europe. The ANPA Radio Committee noted that "in several European countries the radio has been used by the party in power to *destroy the confidence of the public in the press*," and explained that the ultimate outcome of this in those countries "has been the suppression of the press and the destruction of the newspapers."[36]Edward Harris observed that "in some European countries, radio was the medium through which the press was destroyed."[37] "If we accept dictation and domination of radio by those in governmental power," he warned, "it will not be a far step until our governmental leaders may seek to influence the presentation...of news in our daily press."[38]

In their warnings of the dangers that radio posed to democracy, print journalists did not limit themselves to predictions of government censorship. They also called upon the argument that inherent differences between the spoken and the printed word made radio a medium that could be exploited for propaganda purposes far more easily than the newspaper. As described in Chapter 3, many journalists took the position that there were intrinsic qualities that made the printed word superior to the spoken as a means of communicating news. According to them, the printed word is more rational and logical, and thus appeals to the intellect of the reader, while the spoken word arouses the passions and emotions of the audience. In matters of propaganda and persuasion, the implications of this deterministic perspective on inherent media differences were obvious. Clearly, the journalists warned, the "intrinsically emotional" nature of the spoken word meant that the airwaves were the perfect means by which skillful political orators could sway the passions of the masses. A number of journalists took this position, warning that the "inherent" power of the human voice to convey emotion made radio a tool that was particularly suited to appealing to the feelings of the crowd rather than the rational mind of the individual.

In his book *Propaganda and the News*, Will Irwin wrote that "The radio, through the *magic* inherent in the human voice, has means of appealing to the *lower* nerve centers and of creating emotions which the hearer mistakes for thoughts."[39] Here radio is portrayed as having magical powers over the audience. In the context of propaganda such forces are particularly dangerous, for they conjure up images of hypnosis. Here is a force that cannot be battled with the rational mind, for it leaves the listener helplessly controlled by emotions, that, while they may be "lower" than thoughts, are apparently far more powerful.

Similar imagery about the "magical" powers of the spoken word was invoked in an editorial about radio news commentators, who were described as "soothsayers" using "suave voice tones" to "deftly slip their politics between the layers of the news cake." Here again are images of surreptitious manipulation of the listeners through the subtle powers of the spoken word. In this case it is not the politicians but the radio news commentators who are portrayed as exploiting the magic of the voice, subtly shaping public opinion in a way that is undetected by the listener. The editorial asserted that the radio commentators have developed a large public following through "the sound of their voices," explaining that "their appeal is made unconsciously through intonation, diction, mannerism, humor, irony and the ability to sustain a story." Once again, note here the use of the word "unconscious." The effect of radio is continuously portrayed as something over which the listener has no control because it goes undetected. It was predicted that continued use of radio in this way would result in a *"subtle perversion* of the news and editorial function that radio *presumes* to perform," therefore justifying *"serious distrust of radio's strength as a medium of public information."*[40]

If radio speakers could mesmerize the audience with their suave voice tones, another danger was that they could captivate them with showy oratory. As Edson Bixby, editor of the *Springfield (Mo.) News-Ledger* put it in a talk he gave at a meeting of the American Society of Newspaper Editors (ASNE), "the press has only logic and common sense upon which to predicate its appeal", while the radio *"opens the door to showmanship."* The entertainer, like the magician, derives his or her power, in part, from the ability to successfully create illusion. It was this quality which Bixby feared could open the doors to the abuse of radio's power. He suggested that it was with the help of the radio that "the demagogue may become a more successful charlatan." The danger was that by creating an entertaining diversion, the clever speaker might fool or mislead the public. In Bixby's view, the emergence of broadcast news would fundamentally alter the way political discourse takes place in America. He predicted that radio "will fan heated political discussions and excite prejudices...it shall lead the mob, turn black to white, and mislead and deceive." Unfortunately, he warned, *"it will contribute little, if anything, to thought that is fundamentally sound."*[41]

Similar concerns were voiced by Edward Harris, who warned that "reason may be unseated" by the "continuous application of an emotional appeal through insidious propaganda by means of radio broadcasting, similar to that applied in Germany...We have in Germany," he observed, "a glaring example of the result of such a power."[42]

The imagery in these attacks on radio is consistent and quite clear. According to the print journalists, news by radio would create an audience that is mesmerized and entertained but incapable of thinking clearly. It would open a channel through which clever speakers can manipulate the people. It would rouse passions but would not contribute to intelligent dialogue about key public issues. In short, according to the print journalists' argument, because of the "inherent" emotional nature of the spoken word, radio was disqualified from being able to effectively serve the communication functions of the press in a democracy.

It is, of course, impossible to know how seriously the print journalists took their own arguments. It is quite legitimate to wonder whether there was any substance to any of this democratic rhetoric. It all sounds grand and dramatic, but did they mean any of it? Did they really think that inherent differences between radio and newspapers made the new medium well-disposed for propaganda purposes? Did they actually believe that radio might open the door to dictatorship? Did they truly worry that an American president might follow in the footsteps of Hitler or Mussolini? We may never know. We do know that this is the way they chose to defend themselves, which means that even if they didn't believe the rhetoric, they believed that it would or at least should have power as an argument. They felt that these were the words that should be invoked in self-protection.

This tactic was obviously not an invention of the print journalists. The technique of wrapping oneself in the flag is one that has long been used by politicians. It is self interest masquerading as public interest. In their attempts to look out for their own interests print journalists tried to create the impression that they had only the interests of the nation at heart. They called upon those concepts and values they felt would serve them in their attempts to preserve their role in the political communication process.

Their argument was actually quite simple. They warned that unless the press remained the primary channel for the transmission of news and for communication between politicians and the public, the stability of democracy in America was in serious jeopardy. They hooked the future of our political system on the preservation of the communication status quo. The print journalists may or may not have believed that radio was dangerous to democracy, but they clearly believed that saying so was a way to protect themselves.

"Proof" At Home

If events in Europe gave the press ammunition for their attacks on radio, they found further "proof" for their argument right here at home. It is not for nothing that Franklin Roosevelt is known as "the radio president."[43] While Herbert Hoover gave occasional broadcasts, Roosevelt was the first president to make extensive use of this new medium. When he ran for office in 1932, the level of radio ownership was high enough that he could reach fifty-six percent of American households. By the time of the re-election campaign in 1936, radio penetration was more than seventy-three percent.[44] Roosevelt made particularly effective use of the radio. He developed an informal, chatty style of address that conveyed a message of personal availability and concern for the needs and feelings of the average American.

The president's unique powers to reach the people through radio were noted by many at the time. He was praised for "his ability to create a feeling of intimacy between himself and his listeners, his skill in placing emphasis on key words, [and] his adroitness in presenting complicated matters in simple terms that the man on the street could understand."[45] In a 1936 article assessing the "'Radio Personalities' of the Presidential Prospects," *Broadcasting* described Roosevelt as having the most "pleasing and persuasive microphone manner" and rated him as being "far and away the most striking radio personality who has ever occupied either the White House or any high federal office" in the dozen years since radio broadcasting began on a national scale.[46]

With the help of radio, Roosevelt was able to establish a special relationship with the American people. Stanley High, a radio commentator for NBC, noted that Roosevelt's radio speeches "were something new in the recent annals of our democracy." He explained that "there was a 'latch-string-is-always-out' quality about them", and that "all of a sudden, a lot of Americans who never realized before that they mattered to anybody, least of all the President of the United States, awoke to believe that they mattered a great deal."[47] His fireside chats in particular brought many letters and gifts to the White House from listeners across the country expressing their affection and support for the president. For example, after one of Roosevelt's first radio addresses in March of 1933, James Baudo of Brooklyn, New York wrote:

> As I listened to the President's broadcast, I felt that he walked into my home, sat down and in plain and forceful language explained to me how he was tackling the job I and my fellow citizens had given him. I thought what a splendid thing it would be if he could find the time to do that occasionally. [48]

And find the time he did. During the first ten months he was in the White House, Roosevelt went to the American people via radio over twenty times.[49] By the end of his time in office he had made nearly 300 broadcasts, thirty of which were fireside chats.[50]

One of the reasons that the president made such extensive use of the radio was that it gave him direct control over the message that reached the public, something that was not available through the pages of the newspaper. In a letter to Merlin Aylesworth, president of NBC, Roosevelt explained his preference for radio over newspapers as a means of addressing the people.

"Radio is now one of the most effective mediums for dissemination of information," he wrote, because "it can not misrepresent nor misquote."[51] At this time radio broadcasts were live, so there was no opportunity for newscast producers to edit the president's words down to convenient sound bites. Thus radio gave the politicians direct access to the people, free from editorializing or critical comment.

It was precisely to counteract strong newspaper opposition to his New Deal policies that Roosevelt became so reliant on broadcasting as a means of reaching the public. One of the many challenges facing him in his efforts to revive the American economy was that he was operating in an especially hostile media environment. The majority of the nation's newspapers at this time were owned by Republicans, and most papers were staunch critics of the New Deal.[52] The president took to the air in an effort to bypass the critical editorial pages of the press and deliver his message directly to the American people.

Roosevelt and his staff made no secret of the fact that they were intentionally using radio to counteract press criticism. A White House spokesman told *Broadcasting* that it was because "eighty-five percent of the metropolitan press was 'anti-New-Deal'" that "the president has relied upon radio as a means of going direct to the people with his vivid accounts of his stewardship."[53] Roosevelt explained that it was necessary for him to make extensive use of broadcasting because "in some communities it is the unhappy fact that only through the radio is it possible to overtake loudly proclaimed untruths or greatly exaggerated half truths." Upon initiating a series of radio reports in which his cabinet members would address the public, Roosevelt stated emphatically that these broadcasts would be "entirely factual...*to correct the kind of misinformation that is sometimes given currency.*"[54]

Commenting on the power of radio to help the Roosevelt administration counteract press opposition was Jim Farley, the Democratic National Chairman. He observed in his autobiography that "the influence of the radio in determining the outcome of the 1936 election can hardly be overestimated." "Without that unrivaled medium for reaching millions of voters," he wrote, "the work of overcoming the false impression created by the tons of written propaganda put out by foes of the New Deal...might conceivably have been an impossible job." He went on to state that no matter what the opposition papers wrote about Roosevelt, "the harmful effect was largely washed away as soon as the reassuring voice of the President of the United States started coming through the ether into the family living room."[55]

This tactic proved quite effective, for despite consistently negative press coverage, Roosevelt was able to achieve tremendous and continuing popular support. Roosevelt's political success in the face of such extensive opposition from the nation's newspapers signaled a significant change in the power of the press over the political process. The long-established flow of political communication had been disrupted. Newspapers, which had always been the primary link between the government and the people, now faced competition from a medium that allowed politicians to address the voters directly. For the first time in American political and journalistic history, the nation's leader could reach the public without the help or influence of the press. No longer the exclusive channel of news and information, the press was also no longer the only medium shaping public opinion. Newspapers had lost their exclusive control over the flow of political information in this country. As journalism critic Oscar Garrison Villard wrote of the period, "The newspaper reader pays less and less attention to what the editors are saying and to their advice on the conduct of the nation's affairs." 56 Newspapers were losing their influence over public opinion.

Proof of this came when Roosevelt was reelected by a forty-six-state landslide in 1936. A few months after the election, journalist Hendrik William Van Loon observed that despite the fact that "the greater majority of all the newspapers were against him", Roosevelt, "by means of radio, was able to speak directly to his fellow citizens while they were sitting in their own homes." Van Loon explained that the new medium allowed Roosevelt to "step across all the intervening barriers of newspaper opposition" and go on to "a victory such as our country has ever witnessed."57 In fact, the degree to which the people ignored the press was so overwhelming that the election was called "a vote against the newspapers, a judgment day for America's daily press,"58 and was cited as "evidence that newspapers have lost their influence with the people."59 As *Fortune* magazine put it, the results of the 1936 election "made painfully clear that the press had lost even the illusion of leadership of public opinion."60

Losing their position of public opinion leadership did not sit well with many print journalists. This was a role they had occupied for a long time, and it was not one they were willing to give up. In an attempt to protect their established position, they responded by attacking. Once again, their approach was one of invoking democratic rhetoric. In the Roosevelt administration's extensive use of the airwaves, the print journalists found evidence that the European trend of government-controlled airwaves had indeed found its way to the United States. Thus, in their criticism of Roosevelt's use of radio, the press raised the specter of propaganda and dictatorship.

Ogden Reid, editor of the *New York Herald Tribune*, complained that in the debate about the National Recovery Act, which most newspapers opposed, "the radio, controlled by the Administration through its licensing power, was made the spokesman of the New Deal and was largely restricted to government propaganda."61 Edward Harris expressed "grave reservations about the constant use of radio broadcasting by the Federal Government to get its message across to the people."62 The ANPA Radio Committee pointed out that "the present national Administration has made very extensive use of the radio to explain and defend its policies," noting that only recently Roosevelt had made one of his fireside talks, "using 400 out of the 700 radio stations in the country for the purpose." "*This is a precedent*," the report warned, "*which in future years might encourage dictatorship.*"63

Roosevelt was not the only politician to provoke these reactions from the press. Other political figures of the day had also discovered radio, much to the distress of the press. *The American Press* noted with some concern that "many politicians are now thoroughly 'sold' on radio as a medium for getting their political appeals across," because "they object to the nasty habit" that newspapers have "of cutting speeches down to their essentials."[64] One of these politicians was Senator Huey Long of Louisiana. Long, like the president, was noted for his highly effective radio techniques. He delivered speeches that were quite emotional, filled with "earthy figures of speech" and quotations from the Bible. As Edward Chester explains in his book *Radio, Television and American Politics*, "Long deliberately violated the canons of good usage in grammar, articulation and pronunciation so as to appeal more effectively to the masses."[65] Using simple and familiar language, he targeted his message to arouse the passions of the people.

Long was keenly aware that he could use radio as a means of bypassing the press and going directly to the public. On one occasion, he barred the press from the sessions of the Louisiana legislative committee where an investigation was being held into alleged improprieties in the New Orleans city government. Invoking a "gag rule", Long prevented print journalists from entering the chambers, but broadcast his questions and the answers of the witnesses on station WDSU. In an editorial objecting to this, *Editor and Publisher* complained that Long had "managed to get publicity and yet *retained an effective control over what part of the proceedings was to reach the public."* The editorial warned that this practice on the part of politicians could have potentially dire consequences. "It seems to us," *Editor and Publisher* observed,

that the press owes it to itself to make clear to the public the menacing possibilities of radio in the wrong hands. *If democratic institutions are to be preserved*, some system must be devised whereby *demagogues cannot seize radio and by reason of the contact provided lead the people into a dictatorship.*[66]

It was this direct contact between the politicians and the people that many journalists seized upon in their attacks on radio. Opening this channel, they warned, posed a serious threat to the stability of democracy because it placed the public in grave danger of being manipulated. Karl Bickel explained that the problem with radio was that "the speaker before the microphone necessarily presents only his own interpretation of any situation he is dwelling upon. He is solely in charge of the selection of the facts and the relative emphasis placed upon them." Thus when politicians speak directly to the public without the intermediary of the print journalist, Bickel explained, the danger is that "the keen, incisive, often hostile questioning of the newspaper correspondent, provided in the press conference or interview is entirely lacking in the broadcast".[67]

Here Bickel invoked one of the central concepts inherent in the idealized model of the function of the press as the fourth estate--an adversarial relationship between the public and the government. In such a relationship, the press is needed to protect the people from the deceptions of the politician by asking "keen, incisive and often hostile questions", cutting through political rhetoric and revealing the truth. Implicit in his statement is the assumption that when the politician uses radio to bypass the press, this key watchdog function is not served, thereby leaving the people vulnerable to manipulation and abuse of power by the government.

The print journalists' argument was quite simple: Without the watchful eye of the press the people were in grave danger of being manipulated by their political leaders. In the words of Frank Stockbridge, "Once the public gets into the habit of depending upon radio for its news, without critical comment or interpretation, what a playtime that would make for the politicians!"[68] Similar views were voiced by Julian Mason, editor of the *New York Evening Post*, who observed that in a press conference, reporters have the opportunity to ask politicians questions in order to clarify and interpret statements made by the speaker. However "a radio discourse," he warned, "is absolutely unchecked," which is the "danger, therefore of denying interpretation to the press."[69] In other words, the danger of radio is that it does not serve the function of "checking" political discourse.

Similarly, Arthur Robb, a columnist for *Editor and Publisher*, warned that the danger of radio is that "it has no editorial page" and thus "can neither curb perilous policy of government nor guide the public thought into safe channels." "In a democracy," Robb reminded his readers, "nothing else matters much."[70] Again and again the same themes were repeated. Radio cannot serve the functions of the press in a Democracy. It cannot serve to check governmental excesses, and it cannot effectively guide the people in their voting choices.

Another repeated theme was that the government is a dangerous force from which a vulnerable public needs protection. Robb, for instance, spoke of "guiding public thought into safe channels." Comments like this reveal a rather paternalistic attitude in which the members of the public are seen as helpless and unable to formulate their own opinions safely without assistance. This made it essential for someone to serve the function of guiding them, and it is clear that the print journalists felt that they should fill that role. It is also interesting to note that the journalists' perspective was one according to which the newspapers constitute benevolent thought control while radio was seen as a dangerous, propagandistic force. The concept of press manipulation, reporter bias or distortion in print journalism never seems to have come up. Radio was portrayed as a source of great evil for the republic, while the press was continually painted as the paragon of virtue, the solution to the radio problem.

CONTROLLING RADIO IN THE NAME OF DEMOCRACY

What exactly were the print journalists' suggestions for solving the radio problem? Quite simply, they thought it would be best if they just took over. Throughout their warnings about the dangers of broadcasting to our political system, the journalists continually stated or implied that newspapers were the only medium that could properly serve the essential political communication functions in a democracy. The logical extension of their argument was that newspapers should assume control over radio to protect the people from the potential abuse of the airwaves by the government. Since the press, unlike radio, was free from government control, it was free to act in the public interest. Thus, journalists argued, it was the duty of the nation's newspapers to assume this control in order to protect the public from the misuse of radio by the state. Once again, using their best democratic rhetoric, they masked a plan that was clearly designed to serve their own interests in claims that they had only the public interest at heart.

An editorial titled "Freedom of the Air," for example, stressed the responsibilities of the press to protect radio from government control. Taking the position that the press and radio "have the common cause of free speech, to be defended at all costs against coercion, open or implied, by the administration," the writer argued that *the press*, serene in its right to select and reject what it offers to the public, *must not permit the radio instrument to become the political football of politicians.*"71 Another article noted the rise of communism and fascism in Europe, and stated that "if popular government is to remain with us and to be worth keeping, the *job of preservation must in large measure be done by the journalist.*" 72 Karl Bickel put it this way: "the newspapers of America should never make the supreme mistake of standing idly by and permitting broadcasting to become a bureaucratic creature." 73

Edward Harris also described the press as bearing the responsibility to protect democratic liberties. Speaking before the Inland Daily Press Association in Chicago, he warned that "if our form of government is to escape the fire of dictatorship which has burned through many of the countries of Europe, *the newspapers of American must assume the burden of the battle.*" Harris explained that this responsibility should be borne by the newspapers because "*they are organized* as free agencies to gather the news and *to preserve democracy.*"74

Echoing Harris' sentiments, the ANPA Radio Committee worried that radio could easily become a tool for whatever party happened to be in power, arguing that since "the future welfare of this country may depend upon the continuance of both of these media [the press and radio] as free institutions, *it is the duty of publishers* to see that the regulation of broadcasting is kept free from political domination, and without bias or prejudice."75 On another occasion, the committee stated simply that "*the inescapable task of the American press* is to guard against any encroachment upon American Democracy by the Federal government with radio as an instrument of political power."76

Again and again the press was described in virtuous tones as having the solemn responsibility to serve the public by selflessly assuming control over radio. Never was it mentioned that such a press takeover of broadcast news might also serve the interests of the newspapers. Just how did the press plan to carry out its solemn "responsibilities" of protecting the people from government propaganda by radio? While only a few articles addressed the specifics of how these duties were to be carried out, it seems that two approaches were offered. One was for newspapers to assume ownership of radio stations. The other was a plan by which newspapers would control the flow of news that reached the people via the airwaves.

Newspaper Ownership of Radio

Calls for press control of radio stations were issued as early as 1930. In an article titled "Radio versus the Press: Will the Newspapers Control Broadcasting?" Frank Stockbridge suggested that the press should indeed take over radio. Like his colleagues, he employed democratic rhetoric to justify such a move. Stockbridge argued that "the reason newspapers must take over broadcasting in America is to forestall government censorship." The way to prevent the abuse of the airwaves by the government, he explained, is the "ultimate control of radio broadcasting by the newspapers of the United States," to protect "*the interest not primarily of newspapers but of the radio audiences.*"[77]

Despite Stockbridge's claims to the contrary, it was definitely in the interest of the newspapers to assume ownership of the nation's radio stations. Such an arrangement would not only be beneficial to them economically, but would also allow them to retain their monopoly over the kinds of ideas and information that reached the American people. Control over radio newscasts would also have allowed newspapers to remain the primary channel by which the government could address the nation, thereby preserving the primacy of the influence of the press over public opinion. Thus, newspaper ownership of radio stations was one important way for the press to preserve the communication status quo.

As described in Chapter 2, an increasing number of newspapers began buying radio stations during the mid-thirties. In 1930, when Stockbridge issued his call for newspaper control of broadcasting, only sixty out of approximately 600, or ten percent, of all radio stations were owned by newspapers. By the end of the decade newspaper ownership was up to thirty percent, or 250 out of approximately 800 stations.[78] It is impossible to know the exact motives of the newspaper owners for purchasing these stations, and it is certainly possible that their desires to move into broadcasting were strictly economic. There is, however, some evidence that newspaper involvement in radio station ownership may have been motivated by a desire to retain and/or regain the influence over public opinion that the press was losing to radio. This is suggested by the nature of the government's reaction to increasing newspaper involvement in broadcasting. Once the newspapers began to take over radio they started to use it to editorialize against the Roosevelt Administration. It didn't take long, therefore, before the government began questioning the wisdom of granting publishers the license to broadcast.

Shortly after Roosevelt's sweeping victory, achieved with the help of radio in the fall of 1936, several Democratic congressmen introduced bills to limit or prohibit newspaper ownership of radio stations. Sounding much like the print journalists themselves in their attacks on radio, Montana Senator Burton Wheeler argued that newspaper control over radio would limit freedom of expression and lead to "monopoly, or the tendency towards monopoly of the two most popular forms of communications." Making reference to the fact that many of the nation's newspapers had ties with the Republican Party, Wheeler warned that joint ownership of newspapers and radio stations would mean that "the twin fountains of public information would be under the control of one party, to operate as it saw fit to do so."[79]

It is interesting to note that both politicians and journalists employed the same public interest rhetoric when trying to justify why they, and not someone else, should have control over radio broadcasting. In the tension between the press and government, each saw the other as the enemy, posing a monopolistic threat over the channels of communication through which the voting public can be reached. Print journalists, many of whom were opposed to the Democratic Administration in office at the time, cautioned that government control over broadcasting would lead to the use of radio for political propaganda. Similarly, Democratic politicians of the day warned that newspaper ownership of radio would allow the press to limit the kinds of news and information that reached the people. Each side saw itself as benevolent and argued that if it were in control of radio, the people would be safe.

Many journalists felt the efforts to limit newspaper ownership of radio were indeed politically motivated. In discussing whether the legislation proposed by Senator Wheeler would find support in Congress, *Editor and Publisher* speculated that "one of the factors that may have some influence is the fact that many of the newspapers that were strongly opposed to the New Deal before the election are major operators in the radio field."[80] David Lawrence, a syndicated Washington columnist, took the position that the measure was an effort on Roosevelt's part toward "control of radio and the press."[81]

Similarly, *Broadcasting* observed that "it is generally understood" that the strong newspaper opposition to Roosevelt during the 1936 election "has had considerable to do with administration sentiment against newspaper 'domination' of radio and indirectly may have resulted in the crystallization of plans for legislation."[82] In an editorial on the matter, *Broadcasting* argued that the move to enact legislation on newspaper ownership of radio was "largely political," explaining that it was an effort motivated "by an overpowering desire to prevent publishers from dominating the 'editorial policies' of radio stations as they do those of newspapers." The editorial observed that "with newspapers applying by the score for new stations, politicians are becoming uneasy" and are seeking protection from "the domination of the editorial capacity of the microphone by hostile newspaper publishers."[83]

Despite much discussion of the issue in the late 1930s, no legislation was enacted at that time. One of the questions involved was whether the FCC had the authority to single out a particular group of radio license applicants, in this case newspaper owners, as being ineligible for broadcast licenses.[84] In June of

1937 it was determined that only Congress had the power to "divorce" the two media and exclude newspapers from radio ownership.[85] However, Congress took no further action on the matter, and the issue seems to have lain dormant for a time. In 1941, several years after active tension between radio and the press had ended, there was revival of government interest in joint newspaper-radio ownership. This time the FCC conducted an extensive investigation of the matter.

Commenting on this renewal of activity, the *Journal of the Federal Communications Bar Association* wrote that "the reason why the question became a major consideration in 1941 is a matter of conjecture," but speculated that "it would not be too difficult to reach the conclusion that the presidential campaign of 1940 bore more than a passing relationship to the revival of this question." The *Journal* noted that the majority of the newspapers in the country had once again opposed Roosevelt's re-election, and suggested that the new interest in the joint ownership issue stemmed from concern on the part of the administration that the press would control radio in such a way that "only one side of public issue would have an adequate hearing in the public forum."[86]

The FCC hearings lasted for over a year, with extensive witness testimony on the issues of press freedom and monopoly ownership. Ultimately, the Commission adjourned the hearings, without making any statement of policy. It was determined that rather than adopting an official stance on the issue of newspaper ownership of stations, individual applications for licenses would be considered on a case-by-case basis, "under the guiding rule of as much diversification of ownership as feasible."[87] Despite the fact that no policy decisions emerged from all of this investigation, it seems clear that the extensive energy that the government devoted to the issue of newspaper ownership of radio was motivated by a desire on the part of the Roosevelt administration to prevent the opposition press from gaining control of the broadcast channels through which the New Deal was so successfully appealing to the people. There is no direct evidence to prove that newspapers were acquiring radio stations in order to regain their political influence. Nonetheless, publishers and print journalists were undoubtedly aware that involvement in broadcasting would allow the press to regain some of the control over political communication that it was losing to radio.

Press Control of Radio News

If owning radio stations was one solution to the problem of possible government control over radio news, the other was for newspapers and wire services to supply the broadcasters directly with news bulletins. The idea was that if the news services wrote the newscasts themselves, the danger of federal influence over the news would be eliminated or at least greatly diminished. Ironically, print journalists were essentially saying that in order to protect radio's freedom, the press should have control over broadcast news. They attempted to do just that through the establishment of the Press-Radio Bureau. As described in Chapter 2, the Press-Radio Bureau was an arrangement to which representatives from the wire services, newspapers and networks agreed at the Biltmore Conference in December 1933. According to the arrangement, the wire services agreed to supply the networks with brief news bulletins through the newly established Press-Radio Bureau in exchange for which the networks agreed to dismantle their own news-gathering divisions. It was an agreement that gave the press associations full control over the form and content of network radio news for the three years in which the plan was in operation. Thus the fourth estate, the long-time champion of First Amendment rights, had taken over another medium in the name of preserving free speech.

In their arguments justifying this deal, the print journalists once again invoked democratic rhetoric that portrayed the Press-Radio Bureau as serving the public interest. Their many comments about how beneficial this arrangement would be for the people almost sound as if the press were engaged in a grand gesture of self-sacrifice by agreeing to supply radio with news. For example, Edward Harris said that the press associations had agreed to provide radio with news bulletins because "*it is the obligation of the newspapers and the press associations* to preserve for the citizens the freedom of the press and the freedom of expression which are inherent rights of every citizen." He described the arrangement as a "*public service* being performed for the American people by the wire services," explaining that "if the broadcasters are permitted to form their own newsgathering organization for general news broadcasts they can never evade governmental supervision over their output."[88] On another occasion, Harris told the *New York Times* that as long as radio news is "supplied by agencies that are not operating under government license, there is no danger that the news will be censored or controlled in the slightest degree by the government." He went on to explain that the nation's press felt it was "*performing a patriotic service*" in providing radio with news "which has originated from sources that cannot be controlled, directly or indirectly, through fear of revocation of license."[89]

Similar public interest rhetoric was offered as a justification for the Press-Radio Bureau by other journalists, particularly when they found the bureau under attack by an outspoken opponent of the arrangement, Senator Clarence Dill. Shortly after the Press-Radio Bureau commenced operations in 1934, Senator Dill, a Democrat from the state of Washington, issued strong objections, complaining that the agreement was unfair to the broadcasters and that it constituted an effort on the part of print journalism to control radio news. As he put it, the Press-Radio Bureau "now censors all national and world news by radio. Press associations and they alone determine what news may be broadcast. They write the language in which it is broadcast." Dill argued that the press was limiting the free speech of the broadcasters and suggested that the broadcasters establish their own independent news service. He explained that since radio "can combat the abuse of the power of the press...we must make freedom of speech by radio as sacred as freedom of speech on the platform."[90] As an alternative, Dill proposed that the broadcasters start their own independent news-gathering service so that they would no longer be dependent upon the press associations for their news.

Here was a Democratic politician fighting to preserve "freedom of speech" for the broadcasters. By its very nature, the Press-Radio Bureau cut the politicians off from the people. Now, as it was in the days prior to the advent of radio, political speeches would have to filter through the (primarily Republican) press before reaching America's radio audience. Dill's proposal, had it been pursued, would have opened a clear channel between the politicians and the people once again. Like the print journalists, however, Dill couched his proposal in democratic rhetoric, this time invoking the First Amendment. Like the print journalists, Dill suggested a plan that would serve his own interests, but presented it as if it were designed solely to serve the interest of the people. He claimed to be interested only in preserving freedom of speech, and never mentioned the ways in which his proposal might be beneficial to politicians, particularly the Democrats.

The print journalists, not surprisingly, responded in kind. Just as Dill used free speech as an argument for why broadcasters *should* control their own news gathering, print journalists invoked free speech to explain why radio *should not* gather its own news. Federal regulation of radio, they argued, would render a news-gathering organization organized and run solely by the broadcasters vulnerable to government control. Newspaper publishers interviewed on this issue said that since the broadcasters are "dependent for their very existence upon the licensing power of the government, they should not be entrusted with the exacting task of informing the public." *Editor and Publisher* also took a stand on this matter in an editorial that warned its readers to "Keep an Eye on Dill," complaining that the senator's proposal showed that he "has no respect for *the integrity and public service value of the independent press* as distinguished from *a radio service that would be dictated to by government bureaucrats.*"[91] James Stahlman, editor of the *Nashville Banner* warned that a news agency "operated and controlled by radio broadcasters, whose very existence is at the will of the government through license, would be, at best, nothing more nor less than an agency of propaganda," and called Dill's idea "*repugnant to the fundamentals of Americanism,* inimical to freedom of expression and the very existence of our democratic institution."

Other journalists had similar things to say. George Longan, editor of the *Kansas City Star* argued that it was "beyond comprehension" that anyone would want to "take away from private agencies [i.e., the press] *which are serving the people with news* in order to turn that news over to government controlled radio outlets." This implication that radio news and free speech are safer in the hands of the press than in the hands of the government can also be heard in the comments of Paul Patterson, publisher of the *Baltimore Sun.* Patterson explained that the newspapers had agreed to form the Press-Radio Bureau "because they felt that they, being reasonably free of government supervision, could *provide a more disinterested news service* than could the radio stations, which are under such close Federal regulation."[92]

The language of self-sacrifice and public service is consistent here. Again and again the print journalists described themselves and the Press-Radio Bureau in altruistic terms. To listen to them it sounds as if they established the bureau merely out of magnanimous concern for the sanctity of free speech and in the interests of serving the citizens of this Democracy. Never is there a hint that the arrangement might also be beneficial to them, or an acknowledgment that newspapers might also be vulnerable to the influence of political pressure. Never is there the admission that public opinion might be manipulated by the printed word as well as the spoken word, or any recognition that by attempting to control radio news the press was actually infringing upon the broadcasters' freedom of expression. Instead, the print journalists cloak themselves in a mantle of self-sacrificing virtue and depict the broadcasters and the government as enemies of the most essential values of our political system.

Throughout these journalistic criticisms of radio is an appeal to an idealized model of the press, in which newspapers dutifully protect the people from the abuses of governmental excess or political propaganda. The radio, in contrast, is portrayed as a medium through which the public could be manipulated and exploited. This is an argument that predicates the survival of our political structure upon the preservation of the communication status quo. By linking the survival of democracy to the maintenance of their own role in the political communication process, the print journalists depicted themselves as indispensable, and portrayed the preservation of their own power as essential to protecting our form of government.

That the print journalists of the 1930s attempted to defend the long-established functions of their institution is not surprising. Much of the power enjoyed by the institution of journalism derives from the functions it serves in our lives. The arrival of a new communication technology threatened to replace newspapers, thereby robbing the print journalists of their powerful position in the stream of political discourse.

New communication technologies threaten to replace older ones. By definition this means that they threaten to render the established media institution functionally obsolete. If the new technology can perform the same communication function as the older one, and do a faster, more efficient job of it, the older institution is no longer needed. Not only is this an economic threat, but it is also quite threatening to the social, cultural, and political power enjoyed by the established institution. The established media institution fights back in self-defense. One of the best ways to defend one's own interest is to link it to the interests of society at large. The use of democratic or other "sacred" rhetoric effectively masks the self-interested nature of the argument, for who can argue with someone claiming to be protecting democracy?

At stake in battles between old and new media is the struggle for the enormous power that comes with controlling the channels of communication. It is a power that derives from serving certain communication functions in a society. The story of the Press-Radio War suggests a pattern: Faced with the possibility of being displaced from a long-established role, communication institutions are likely to fight back by accusing the new medium of being dangerous to one of society's sacred values. They will wrap their own interests in the flag of democracy, the family, the church, or whatever appears to be the best ideal to hide behind. They will take this sacred rhetoric to Congress, the FCC, the courts, or whatever regulatory or legal body has the power to protect the communication status quo, and they will argue that unless they retain their role and continue to serve "their" institutional function, this sacred ideal will be endangered or destroyed entirely.

NOTES

1. Isabelle Keating, "Pirates of the Air," *Harper's*, (September 1934): 463 (emphasis added).

2. Charles Wright, *Mass Communication: A Sociological Perspective*, 2nd edn. (New York: Random House, 1975).

3. For further discussion of the ANPA/Baby Bell fight, see for example, John Rodden, "Ma Bell, Big Brother and the Information Services Family Feud," in *Media Studies Journal*, Freedom Forum Media Studies Center, New York: Columbia University, Spring 1992.

4. For a discussion of press response to television coverage of the Gulf War, see for example, Freedom Forum Media Center, *The Media At War: The Press and the Persian Gulf Conflict*, A Report of the Gannett Foundation, (New York: Gannet Foundation), 1991.

5. For a full discussion of the functions of the press in a democracy, see Fred Siebert, Ted Peterson and Wilbur Schramm, *Four Theories of the Press* (Urbana: University of Illinois Press, 1956).

6. Ibid., 56.

7. Ibid., 56

8. The term "fourth estate" is variously attributed to either Edmund Burke (an English statesman in the late 1700s) or Thomas Babington Maccaulay (a British historian writing in the first half of the nineteenth century). The British government, like the American, is comprised of three divisions. Edmund Burke is reported to have stood up in the House of Commons, pointed to the public gallery where reporters were seated, and declared that "there are Three Estates in Parliament; but in the Reporter's Gallery yonder there sits a Fourth Estate, more important by far than they all." The other three estates, in England, were "the Lords Spiritual [the Church], "the Lords Temporal" [the Aristocracy], and "the Common" [the representatives of the rising commercial civilization of the towns]. See Herbert Brucker, *Freedom of Information* (New York: Macmillan Company, 1949), 27.

9. Siebert, Peterson and Schramm, *Four Theories.*

10. "Enter Radio News," Editor and Publisher, (March 2, 1929): 38 (emphasis added).

11. "Radio in Politics," *Editor and Publisher*, (November 19, 1932).

12. "The Radio Question," *Editor and Publisher*, (December 22, 1928):28 (emphasis added).

13. "News in Advertising," *New York Times*, (April 25, 1931), 18:3.

14. "Irresponsible Radio News," *Editor and Publisher*, (May 26, 1934):22 (emphasis added).

15. Proceedings of the 11th Annual Convention of the ASNE, April 28-29, 1933.

16. "News Service for Radio Organized," *ANPA Bulletin*, (September 21, 1933): 507.

17. "Publishers Oppose Gallery Rights For Radio Reporters", *Editor and Publisher*, (December 2, 1933):8 (emphasis added).

18. "Radio to Carry Fight to Congress for Admission to Press Gallery," *Editor and Publisher*, (November 11, 1933): 8.

19. "Press Radio Extended One Year," *Editor and Publisher*, (April 25, 1936): 120.

20. "Press Drops Cudgels, Ends Radio Feud", *Editor and Publisher*, (May 1, 1936): 9 (emphasis added).

21. Will Irwin, *Propaganda and the News*, (New York: McGraw-Hill Book Co., 1936): 263.

22. "Press-Radio Extended One Year,"

23. Edward Harris, "Radio and the Press," *Annals of the American Academy*, (January 1935): 163.

24. Ibid., 164.

25. "Harris Rebukes Agencies Selling News for Radio Sponsorship," *Editor and Publisher*, (January 25, 1936).

26. Ibid., (emphasis added).

27. *Nashville Banner*, January 25, 1936.

28. Karl Bickel, *New Empires: The Newspaper and the Radio* (Philadelphia: J.B. Lippincott, 1930), 78.

29. Harris, "Radio and the Press," 163, (emphasis added).

30. O.W. Riegel, *Mobilizing for Chaos: The Story of the New Propaganda*, (New Haven: Yale University Press, 1934), 17.

31. Ibid., 1.

32. Ibid., 87 (emphasis added).

33. Ibid., 214.

34. Frank Stockbridge, "Radio vs. the Press: Will the Newspapers Control Broadcasting?" *Outlook and Independent*, (December 31, 1980): 692.

34. Frank Stockbridge, "Radio v the Press: Will the Newspapers Control Broadcsting?" *Outlook and Independent*, (December 31, 1980): 692.

35. "Dailes Must Oppose Use of Radio to Impair Democracy," *Editor and Publisher*, (April 30, 1936): 18.

36. "Press Drops Cudgels, Ends Radio Feud," *Editor and Publisher*, (May 1, 1936): 9 (emphasis added).

37. "Harris Rebukes Agencies Selling News for Radio Sponsorship," *Editor and Publisher*, (January 25, 1936).

38. "Radio is 'Pure News' Channel", *Editor and Publisher*, (October 13, 1934): 5.

39. Will Irwin, *Propaganda and the News*, (New York: McGraw Hill,

1936): 252 (emphasis added).

40. "News Commentators," *Editor and Publisher*, (July 25, 1936):26 (emphasis added).

41. "Growth of Radio's Influence Places Heavier Burden on Press, Says Bixby," *Broadcasting*, (1 May 1937): 15 (emphasis added).

42. Ibid.

43. See, for example, Michael Emery and Edwin Emery, *The Press and America*, (Englewood Cliffs, N.J.: Prentice Hall, 1988), 355; and Arthur Molella and Elsa Bruton, *FDR: The Intimate Presidency: Franklin D. Roosevelt, Communication and the Mass Media in the 1930's*, (Washington, D.C.: Smithsonian Institution, 1981, 4). For a particularly in-depth and comprehensive discussion of Roosevelt's use of radio and his relationship with the press, see Betty Houchin Winfield, *FDR and the News Media*, (New York: Columbia University Press, 1994).

44. "Radio's Reach to Masses and Classes," *Broadcasting*, (November 11, 1933): 9;   "Four Out of Five Homes Now Have Radios," *Broadcasting*, (May 1, 1937): 1.

45. Quoted in Edward Chester, *Radio, Television and American Politics*, (New York: Sheed & Ward, 1969): 31.

46. "Radio Personalities of the Presidential Prospects," *Broadcasting*, (March 1 1936).

47. Stanley High, NBC broadcast, March 22, 1935; NBC MSS files, Box 37, folder 42.

48. Mollela and Bruton, *FDR: The Intimate Presidency*, 51.

49. Chester, *Radio, Television and American Politics*, 33.

50. Molella and Bruton, *FDR: The Intimate Presidency*, 49.

51. Ibid.

52. Winfield, *FDR and the News Media*.

53. Sol Taishoff, "Election Augurs Well For American Radio," *Broadcasting*, (November 11, 1936): 1.

54. Quoted in Molella and Bruton, *FDR: The Intimate Presidency*, 129 (emphasis added).

55. Jim Farley, *Behind the Ballots: Personal History of a Politician* (New York: Harcourt Brace, 1938): 319.

56. Oswald Garrison Villard, *The Disappearing Daily*, (New York: Knopf, 1944), 8.

56. Villard, *The Disappearing Daily*, 9.

57. Hendrik Willem Van Loon, "Man's Mightiest Weapon -- For Good or Evil," *Broadcasting*, (January 1 1937): 13.

58. Quoted in Robert Rutland, *The Newsmongers:Journalism in the Life of the Nation, 1690-1972*, (New York: Dial Press, 1973), 346.

59. Villard, p 9.

60. "The Press and the People -- A Survey," *Fortune*, (August 1939): 64.

61. "Nevermore," *New York Herald Tribune*, (May 12, 1934): 12.

62. "Radio News Service Seen as Threat," *Editor and Publisher*, (October 7, 1933).

63. "Dailies Must Oppose Use of Radio to Impair Democracy," (emphasis added).

64. "Politicians Like to Talk on Radio," *American Press*, (August 1932): 3.

65. Chester, "The Press-Radio War," 35.

66. "Long's System," *Editor and Publisher*, (September 8, 1934) (emphasis added).

67. Bickel, *New Empires*, 77.

68. Frank Parker Stockbridge, "News Broadcasting and the Newspapers," *American Press*, (October 1934): 1.

69. Bickel, *New Empires*, 77.

70. Arthur Robb, "Shop Talk at Thirty," *Editor and Publisher*, (November 1937): 40.

71. "Freedom of the Air," *Editor and Publisher*, (January 18, 1936): 34.

72. Frank Scott, Some Notes on Ethics and Taste for Journalists," *Journalism Quarterly*, vol 1 #2, 1929 (emphasis added).

73. Bickel, *New Empires*, 80.(emph added).

74. "Foreign Air Propaganda is Threat," *Editor and Publisher*, (June 6, 1936), 11. (emph added).

75. "Press Drops Cudgels, Ends Radio Feud," *Broadcasting*, (May 1, 1936), 9.

76. "Dailies Must Oppose Use of Radio to Impair Democracy," *Editor and Publisher*, (April 30, 1938), 18.

77. Stockbridge, "Radio vs. the Press,"(emphasis added).

78. *Broadcasting Yearbook* 1935-1940 and *Editor and Publisher Yearbook*, 1935-1940.

79. "Legislation May Divorce Press From Radio Interests," *Editor and Publisher*, (December 5, 1936), 8.

80. "Press-Radio Divorce Up to Congress," *Editor and Publisher*, (February 20, 1937): 9.

81. "Wheeler Radio-Press Bill Gets Reaction," *Broadcasting*, (March 1, 1937): 15.

82. Sol Taishoff, "Newspaper-Radio Problem Out in the Open," *Broadcasting*, (Feburary 15, 1937): 1.

83. "Politics or Public Service--The Newspaper-Radio Issue," *Broadcasting*, (March 1, 1937).

84. Frank Arnold, "Radio and the Newspaper," *Editor and Publisher*, (Feburary 27, 1937): 22.

85. "The Newspaper-Radio Decision," *Federal Communication Bar Journal*, 7 (4), February 1944; "Joint Press-Radio Ownership Up to Congress, FCC Suggests," *Broadcasting*, (June 1, 1937): 23.

86. "The Newspaper-Radio Decision," Ibid.

87. Edwin Emery, *The History of the ANPA*, (University of Minnesota Press, 1950): 210.

88. Edward Harris, "Radio and the Press," *Annals of the American Academy*, January 1935: 166-9.

89. "Radio Press Fails, Senator Dill Says," *New York Times*, (September

18, 1934): 3.

90. "Press Radio Pact has Failed, Says Dill," *Editor and Publisher*, (September 22, 1934): p 5.

91. "Keep an Eye on Dill," *Editor and Publisher*, (September 22, 1934):26 (emphasis added).

92. "Dill's Radio News Service Assailed As Repugnant to Americanism," *Editor and Publisher*, (September 22, 1934): 1   (emphasis added).

Epilogue

The history of media is never more or less than a history of their uses, which always lead us away from them to the social practices and conflicts they illuminate.[1]

Carolyn Marvin
University of Pennsylvania

This has been a study of resistance to change. More specifically, it has been an examination of ways in which an established media institution responded to a technological innovation in communications.   As Carolyn Marvin has observed, media history is not so much a study of the technologies as it is the study of the uses to which people put those technologies, and the social practices these uses reveal. Wars, whether actual or metaphoric, are quite costly. At the very least they cost time, money and other valuable resources. Sometimes the cost is much higher. Thus people or institutions tend to declare war only when there is, at least in their eyes, just cause. In general, wars are waged only when people feel there is something worth fighting for. To justify the risk there must be sufficient incentive. Thus, the study of media wars is ultimately the study of values, for the things over which people are willing to go to war are truly those things that they hold most dear. By exploring resistance to new media, we are studying not the new technologies but the values of those who reacted to them. Revealed here is what they were afraid of, and why they were willing to fight for it. Studies of this nature are ultimately studies of the ways in which new communication technologies can be threatening, to whom, and with what consequences.

Reactions to new media are the place where technology and culture meet. In the hopes and fears of those living at the time of a particular technological innovation can be heard the social imagination at work. Having been presented with a new technology, contemporary social actors voice their concerns about how the new medium will change their lives, and in so doing they reveal their vulnerabilities. In their hopes of technological deliverance is reflected the ways in which their current lives fall short. In their fears of technological danger can be heard what they hold sacred and are most afraid of losing. Listening to fears about the impact of new media is much like interpreting dreams. These are the collective nightmares of a people, or an institution, about the potential dangers of changing the familiar media ecology. Whether or not the fears are realistic is much less important than the simple fact of the fears themselves. The fears point to the deeper issues at stake in resistance to new media. In Marvin's words, they point us away from the technologies "to the social practices and conflicts they illuminate."

The story of the Press-Radio War provides insights into the deeper social issues over which Media Wars are waged. This is a not a story about radio or newspapers, but about the struggle for control over the channels of news gathering and dissemination, and for the power that comes with that control. It is a story about how those with that power respond when they find their position in jeopardy, and it reveals the various ways in which new media threaten the power of established media institutions.

Institutional power is derived from a number of sources. Three key sources of an institution's power are its identity, its structure and its function. Institutional identity is the way in which the institution defines itself, generally determined by a set of standards or operating procedures governing its performance. Institutional structure is the internal division of labor that organizes the institution, and the laws and regulations that govern its operations. Institutional function is the role or roles that the institution plays in society. Together these three areas are the sources of much of a media institution's power.

New communication technologies are threatening to these three components of institutional power because they bring with them the possibility of communicating in a new way. New media offer new ways of sending, receiving, storing and accessing information. Since the identity, structure, and function of the established media institutions are defined, at least in part, by the technology available to them, the arrival of new technology carries with it the seeds of potential institutional redefinition. If information can be processed in a new way, the identity of the institution might change, and with it the division of labor and rules governing its operations, and the function(s) it serves in society. Changes in any of these areas could mean a loss of institutional power.

Thus, media wars are waged by communication institutions to preserve the power they derive from their established identity, structure, and function. They are battles waged in response to threats posed to this power by the introduction of new communication technologies. In the case of the Press-Radio War, the print journalists attempted to defend their institution from radio on each of these three levels. Radio threatened the established identity of the institution of print journalism because it provided a new way of delivering the news. The arrival of this new technology raised questions about who should be considered a journalist, and what standards should govern the practice of journalism. This new technology also threatened the established structure of the institution of print journalism. With the arrival of a new way to transmit information, the established patterns of division of labor that organized the institution, and the laws and regulations that had been written to protect this organizational structure were in danger of being rendered obsolete. Finally, the availability of a new channel of communication raised the possibility that the various essential functions that newspapers had so long served in the democratic political process might be served by radio.

Faced with threats to three key sources of their power, the print journalists fought back. Their efforts at self-defense included action on the legal, political, and regulatory levels in an attempt to block the emergence of broadcast journalism. Perhaps their most consistent weapon in this battle was not action, however, but rhetoric. In the invocation of sacred rhetoric as a form of self-defense, an established media institution puts forth an argument claiming that one or more of the culture's most cherished ideals or values is threatened in some way by the new medium. This is in some ways a brilliant self defense strategy, for it links preservation of these sacred values with the preservation of the established media institution. In wrapping self-interest in a cloak of public interest, one can argue that the way to preserve cherished ideals is to maintain the communication status quo.

The print journalists of the 1930s, fighting to protect their institution from the threats of radio, issued warnings that the journalistic ideals of objectivity, the capitalist ideals of protecting intellectual property, and the political ideals of democracy would be compromised by the emergence of broadcast journalism. Fifty years later, the print journalists of the 1980s, fighting to protect their institution from the threats posed by the attempts of the telephone companies to enter the business of on-line news transmission, issued warnings of monopolistic thought-control, in which the Baby Bells were portrayed as the enemies of both the free market and free speech. Other Media Wars, such as that between cable and broadcast television, or between cable television and the telephone companies, have called forth similar predictions of threats posed to capitalist or democratic ideals.

At first glance it may appear easy to dismiss these doomsday warnings as simply a clever way to disguise economically motivated self-defense. To contemporary ears, so attuned to the masterful devices of advertising, public relations, and propaganda campaigns, it almost seems hard to believe that print journalists thought that radio would really bring about the downfall of democracy. We might argue that this was just a clever way for them to disguise their own financial self-interest. In a sense, this may be quite true. But notice how this strategy is continually used in these Media Wars. There are many ways to sell an idea. The invocation of "sacred" rhetoric is only one approach. Why does it continually reappear when established media institutions find their power threatened?

New communication technologies are potential agents of social change.[2] They bear the seeds of subversion. By carrying with them the possibility of disrupting established patterns of communication, they bear the power to displace some of the basic building blocks of social reality. Much of the way in which we define our world is reflected in the way we organize the movement of information, and the ways we communicate with each other. Written and unwritten rules governing who speaks to whom, about what are manifestations of deeper social beliefs about power, control and the hierarchy of social relations.   Rules governing who has access to which kind of information and who should control its distribution are similar reflections of social priorities. When it becomes possible to disrupt these established communication patterns, it also becomes possible to rebuild them in ways that no longer serve to support and preserve the status quo. No wonder the arrival of new media provokes "sacred" rhetoric. We seem to sense intuitively the potential for these new communication technologies to be used as powerful tools for reshaping patterns of human relations. If we begin to relate with each other in new ways, then society itself may be reshaped. For those interested in preserving the established social structure, this is a grave danger indeed. It is not surprising that they issue warnings that new media pose a threat to some of the culture's sacred values, because they do, or so it seems.

In ascribing to new media the power to disrupt fundamental social values, established media institutions make an error common to many critics of new technologies. They are accusing machines of being the cause of social problems. What they seem to forget is that while new media make it possible to disrupt established patterns of communication, the technologies themselves do not determine the way in society makes use of them. If democracy falls, if the telephone companies assume the role of Big Brother, or if the ideals of free speech are abandoned, it will be the result of human choice, not technological imperative. New media cannot reshape society on their own. They can only be used by people who are interested in doing so.

When we hear warnings that new media will lead to the destruction of one of our sacred values, what we are hearing is the fear that this new tool may be used to redirect communication patterns in ways that no longer support the current social structure. From this perspective, Media Wars are not waged by established media institutions just to protect their economic stability; they are conflicts of a far more serious nature. These are battles fought by those who control the channels of communication, to retain that control. With that control comes the power to ensure that established patterns of communication are preserved, and the preservation of those patterns helps insure that the deeper social structure they reflect will be protected.

What does this mean for us as we face the inevitable media wars of tomorrow? The introduction of new media appears to be one of the "givens" in our world. Indeed, technological innovation in communication continues to occur at an increasingly rapid rate. We have become very skilled at inventing newer, better ways of communicating farther and faster, to more people, in ever novel ways. What we are still not very good at is accommodating these changes with ease. We continually balk and hesitate, reacting with fear and concern. This resistance to change is particularly marked from established media institutions, for they have perhaps the most to lose. Yet if they are to survive in today's ever changing media ecology, it is essential that they develop the ability to adapt.

By studying the media wars of yesterday, today's communication institutions can become prepared for the ways in which they might feel threatened by the introduction of new media. They can develop institutional identities that are not so technologically dependent, and that can accommodate technological change more easily. Similarly, they can develop institutional structures based less on the demands of current technology, and more on patterns of organizational relationship that permit flexibility. This will allow the institution to serve various social functions as its identity and structure evolve with time and technology.

Ultimately, the waging of Media Wars is a tremendous waste of institutional and social resources. The time, energy, and money spent attempting to block the inevitable tide of change could be far better spent developing ways to better adapt to it. The key to understanding why these futile battles are continually waged is to listen closely to the sacred rhetoric that gets invoked in response to new communication technologies. The repeated use of this kind of language reveals fears that these new media will dislodge the very building blocks of society. It also reveals a fear that the stability of the social foundation is very vulnerable, and could be dislodged simply with the introduction of a new technology. But in ascribing technology with the power to dismantle the political system, we forget that it was not the technology of yesterday that built democracy, it was human beings, with a dream of freedom. If the values of our political structure, or any other values we hold dear are dismantled, it will not be the work of robots, but of those who programmed them. Similarly, if some of the building blocks need to be reset, to provide a stronger foundation, that is work that only we, and not our inventions can accomplish.

It is far easier to blame the box than to take responsibility for building it, deciding who should use it, and in what ways. When sacred rhetoric gets invoked as a response to the introduction of new media, that is a signal that people are frightened. It is a sign that those who enjoy power as a result of their position in the current social structure feel threatened in some way. But that does not mean it is time to go to war, taking legal, economic or regulatory action against the 'invasion' of the new technological enemy. It means that it is time to take steps to make sure that the new media institution gets defined and structured in ways that allow it to serve the function of supporting those values to which we are committed. It may be, of course, that we are unsure about the nature of those values. It may be that competing groups with contrasting visions of the ideal social structure are all attempting to control the channels of communication. In that case, it is time to turn our attention to the deeper issues at stake, which are not about the communication technologies at all, but the social values their use reflects. Once we are in agreement about what we want our world to look like, we will have far fewer battles over how to use our media.   Until then they will serve as pawns in the much larger war that we are continually waging: the ongoing struggle to control and define social reality.

NOTES

1. Carolyn Marvin, *When Old Technologies Were New: Thinking About Communications in the Late Nineteenth Century* (New York: Oxford, 1988).

2. For further discussion of this concept, see Elizabeth Eisenstein, *The Printing Press as an Agent of Change: Communications and Cultural Transformations in early-modern Europe* (New York: Cambridge University Press, 1979).

Bibliography

BOOKS AND ARTICLES SINCE 1950

Barnouw, Eric. *A Tower in Babel*. New York: Oxford University Press, 1966.
_____. *The Golden Web*. New York: Oxford University Press. 1968.

Bessie, Simon Michael. *Jazz Journalism: The Story of the Tabloid Newspapers*. New York: Russell & Russell, 1969.

Bledstein, Burton. *The Culture of Professionalism: The Middle Class and the Development of Higher Education in America*. New York: W. W. Norton, 1976.

Bliss, Edward. *Now the News: The Story of Broadcast Journalism*. New York: Columbia University Press, 1991.

Briggs, Asa. *The Birth of Broadcasting: The History of Broadcasting in the United Kingdom*. New York: Oxford University Press, 1961.

Burlingame, Roger. *Don't Let Them Scare You: The Life and Times of Elmer Davis*. Philadelphia: J. B. Lippincott, 1961.

Carey, James. "The Problem of Journalism History." *Journalism History* 1 (Spring 1975): 3.

Clanchy, Michael. *From Memory to Written Record: England, 1066-1307*. Cambridge, Mass.: Harvard University Press, 1979.

Cook, Joe, and Sam Slate. *It Sounds Impossible*. New York: Macmillan, 1962.

Czitrom, Daniel. *Media and the American Mind: From Morse to McLuhan*. Chapel Hill, N.C.: University of North Carolina Press. 1982.

Danna, Sammy. "The Rise of Radio News." In *American Broadcasting: A Source Book on the History of Radio and Television*. Lawrence Licthy and Malachi Topping, eds., New York: Hastings House, 1975, p. 338.

Douglas, Susan. *Inventing American Broadcasting, 1899-1922*. Baltimore: Johns Hopkins University Press, 1987.

Eisenstein, Elizabeth. *The Printing Press as an Agent of Change*. Cambridge, England: Cambridge University Press. 1979.

Emery, Edwin. *The History of the ANPA*. Minneapolis: University of Minnesota, 1950.

Emery, Edwin, and Michael Emery. *The Press and America*, 7th ed. Englewood Cliffs: Prentice Hall, 1992.

Fang, Irving. *Those Radio Commentators!* Ames, Iowa: Iowa State University Press, 1977.

Gitlin, Todd. *Deciding What's News*. New York: Vintage 1979.

_____. *The Whole World Is Watching*. Berkeley: University of California, 1980.

Goody, Jack. *The Logic of Writing and the Organization of Society*. Cambridge, England: Cambridge University Press, 1986.

Heyer, Paul. *Communications and History: Theories of Media, Knowledge, and Civilization*. New York: Greenwood Press, 1988.

Innis, Harold. *Empire & Communications*. Toronto: University of Toronto Press, 1950.

Jensen, Joli. *Redeeming Modernity: Contradictions in Media Criticism*. Newbury Park. Calif.: Sage, 1990.

Jowett, Garth. "Toward a History of Communication." *Journalism History* 2 (Summer 1975): 4.

Kitross, John, and Christhoper Sterling. *Stay Tuned: A Concise History of American Broadcasting*. Belmont, Calif.: Wadsworth, 1978.

Klaidman, Stephen, and Tom Beauchamp. *Virtuous Journalist*. New York: Oxford University Press, 1987.

Klurfeld, Herman. *Winchell: His Life and Times*. New York: Praeger, 1976.

Levin, Harvey. *Broadcast Regulation and Joint Ownership of Media*. New York: New York University Press, 1960.

Levine, Lawrence. *Highbrow, Lowbrow: The Emergence of Cultural Hierarchy in America*. Cambridge, Mass.: Harvard, University Press, 1988.

Lichty, Lawrence, and Malachi Topping, ed. *American Broadcasting: A Source Book on the History of Radio and Television*. New York: Hastings House, 1975.

Logan, Robert. *The Alphabet Effect: The Impact of the Phonetic Alphabet on the Development of Western Civilization*. New York: St. Martin's Press, 1987.

Lott, George. "The Press-Radio War of the 1930's," *Journal of Broadcasting* 14 (3) (Summer 1970): 277.

MacLaurin, W. R. *Invention and Innovation in the Radio Industry*. New York: Macmillan: 1949.

Mander, Mary. "The Public Debate About Broadcasting in the Twenties: An Interpretive History." *Journal of Broadasting* 28 (Spring 1984).

Marvin, Carolyn. "Space, Time, and Captive Communications History." In *Communications in Transition*. Edited by Mary Mander. New York: Praeger, 1983.

_____. "Constructed and Reconstructed Discourse: Inscription and Talk in the History of Literacy," *Communication Research* 11 (4) October 1984.

_____. "Experts, Black Boxes and Artifacts: New Allegories for the History of Electric Media." In *Paradigm Dialogues*. Edited by Brenda Dervin and Larry Grossberg. Newbury Park. Calif.: Sage, 1987.

_____. *When Old Technologies Were New*. New York: Oxford University Press, 1988.

_____. "Literacy." In *International Encyclopedia of Communications*. New York: Oxford University Press, 1989.

Marzolf, Marion. "Operationalizing Carey--An Approach to the Cultural History of Journalism." *Journalism History* 2 (Autumn 1975.)

_____. "American Studies -- Ideas for Media Historians?" *Journalism History* 5 (Spring 1978.)

McChesney, Robert W. "Towards a Reinterpretation of the American Press-Radio War of the 1930's." *Proceedings of Journalism Annual Convention: Association for Education in Mass Communication.* August 1990, Minneapolis.

_____. *Telecommunications, Mass Media, & Democracy: The Battle for the Control of U.S. Broadcasting, 1930-1935.* New York: Oxford University Press, 1993.

_____. "Press-Radio Relations and the Emergence of Network, Commerical Broadcasting in the United States, 1930-1935." *Historical Journal of Film Radio and Television* 11 (1) 1991): 47.

McLuhan, Marshall. *The Gutenberg Gallaxy.* Toronto: University of Toronto Press. 1962.

McLuhan, Marshall. *Understanding Media: The Extensions of Man.* New York: McGraw-Hill, 1964.

Meyer, Philip. *Ethical Journalism.* New York: Longman, 1987.

Meyerowitz, Joshua. *No Sense of Place: The Impact of Electronic Media on Social Behavior.* New York: Oxford University Press, 1985.

Molella, Arthur, and Elsa Bruton. *FDR, The Intimate Presidency: Franklin D. Roosevelt, Communication and the Mass Media in the 1930's.* Washington, D.C.: Smithsonian Institution, 1981.

Ong, Walter. *Orality and Literacy: The Technologizing of the Word.* New York: Methuen, 1982.

Pitts, Alice Fox. *Read All About It!: 50 Years of ASNE.* New York: ASNE, 1974.

Postman, Neil. *Amusing Ourselves to Death: Public Discourse in the Age of Show Business.* New York: Viking. 1985.

Rosen, P. T. *The Modern Stentors: Radio Broadcasting and the Federal Government, 1920-1934.* Westport Conn.: Greenwood Press, 1980.

Schiller, Dan. *Objectivity and the News: The Public and the Rise of Commercial Journalism.* Philadelphia: University of Pennsylvania Press, 1981.

Schoenful, Clarence. *Effective Feature Writing.* New York: Harper, 1960.

Schudson, Michael. *Discovering the News: A Social History of American Newspapers*. New York: Basic Books, 1978.

Shuman, Amy. *Storytelling Rights: The Uses of Oral and Written Texts by Urban Adolescents*. Cambridge, England: Cambridge University Press, 1986.

Siebert, Fred, Ted Peterson and Wilbur Schramm. *Four Theories of the Press*. Urbana, Ill.: University of Illinois Press, 1956.

Slate, Sam, and Joe Cook. *It Sounds Impossible*. New York: Macmillan, 1963.

Stephens, Mitchell. *A History of News: From the Drum to the Satellite*. New York: Viking, 1988.

Stock, Brian *The Implications of Literacy: Written Language and Models of Interpretation in the 11th and 12th Centuries*. Princeton, N.J.: Princeton University Press, 1983.

Sullivan, Paul. "News Piracy: Unfair Competition and the Misappropriation Doctrine." *Journalism Monographs,* Association for Education in Journalism and Mass Communication, May, 1978.

Thomas, Lowell. *Good Evening Everybody*. New York: Morrow, 1976.

Tuchman, Gaye. *Making News: A Study in the Construction of Reality*. New York: Free Press, 1978.

United States Department of Commerce. *Historical Statistics of the United States: Colonial Times to 1970*. Washington, D.C.: Bureau of the Census, 1975.

MATERIALS PRIOR TO 1950

Associated Press v. KVOS, Decree, 9th Cir., 1935, p. 11.

Associated Press v. KVOS, Inc. 9th Cir. 1935, Brief for Appellant, p. 5.

Bickel, Karl. *New Empires: The Newspapers and the Radio*. Philadelphia: J.B. Lippincott, 1930.

Bickford, Leland. *News While It Is News: The Real Story of the Radio News*. Boston: Manthorne & Co., 1935.

Borden, Neil. *National Advertising in Newspapers*. Cambridge, Mass.: Harvard University Press, 1946.

Brooks, William. *Radio News Writing*. New York: McGraw Hill, 1948.

Carskadon, T. R. "The Press-Radio War." *The New Republic* (March 11, 1936):133.

Charnley, Mitchell. *News by Radio*. New York: Macmillan, 1948.

Chester, Giraud. "The Press-Radio War: 1933-1935." *Public Opinion Quarterly* (Summer, 1949): 252.

Desmond, Robert. *Professional Training of Journalists*. Paris: UNESCO, 1949.

Dunlap, Orrin. *Talking on the Radio: A Practical Guide for Writing and Broadcasting a Speech*. New York: Greenburg Publishing, 1936.

International News Service v. The Associated Press. Certiorari to the Circuit Court of Appeals for the Second Circuit, Case #221., December 23, 1918, p. 236.

Irwin, Will. *Propaganda and the News*. New York: McGraw Hill, 1936.

Lawton, Sherman Paxton. *Radio Continuity Types*. Boston: Expression, 1938.

Lazarsfeld, Paul, and Harry Field. *Radio and the Printed Page*. New York: Duell, Sloan & Pearce, 1940.

Lippman, Walter. *Liberty and the News*. New York: Harcourt, Brace and Howe, 1920.

_____.*Public Opinion*. New York: Harcourt, Brace and Howe, 1920.

Newsom, Phil. *United Press Radio News Style Book*. New York: United Press Association, 1943.

Parker, George. *Detroit Free Press Style Book*. Detroit: Detroit Free Press, 1943.

Readability in News Writing. New York: United Press Associations, 1945.

Schechter, Abe. *I Live On Air*. New York: Stokes 1941.

Seldes, George. *Freedom of the Press*. New York: Bobbs Merrill, 1935.

Sinclair, Upton. *The Brass Check*. New York: Johnson Reprint Corp, 1970.

Sutton, Albert. *Education for Journalism In the U.S. from Its Beginning to 1940*. Evanston, Ill.: Northwestern University Press 1945.

Villard, Garrison. *The Disappearing Daily*. New York: Knopf, 1944.

Wagner, Paul. *Radio Journalism*. Minneapolis: Burgess Publishing, 1940.

Wakelee, Arthur. *News Broadcasting*. M.A. Thesis, Columbia School of Journalism, Columbia University, 1932.

Warren, Carl. *Radio News Writing and Editing*. New York: Harper Bros. Pubs., 1947.

Weaver, Luther. *The Technique of Radio Writing*. New York: Prentice Hall, Inc., 1948.

White, Paul. *News on the Air*. New York: Harcourt Brace, 1947.

ORAL HISTORIES

Bragdon, Everett. *Reminiscences*. New York: Columbia University Oral History Collection, 1950.

Haeffner, Joseph. *Reminiscences*. Broadcast Pioneers Project, New York: Columbia University Oral History Collection, 1950.

Kaltenborn, H. V. *Reminiscences*. Radio Pioneers Project. New York: Columbia University Oral History Collection, 1950.

Schechter, Abe.   *Reminicenses,* Broadcast Pioneers Project, New York: Columbia University Oral History Collection, 1950.

Index

About the Author

GWENYTH L. JACKAWAY is an Assistant Professor of Communication at Fordham University in New York, where she teaches courses in media history, mass culture, and research methods.

ISBN 0-275-95257-6

90000>

EAN

9 780275 952570

HARDCOVER BAR CODE